Radical State

Radical State

*How Jihad Is Winning Over
Democracy in the West*

ABIGAIL R. ESMAN

Praeger Security International

PRAEGER

AN IMPRINT OF ABC-CLIO, LLC
Santa Barbara, California • Denver, Colorado • Oxford, England

Library of Congress Cataloging-in-Publication Data

Esman, Abigail R.
   Radical state : how Jihad is winning over democracy in the West / Abigail R. Esman.
      p. cm.
   Includes bibliographical references and index.
   ISBN 978-0-313-34847-1 (hard copy : alk. paper) — ISBN 978-0-313-34848-8 (e-book)
1. Terrorism—Netherlands. 2. Islamic fundamentalism—Netherlands. 3. Jihad.
4. Gogh, Theo van, 1957-2004—Assassination. 5. Islam and politics—Netherlands. I. Title.
   HV6433.N4E86 2010
      305.6'9709492—dc22   2010001086

ISBN: 978-0-313-34847-1
EISBN: 978-0-313-34848-8

14 13 12 11 10   1 2 3 4 5

This book is also available on the World Wide Web as an eBook.
Visit www.abc-clio.com for details.

Praeger
An Imprint of ABC-CLIO, LLC

ABC-CLIO, LLC
130 Cremona Drive, P.O. Box 1911
Santa Barbara, California 93116-1911

This book is printed on acid-free paper ∞

Manufactured in the United States of America

This book is gratefully and humbly dedicated to those
who have sacrificed their lives
so that the rest of us might freely speak.

Contents

Preface	ix
Acknowledgments	xv
Introduction	1
Chapter 1	6
Chapter 2	12
Chapter 3	24
Chapter 4	31
Chapter 5	41
Chapter 6	48
Chapter 7	58
Chapter 8	65
Chapter 9	76
Chapter 10	84
Chapter 11	92
Chapter 12	101
Chapter 13	111
Chapter 14	125

Chapter 15   135

Chapter 16   149

Chapter 17   157

Chapter 18   169

Chapter 19   182

Chapter 20   195

Chapter 21   204

Chapter 22   215

Notes   229

Index   239

Preface

On the morning of January 17, 2005, I received an e-mail with the following subject line: "The Next Victim?" and a link to a conversation on a Webboard about the latest art scandal in the Netherlands: an exhibition of cartoon-like paintings by Rachid Ben Ali, a Moroccan-born Dutch artist, that included images of what seemed to be a Muslim cleric either, as it were, eating shit or speaking it. The phrase "next victim" referred to the murder of another artist, the filmmaker Theo van Gogh, who had been slaughtered two months earlier by a Muslim extremist angered by a film Van Gogh had made about the abuse of Muslim women. The question of the day was, of course, whether Ali would be the next target of a Muslim extremist killing, or whether this was harmless enough that it wouldn't really matter.

There was a time, not long ago at all, when "the next Van Gogh" was a phrase used to describe an up-and-coming Dutch artist, when wondering who the next Van Gogh would be was about hoping that, in the meager pickings of the Dutch art scene, someone would emerge of international quality and capture the imaginations of the world.

But when Theo van Gogh was shot twenty times by a jihadist, his body stabbed, and his throat slashed open, the phrase gained a whole new meaning.

In the United States, it was Election Day when Theo van Gogh was murdered—the day when the country would choose either to keep in office the man who had sworn to fight Islamic extremism and oppression by spreading democracy across the Muslim world, or to be rid of him. What no one realized was that even before the polls had opened, whether George W. Bush won the election that day or not, that morning on the streets of Amsterdam, democracy had already lost.

I moved to Amsterdam from New York City because of the canals, because the streets were laid out in a plan that made it difficult to get lost, because you could see time move with the clouds across the sky, so real, so *there*, you thought maybe you could touch it, and if you could touch it, maybe even hold it still. I moved to Amsterdam because, in some ways, time there always *had* held still.

It was summer when I first visited, one of the rare summers when the air is actually hot, and the sun on the canals so bright that the reflections of windows in the water sting your eyes, and the ducks clamor joyously until late into the night because it doesn't get dark until nearly midnight and the entire city—*de gehele stad*—is out on café terraces, or on chairs dragged out to the sidewalk from living rooms, drinking Grolsch and jenever and laughing loud enough to be heard in third-floor apartments, if anyone were home to hear them, which, mostly, they are not. It was the summer before the crash of '89, when everyone was buying art and whoever didn't paint or sculpt had a gallery and traveled country to country, art fair to art fair, buying one another's goods and selling them again. Roy Lichtenstein and Jerry Garcia and Michael Jackson all were still alive. Answering machines were just coming into the market in Holland, and only the coolest people had them. *Dallas* reruns played nightly on TV. At the jazz clubs on the Leidsedwarsstraat, Hans and Candy Dulfer played the saxophone; and in the United States, Ronald Reagan was still the president, and in Berlin, the wall still stood immobile, we thought then, impenetrable, in place.

The other Van Gogh was in the news that summer, with a celebration being planned for 1990 to mark the hundredth anniversary of (of all things) his death. The man charged with organizing it all—from concerts of specially-commissioned symphonies to the launching of a new Van Gogh perfume—took me to lunch at the Amstel Hotel, the most impressive—and expensive—spot in town. He told me about the Van Gogh project. He told me about his own art collection and invited me to visit his home outside of Amsterdam to see it. He told me that the Dutch had an expression he held dear: *vrijheid, blijheid*. It means, he told me, "freedom is happiness."

I decided I was coming here to live.

* * *

Radical State is, in part, the story of how Holland lost that freedom and that happiness to the terrors of jihad. In tracing the events of the fifteen years from 1989, when fireworks celebrated the life and the achievements of Vincent van Gogh, to 2004, when the artist's great-grand nephew was slaughtered in the street and plans were made to kill the writer of his film, Ayaan Hirsi Ali, amidst the fireworks of New Year's Eve (so the gunshots would not be heard), this book paints a portrait of a thriving democratic nation and the forces that threaten to bring about its demise. It is about a transition in culture from the celebrations of the art of one Van Gogh to the death caused by the art of the other. And in that moment, *vrijheid* ended in the Netherlands: for not only was Theo van Gogh killed for his embrace of the principle of free speech, but in the aftermath of the killing, laws began to change. National IDs became mandatory for the first time since the German occupation. The Parliament debated house arrests for people suspected, but not convicted, of ties to Muslim extremist groups. The integration minister proposed a ban on all languages but Dutch, not only in businesses and schools, but also on the streets. The Arab European League, comprised of political hopefuls aiming to introduce sharia law to the Dutch system, announced plans for candidates to run in the next parliamentary elections—this when radical Islam smolders and flames among Dutch Muslim youth and Muslims are expected to become the majority population in the Netherlands within the next ten to fifteen years. So concerned are Dutch natives now about the radicalization of Muslims here that they have placed support behind any politician willing to crack down on immigrants and Islam, even knowing that such politicians are equally opposed to many of Holland's most proud traditions: welfare, for instance, or subsidies for the arts. So dramatic has the change, in fact, become, that in June, 2005, Filip de Winter, one of Europe's most extreme-right political leaders, declared the Netherlands "the model country for conservatives and the far-right."

And so the question *Radical State* raises—and explores—is in fact a very basic one: Who is really winning here: Democracy—or Jihad?

Why does this matter?

It matters because, according to a Council on Foreign Relations report, Europe hosts some 15–20 million Muslim immigrants and their descendants, and they are radicalizing at an alarming rate. The children of immigrants, born on European soil, are eligible for visa-free travel into the United States—this, while bin Laden, the report states, "has outsourced planning for the next spectacular attack on the United States to an 'external planning' node. Chances are it is based in Europe and will deploy European citizens." Moreover, in the words of Francis Fukuyama, "There is good reason for thinking . . . that a critical source of contemporary radical Islamism lies not in the Middle East, but in Western Europe. . . . Many Europeans assert that the American melting pot cannot be transported to European soil. Identity there remains rooted in blood, soil, and ancient shared memory. This may be true, but if so, democracy in Europe will be in big trouble in the future as Muslims become an ever larger percentage of the population. And since Europe is today one of main battlegrounds of the war on terrorism, this reality will matter for the rest of us as well." [1]

And it matters, too, because Holland is not the only one: America, Canada, England, Germany, and France all wrestle with similar dilemmas, from the creation of the USA Patriot Act to the banning of headscarves in France and the possible official introduction of sharia law in Canada and the United Kingdom. Indeed, some warn that lack of assimilation by Muslims in America—and incidents like the "Virginia Jihad" and Washington sniper cases—may be making the United States vulnerable to its own brand of home-grown Islamic terrorism. It matters because throughout history, Holland has been a bellwether for socio-political change worldwide, from being among the first European countries to accept and integrate the Jews as early as the 17th century to legalizing marijuana, gay marriage, and euthanasia in the 20th. It matters because, in the words of England's former Home Minister, Mike O'Brien, multiculturalism—the social fabric that holds America and most Western societies together—has become, in many ways, "an excuse for moral blindness."

But most of all, it matters because America's war on terrorism is not just America's war, but a world war; and it is not just a war against terrorism; it is a war for freedom. It is not just about spreading what we have to places that don't have it; it's about merely keeping it alive at all.

And it matters for other reasons. It matters because, before it collapsed, Holland's brand of democracy was possibly the most-admired (and certainly the most liberal) of them all. And yet, as the Dutch grow more restrictive in their policies, recruits for Islamic jihad there increase, leaving us with the critical dilemma: if tolerance allowed extremism to rise in the first place, and intolerance is causing it to spread, what is the solution?

Holland is not the only example of the clash between democracy and Islam in the West, but it has been the most dramatic one. As David Rieff wrote when describing Euro-Muslim alienation in the *New York Times Magazine*,[2] the "eclipse" of the "multicultural fantasy in Europe can be seen most poignantly in Holland, that most self-defined liberal of all European countries." By understanding what the country was—in all its strengths and in the weaknesses that made it fall—we can not only keep democracy safe in the West; we can make it better.

Radical State chronicles the nearly two decades of my life in the Netherlands, incorporating people, places, and reflections on events, both personal and public. Dutch history, at times, occasionally also plays a part in order to provide a comprehensive vision of the cultural foundations that led to the current situation. Further, I have occasionally drawn parallels where possible with American culture, noting global highlights of the times to lend a further sense of atmosphere and place.

However, the years since 2001 form the emphasis of the book, focusing on the rising conflict between Western and Muslim cultures. The disclosure of extremist groups, of domestic violence, and even of honor killings in Dutch-Muslim families, has forced powerful changes in the Dutch—and consequently, to some extent, Euro-American—understanding of Islam as it is often practiced within democratic society. And in Holland, perhaps more than in any other Western country, that "clash of civilizations" has reached a point some believe to be insurmountable.

Through narrative, analysis, and portraits, I have tried to elucidate the struggle between those who seek to Islamize Dutch culture, and those who will do whatever necessary—including compromising democracy—to preserve it. Ultimately, *Radical State* champions the idea of a supportive, secularized, Enlightenment ideal as it chronicles the rise and fall of a free democracy in a clarion call to America.

Acknowledgments

My gratitude, above all, to my parents, Rosa and Aaron Esman, for more reasons and in more ways than I can possibly list here; to my husband, Peter Madden, for his endless encouragement and patience throughout the writing of this book; to my "uchti," Nour Al-Khal and Lisa Ramaci, whose determination and courage are my constant inspiration; to W. Thomas Smith Jr., my editor at *World Defense Review*—much of my work for him formed the foundations and the walls on which this book was built; to Ayaan Hirsi Ali, for her trust; to the many who took the time to lend me their ideas and expertise; and to Barbara Divver, for believing.

INTRODUCTION

There are perhaps as many explanations for Dutch tolerance as there are opinions about it. "The Dutch are open," some say, "like our land."

"The Dutch have a history of trade with other lands," say others, "we have always dealt with other cultures, because we're on the sea." (In fact, the so-called *poldermodel*—a socio-economic system based on a program of consensus that was praised especially during the 1990s by world leaders—is said to be based on Holland's relationship to the sea: only through cooperation and compromise was it possible to reclaim the land that became—and still is now becoming—the Netherlands.)

More cynical types declare there is in fact no Dutch tolerance. "It's indifference," they say—a description which might equally find origins in the Dutch landscape: flat. (There are, in fact, few peaks and valleys of any kind in the Netherlands: a socialist economy prevents the kind of disparity in wealth Americans experience, for instance, and even the weather is usually the same, the temperature rarely reaching extremes of either heat or cold.)

All of these are likely true and related to another important factor: The Dutch penchant for *gezelligheid*, a word often translated as "coziness" but for which there is no real English equivalent. In a land where it is often cold and damp, where winter days are extremely short and winter itself unendurably long, the Dutch settle in. More books are read per capita in this country than anywhere else in the world, they say. Evening meals are heavy, comprised of thick pea soup or potatoes mixed with greens and meat. Always thickly-populated, always eager for *gezelschaap* (company)—and *gezelligheid*—the Dutch have little choice but to get along with one another, to make the best of differences, be it by tolerating or by ignoring them.

This is, of course, more true when an entire economy depends on amiable relations—as was the case in the 17th century, Holland's Golden Age, when merchant sailors traveled the globe, mostly to the East Indies, Africa, and Brazil, returning with sugar, tobacco, silks, and spices to trade with the rest of Europe. With a flourishing culture, the city attracted, in turn, immigrants from neighboring European lands, whose presence both instilled and deepened the spirit of "tolerance" across the lowlands. Jews, particularly, found themselves welcomed— or at least, comparatively so: forbidden to join guilds or own shops, Portuguese Jews immigrating to the Netherlands became publishers, physicians, and a primary force in the Dutch diamond trade.

It is not for lack of activity that the century following the Golden Age had little bearing on the formation of Dutch culture, however; if anything, it is for the abundance of it, with wars fought against the Brits, the Spanish, and the French. Strong in business but lousy on the battlefield, Holland found itself tossed like a softball in the schoolyard, alternately taking and capitulating to its various rivals and neighbors: A country that was Spanish on Thursday could be French by Friday and Austrian next month, making it difficult for a cohesive society to establish a true identity.

And so it continued, almost unabated, until Napoleon I annexed the Kingdom of Holland to the French Empire in 1810. When the Empire fell in 1814, Holland regained the independence it had known from 1579, when William I of Orange had freed the country of Spanish rule under Philip I, until 1648. (Some say that American Revolutionaries were inspired by the Dutch 1581 revolution against Spain and the belief, espoused by William of Orange, that a leader could rightfully be deposed.)

Still, it was about another half-century before Holland regained anything near its former glory. Only towards the end of the 19th century, with the flourishing of Dutch Impressionism and the impact of the Industrial Revolution on an agricultural society, did the Dutch return again to the idea of a national identity and principles on which to define their culture. The division of church and state, for instance, provided for in the Constitution of 1848, led to secularized educational systems. New political parties emerged, divided along both political and religious lines, including a worker's party—the Social Democratic Union. This, in turn, forged a greater political liberalism and the beginnings of what would become the economic structure of the current Dutch state and its strong welfare policies.

That kind of idealism colors the modern history of the Netherlands, from its neutrality during World War I to its stubborn hold on the international gold standard—it was the last country to abandon it—to the fascination with American jazz and fashion of the 1920s. When artist Theo van Doesburg founded the De Stijl movement in 1917, the concept of purity (primary colors, geometric forms, painting pared to its essentials) took on a spiritual, utopian quality, particularly through the art and writings of Piet Mondrian and the architecture of Gerrit Rietveld. "Universal harmony" could, these artists believed, be achieved through purity and the arts. That sentiment in many ways has continued to typify the Dutch: simplicity, directness, and a non-theological spirituality and faith in humanity have shaped Dutch policy as much as Dutch popular culture ever since. Even as Holland fell to German hands under the Third Reich, even as 75 percent of its Jewish population was exterminated during the occupation (1940–1945), even as more Jews died per capita in the Netherlands than anywhere else in Europe outside of Germany, some of that hope remained, manifest in such occurrences as the 1944 rail strike—the only public protest held anywhere in Europe against the persecution of the Jews.

Perhaps it was also this combination of optimism and idealism that made Holland so open to the revolutions of the 1960s and the adoption of the Anglo-American rock and fashion scenes. Utopian in its welfare ideals while wracked with guilt over its treatment of the Jews during the war, Dutch society grasped hold of hippie fever with fervor. The Provo movement emerged mid-decade, instituting programs like "white bicycles"—a system whereby free bicycles were placed for public use throughout the city—and advocating large-scale squatting of abandoned buildings, usually by student or artist's groups. The movement had a profound influence on the political sphere of the Netherlands, not only because of its initiatives but because of the number of Provo-influenced young politicians who emerged in the years that followed. Legalization of hash and marijuana sold in so-called coffee shops, the destigmatization of prostitution, the creation of political programs to support the arts, all find their roots in the spirit of the Provos, and in turn, quite possibly, in the embrace of the new, the progressive, and the "universal beauty" of De Stijl before them.

But somewhere in the 1970s, between the socialist ethic of Provo, the Christian stronghold in the Parliament, and the emphasis on racial integration and civil rights that had swept the United States and parts of Europe, something in the weave of Dutch culture went awry, like a dropped stitch in a knitted sweater, an unsecured stone in the foundation of a great cathedral. It should have all gone perfectly, and for a while, it seemed it did. Immigrants from poorer countries were invited to fill in labor shortages, particularly in blue-collar sectors, as a larger number of Dutch youth began attending university and taking on higher-paying, higher-status jobs. Arriving largely from Turkey and

Morocco with no knowledge of Dutch culture, history, or language, these Muslim immigrants were welcomed with the idea that community builds strength. Rather than force them into an unfamiliar world in which they might well feel ostracized, alienated, even lost, the Dutch created separate neighborhoods where they might live together, open stores that offered the kinds of foods to which they were accustomed, and share their language—and experience—with one another. Mosques were built, and neighborhood schools, some of which conducted all their classes in Turkish or Arabic or Moroccan.

The last fifteen years are the focus of *Radical State*, which traces the Netherlands' decline from a utopian, peaceful democracy to a chaotic, fragmented, increasingly repressive and frightened culture, bracketed by my first meeting with Theo van Gogh in New York City during the summer of 1990 and his death in November 2004. It was a time of optimism and stability at the start: while the U.S. financial situation fell apart, Holland's reasoned economy held strong. It was a culture of *"samenwerking"*—collaboration and cooperation—and *"samenwoning"*—living together—a period of innocence and trust so deeply imbedded into daily life that one rode the trams according to an honor system, punching one's own ticket for the appropriate price on boarding, a time when not only did my roommates not lock the front door to their apartment—they kept it open wide. Visits from repairmen—plumbers, say, or electricians—began and ended with a cup of coffee shared over a kitchen table. At a junk shop on the Vijzelstraat, the aging proprietors offered visitors tea served in china cups and an easy chair to sit in.

But by the time of Theo van Gogh's death, all of that had changed. Stimulated in part by an increasing number of violent incidents and attacks on city transit largely perpetrated by Moroccan youth gangs (most of whom also engaged in fare-beating), conductors were hired to supervise the trams. In 1998, police clashed with young Moroccans on two occasions, leading to riots and rock-throwing. Further demonstrations and conflicts followed. On September 11 and 12, 2001, some Muslim communities openly celebrated the attacks of 9/11. And still, in December of that year, I attended a public forum about September 11 and its significance to the Dutch. A panelist, introduced as one of the country's most "renowned" and "respected" reporters, described his response on the afternoon of September 11 as he prepared to write the story. "I realized," he said, "that as terrible as it was, it was really about America. It had nothing to do with me."

Less than six months later, a flamboyant gay politician by the name of Pim Fortuyn ran for Parliament on a single platform: close the borders. Islam is a backwards culture, he argued, and Muslims do not belong in our democratic nation. Fortuyn became a national hero—the more so after he was assassinated (by a non-Muslim) in May 2002. His cause became the national cause: Holland has been tolerant enough.

Hafid Bouazza, a Dutch-Moroccan writer and outspoken critic of Islamic extremism, contends that its roots were already burrowing into Dutch soil as early as the 1980s, with the "Muslim Brothers" who, banned by Egypt's President Nasser, found asylum in Holland during the 1950s. The "Brothers" regrouped in the Netherlands, distributing, by Bouazza's account, audio and video recordings filthy with "aggressive lectures." Muslim girls were not to be sent to school, but kept locked in their homes and veiled. By mid-decade, the Muslim Brotherhood had begun encouraging its members to leave their jobs—if possible, to be fired, though in the Dutch system, this is in fact difficult to do—"for no Muslim may work for an unbeliever." Instead, Muslims should spend as much time as possible in the Mosque, reports Bouazza in the Dutch national daily, the *NRC Handelsblad*.[1] It was, says Bouazza, the "famous 'back pain period,'" when numerous first-generation Moroccans received disability payments from the state while, in many cases, plotting to destroy the very state that supported them.

By the late 1990s, Saudi Arabia was funding mosques in the Netherlands, along with several of its schools. (Bouazza counted ten of the country's 32 Islamic schools that were Saudi-subsidized, where extremist propaganda circulated among the students.)

"How naïve can the Netherlands be?" wrote Bouazza in 2002, when the Saudi connection was uncovered. "There is a point where naïveté becomes stupidity, and I fear that Holland is getting dangerously close."

Was the Netherlands naïve—even stupid? Theo van Gogh refused government protection in the face of death threats because, he said, "I'm the village idiot. No one is going to kill the village idiot." But they did, and suddenly all of Holland was a village full of idiots, trying to separate idealism from practicality, racism from reality, with some clinging to the libertarian foundations of their culture and others ready to jettison them all and start anew.

Because only through this can the question "What went wrong?"— the very question *Poldergeist* is written to address—be answered. And answering that question is crucial; because to set things right again requires understanding how it all broke apart. And we must set it right, or jihad's victory over democracy will be complete, and sooner than we may realize.

And one has to ask: If Holland has been this naïve, this stupid, even, then in the United States—the country that was first and most horrifically attacked—have we?

CHAPTER 1

I put the woman I am talking to on hold to take another call.

"Theo is dead."

It is my friend and neighbor Fré who lives just two floors down.

"What?"

"Theo is dood. Vermoord." Theo is dead. Murdered.

"Van Gogh," she adds, to make sure I understand. "Someone just now killed Theo van Gogh in Amsterdam."

I tell her I will be right there and end my other call.

Downstairs, we watch the news reports come in over her TV, describing an incident that has taken place just moments past, and just a few short streets from where we live, where we are standing now. Her eyes fill.

"In *Nederland*," she says, her voice husky in its disbelief: In the Netherlands. I put my arm around her, knowing. "You wonder where your country is now," I tell her, and she nods in recognition.

"This is your 9/11."

I know. I live in Amsterdam, but I am a born and bred New Yorker and I was there, in uptown Manhattan, on that clear, earthshaking September day. Upstairs, my own TV is turned to CNN, where I expect to hear the ongoing coverage of the U.S. presidential vote: It is November 2, 2004, and my country's future, too, lies in the balance.

The news pours in: gunshots, stabbings, Moroccan immigrant—no, the son of Moroccan immigrants, Dutch-born. Theo, heard by witnesses, hordes of them on the street as the killing went on at the height of morning rush hour, 8:43 A.M., in fact—the moment the first plane had hit the World Trade Center tower three years earlier. "Don't do it!" he had cried out, running from the bullets, from the calm and unaffected man continuing to approach him, undeterred. "Don't do it! We can talk!"

But Theo's killer didn't want to talk. Everything he had to say, he'd already put in writing in a five-page letter, a manuscript penned in venom and in hate, wrought with threats and indignations, and warnings of what was yet to come; and when Theo collapsed, at last, falling face-up on the sidewalk, his attacker drew a kukri knife and, in a failed effort to behead him, sliced his throat. Then he stabbed the letter into Van Gogh's corpse, as if pinning a "For Sale" sign on a wall, and calmly walked away.

Just like that.

* * *

I remember the night I first met Theo. It was in New York City, 1989. I was 29, he, 32. The Dutch government owned a loft in Tribeca that it handed out to artists for two-week intervals as a kind of fellowship. Theo made films—some said gruesome, anti-Semitic films, or in any case, controversial—and was living there then, which was where my friend Stephen took me to meet him. I remember wall-length windows, wooden floors, and a view across the water. Then we all went out to dinner.

I remember Theo then already was what the Dutch call *slordig*—sloppy, messy, rumpled, his T-shirt wrinkled and too small for his oversized belly, his face unshaven, his hair—blond and curled—uncombed. I remember thinking he had the face that you imagine when you hear a man is Dutch: round and peasantlike, innocent, even, with ruddy cheeks and wide blue eyes and a bit too small a mouth. I remember staring at his hands and thinking the entire evening: Those are the hands of the hands.

Theo's great-great uncle was the painter.

I could not get enough of looking at those hands.

When Theo died, his hands, his mother later said, were positioned by his face, "like a baby." Later, she told a newspaper reporter, "I only hoped he wasn't cold."[1]

* * *

Fré and I absorb the details of the murder as they arrive on radio and TV reports, in phone calls we field from friends, and updates that come by e-mail from the papers. Immediately, my thoughts go to my friend Ayaan Hirsi Ali, a Somali refugee now in the Dutch parliament who wrote the screenplay for *Submission*, the film that was, we all know from the start, the reason Theo van Gogh was killed. Theo had directed the film, an 11-minute drama emphasizing the abuse of Muslim women and the violence against them prescribed in the Koran. Where is she? Is she safe? She is already under guard, a response to death threats she began receiving in the fall of 2002. (This, we will learn later, is in fact why the killer went for Theo: Ayaan was out of reach.)

"I can hear him," I tell Fré as we stand in shock together. Van Gogh's falsetto voice is famous in the Netherlands.

How can it be silent now?

Someone else performs the math: this day, November 2, 2004, marks exactly 911 days since Holland's last political murder, the slaying of right-wing populist politician Pim Fortuyn on May 6, 2002.

"My God," I say, and the words rise from deep within my throat. "To have planned it all so carefully, so systematically, a math problem, a calculation, like at school. Like homework."

* * *

This is our Holland. But there is another, parallel Holland, where the response plays out quite differently. From the moment the first news releases interrupt regular programming on TV, messages fly on online bulletin boards for the Dutch Moroccan (and Muslim) community. At www.moroc.nl, "Berber 21" giggles, "Terrific! A great day—let's party! My treat."

"Dorian" is less certain. "Is the pig really dead," he asks, "or is this a bad joke?"

"Whoever did this," posts someone with the screen name "Grendel," "Thanks."

Eventually Dorian is convinced the "pig" is really, truly dead. "And so," he writes with triumph, "will the Zionists and their servants come to their bloody end."

In our Holland, the one I live in, have lived in since the fall of 1990, the one where we are not, now, celebrating, it takes little time to get the word out: Van Gogh's colleagues will hold a demonstration at the Palace on the Dam tonight at 7:30. It is not to be a quiet wake, as is the custom, but a loud one: Van Gogh stood for free speech, his friends declare, and so tonight, Holland must make noise. The news spreads through the Internet to millions of Dutch homes and families throughout the country: Be there.

"I'm going," Fré tells me resolutely.

"I'm not," I say. There is too much anger. I am certain riots will erupt: angry Dutch, angry Muslims, battles on the streets of Amsterdam. I'll have a better view of it on TV, anyway.

It is testimony to the power of the Internet that only hours after the idea is first conceived, 20,000 Hollanders stand, determined, at the plaza behind the Palace, the World War II memorial rising, stark and white, amongst the huddled families, the tearful faces and the angry ones, children as young as two years old, adults as old as 90. From the podium, Van Gogh's colleague Lennart Booij speaks to all of Holland: "Theo would not want silence. Theo would want people to be heard. Amsterdam: *make noise!*"

And they do: 40,000 stomping feet, 40,000 clapping hands, 20,000 voices. Pots and pans and spoons and bongo drums all bang in unison and cacophony. Someone lights firecrackers. Engineers of trains entering and leaving the city from all directions sound their horns.

And then the politicians speak: Job Cohen, the city mayor; Rita Verdonk, Minister of Immigration and Integration. Cohen is icy. "He had his opinions," he says. "He also had his opinions about me. This is permitted in the Netherlands."

Verdonk is not so philosophical.

"We know two things," she says, her expression cracking with its fury. "Theo van Gogh was murdered this morning. And the man who did it is Moroccan."

Rita Verdonk does not like Moroccans. The Minister of Immigration and Integration confronts a country where the integration of nearly a million Muslim immigrants—particularly Moroccans—has failed.

"To here," Minister Verdonk spits into the crowd, "And no further."

Amsterdam applauds.

At any other time, such words would sound menacing. Not now. On this lost and shocked and fury-filled night, we welcome them. The limits of tolerance have been reached. And we are angry.

We are angry because Theo van Gogh, for all his insults and his name-calling ("goatfuckers," he called the Muslims of the Netherlands; he'd made equally nasty statements about the Christians and the Jews), was innocent, really, of any harm. His tongue was acid and his pen, when he wrote, acerbic, but he himself was a gentle man, the father of a now fatherless 13-year-old boy, a man who hated hate and loved women and art and, above all, freedom. (For this reason, he also loved the United States, and planned to move there when his son, Lieuwe, was older.) He spoke against the Muslim boys in Muslim-only ghettos and then hired them as actors, sending them off with the promise of a future no one else would give them.

We are angry. We are angry at the utter brutality of knifing a man, of shooting him, and knifing him again, and then before departing, taking the time to slit his throat.

We are angry with a fury that has been gathering for years, and our helplessness in the face of a murder it is now too late to stop: not just of a 47-year-old filmmaker, but of a centuries-old culture that for so long led the world in democracy and freedom, and has ended, just this morning, silenced and red and bleeding on the streets of Amsterdam.

And still, on the morning of November 3, a photograph stretched across the front page of national daily *Trouw* revealed a crowd of tearful faces, and hands all raised in unison forming the letter V, for peace.

* * *

Nonetheless, the days, the weeks, in truth, the years after Van Gogh's slaying were—and remain—times not just of anger but of blame and finger-pointing. It was Theo's own fault, most Muslims insisted, for saying things he never should have said, for producing a film like *Submission*, in which the words of the Koran appeared on the bodies of naked women. It was Hirsi Ali's fault, said others of the film's creator: she knew what she was getting him into, but didn't care. The Left blamed the Right—they antagonized the Muslim population. The Right blamed the Left—they had so catered to the Muslims that the Muslims of Holland had never had to learn or adapt to Western norms of tolerance and freedom. Journalists blamed the secret service—the AIVD (Algemene Inlichting En Veiligheids Dienst)—who (it turned out) knew an attack on Theo van Gogh was imminent, and still allowed him to fire his state-provided bodyguards without advising him of the severity of the risk. ("I'm the village idiot," Van Gogh would say. "Who would kill the village idiot?") The public blamed the journalists for creating a hype about the so-called "Muslim problem" in the first place.

Mostly, everyone blamed the Muslims.

And the Muslims blamed them back.

Eight hundred acts of racial violence took place in the three weeks following the murder of Theo van Gogh, including attacks on 104 mosques, 37 churches, and 25 schools—16 Muslim, nine Christian. As early as November 6, the newspaper *Volkskrant* led its front page with the words, "Murder Begins Holy War in The Netherlands," and an article by reporter Janny Groen, "Jihad Fighters Under Our Very Eyes," noted, "Mohammed B. [as he was called in the Dutch press] is not alone. The jihadists have been among us for a while; they are recruited and trained before our very eyes." Were these exaggerations, hysterical responses from a society taken by surprise? Or had Holland finally awakened to a truth it had, despite the insistent ringing of numerous alarms, ignored, longing to hold, instead, to the comfort of what was, in fact, a dream?

They had closed their eyes to too much, the Dutch: the honor killings of Muslim women that they wrote off for decades as accidents or suicides; the distribution of books like *How to Be a Good Muslim* at mosques and community centers and even schools, which call for homosexuals to be thrown off the tops of buildings and then stoned (lest they survive the fall); the abused, lost, neglected children, who, as Ayaan once noted, "everyone ignores until they start acting out, stealing from the local grocer or getting into fights—and by then, it's far too late."

"The World Trade Center," I wrote in my notes at the time, "was the socket of America's eye. Theo van Gogh was Holland's cheek. And Holland will not, does not, turn the other one."

* * *

Mohammed Bouyeri, we soon learn, did not act entirely alone: he was one of a group of radical Muslims known as the Hofstadgroep, which is usually translated as "The Capital Group" but which I've always rather associated with the CNN talk show, *The Capital Gang*. His letter, knifed to Van Gogh's heart, had spelled out everything the Hofstadgroep essentially stood for, though he wrote it speaking only for himself:

I surely know that you, O America, will be destroyed
I surely know that you, O Europe, will be destroyed
I surely know that you, O Holland, will be destroyed

At Van Gogh's cremation on November 8, his friends offer a letter in response. ("When someone writes a letter to you," says Van Gogh's friend, writer Theodore Holman, "the proper thing is always to write back.") They ask him how his leg is doing, as he heals from the gunshots fired by police—gunshots he had hoped would kill him, provide him martyrdom and a paradise of virgins, but—in a great twist of karma and divine justice, did not. "Hang in there," the letter reads. "You'll be needing your sense of humor now."

So, too, would the rest of us.

CHAPTER 2

Though you're not likely to see it stated in the guidebooks, there is perhaps nowhere quite so Dutch in all of Holland as Amsterdam's Westerkerk. Lording over the Prinsengracht, its tower marking the highest point in the city center—and so, casting the longest reflection in the canal waters—the church bears the crown of Austria's Emperor Maximilian—a gift from the ruler to the city in 1478, and the origin of the triple-X insignia that has become the hallmark of Amsterdam. Rembrandt lies buried here, though no one knows precisely where, as does Titus, his son. Footsteps away is the house where Anne Frank and her family hid from Nazi troops, and at its base stands the Homomonument, originally built to commemorate the homosexuals who suffered, too, under the Nazi regime, though now it is considered a monument to gays worldwide who have suffered the effects of homophobia and AIDS. And at its altar, both the wealthy and the poor have prayed, together.

But it's the crown most people notice, and no wonder—canary yellow, crimson red, and cobalt blue, the color of the Dutch pottery known as Delftware, or *Delfts blau*—Delft blue. That these then became the colors associated with Piet Mondrian's De Stijl and, consequently, with characteristic Dutch design, is hard to miss, whether accidental or (unconsciously) deliberate, whether meaningful or not.

And it's the bells, the Westerkerk bells, bells that ring across the city on the half hour, every hour, and if you should happen to live in the neighborhood, as I did from 1990 to 1992, you realize that the melody is not always the same; at some unannounced moment every now and

again, the carillon that has echoed across the carved gables of the
Jordaan 48 times a day for months will disappear, replaced by different
rhythms, different baritones. It is a big event, this changing of the bells;
in the counting of time passing, one is reminded: time is passing.

My first apartment stood within the shadow of the Westerkerk. "It is
the Dutch Quartier Latin," is how a friend had previously described
the area known as the Jordaan, though my orientation placed it more
along the lines of New York City's SoHo, thick with chic bohemian
boutiques and young designers, and with people riding home from the
bars by bicycle at night, whistling things like Fur Elise or Chopin
mazurkas in between the ringing of the bells.

I visited the Anne Frank Huis once, with my parents and my sisters
in the summer of 1965. I've not been back: there's been no need. I
remember it too well. These are the two things I remember best: a yel-
lowing photograph tacked up to a wall (my mind's eye sees a photograph of Anne herself, but it might as well have, in fact, been anyone)
and the growth chart by the kitchen door. I had never seen or heard of
a growth chart before. My father patiently explained the way it
worked, how Anne and her sister would stand against the wall and
their mother draw a line at the height at which they stood. I want a
growth chart, too, I said, when we go home to New York; but I never
got one, and I realize now it's just as well, or I would have confused
myself with Anne. We have shared enough of the same memories as
it is.

Anne Frank wrote about the Westerkerk in her now-immortal diary,
"Daddy, Mummy, and Margot can't get used to the Westertoren clock
yet, which tells us the time every quarter of an hour. I can. I loved it
from the start, and especially in the night it's like a faithful friend."

The same clock that marked the hours of her last days in Amsterdam
marked, too, the first of mine.

* * *

A funny thing happens to expats on the way across the Atlantic: they
become more of wherever it is they're from. In the summer of 1990,
just before I made my final and official move and was living with my
friend Karin on the Stadhouderskade (the Heineken brewery was just
across the street), I held a Fourth of July party. There were two
Americans; everyone else who came—and there were well over 50 of
us—was Dutch. We hung up posters of American flags and a copy of a
Jasper Johns version we found in one of Karin's books. We served hot
dogs out of jars (it was the only way to get them), fried chicken a
Dutch farm girl cooked up in our kitchen, and hamburgers and potato
salad. We toasted the United States and played old Motown tunes.

I went to bed at three A.M., and when I woke again at eight, some guests still remained gathered at the kitchen table, talking. "God bless America," someone said, and toasted me with his tea.

Thanksgiving brought the next occasion, by which time I was already living in the Jordaan. I invited two Americans I knew and the two men who ran a contemporary art gallery I often hung out in on the Binnenkant. One could not buy turkey, not even ordering it from the poulier on the Rozengracht several days ahead. I roasted a chicken and found Ocean Spray cranberries in a corner of the freezer at a health food store and baked an apple brown betty for dessert, and we all sat around the table and drank too much wine with dinner and Courvoisier when it was over and were thoroughly, blissfully, *gezellig.* It was years before I learned one didn't do such things in Holland— invite people to your home for dinner. That was something only foreigners did, or people who had lived abroad. One invited people individually, usually, for coffee and *gebak*—baked goods—like little pink frosted cakes, or waffle cones filled with whipped cream shaped like a tornado. It was another thing that marked us as both exotic and as outsiders, as curiosities of a sort. In the years that a Mexican-American photojournalist friend lived here, she threw such parties nearly every week. Her guests hailed from Brazil as often as from Bulgaria, from the former East Berlin, from Tokyo, from Texas, from New York. They were pot-luck events for which she inevitably made a Caesar salad and a bowl of guacamole, and there was never a Dutch morsel in the lot. "She's crazy," people said about Diana, shaking their heads at the chaos and disorder of it all.

Everyone always had a wonderful time.

* * *

But there are moments in the Netherlands when conviviality reigns, and voices call out festively from balconies and streets. As a Dutch artist friend said to me on one of my early visits here, "The minute the sun comes out, the Dutch think they're on the Riviera." Couches are hauled out to the sidewalk from first- and ground-floor living rooms, or card tables and chairs, and on warmer evenings, full sets of silverware and dishes. I have, on occasion, walked along the Brouwersgracht to find it transformed into an outdoor dining hall, with another table at every doorstep. I study a photograph Diana once took of boats on the canals—teams of them, and on each, a gathering of friends. Look closely, though, and you notice everyone is wearing overcoats. But the sun shines over the city, and that is all that matters.

If one doesn't have a boat in Amsterdam, one has at least one friend who does, and mine were a couple I'd met through an artist in

New York City—Gijs, a wealthy art collector, and his stunning, younger wife, Jacky, an art historian whose dissertation about medieval manuscript illumination she somehow never did complete. Their apartment on the Keizersgracht encircled an enormous private garden, with a living room at its base and a glass-enclosed master suite—with Jacuzzi—at its top. Their boat had been a fire department vessel in the 1930s, large enough to carry six of us quite comfortably with a cooler full of wine.

In the summer of 1991, the big debate in Amsterdam circulated around the Café de Jaren, a new, designer café popular with twenty-somethings, the terrace of which extended out onto the river Amstel, causing uproar among conservationists and others who were less than keen about having a big, post-modernist, commercial *thing* at the center of one of the city's most gracious corners. We drove the boat along its banks, admiring the sun refracting off the windows, and wondering what the fuss was really all about. "These are people," said Gijs, "with nothing at all to do all day but count their pension. There are uglier buildings all over Amsterdam."

"It's a landmark location," his wife countered, "People want it left unspoiled."

Students in large groups crowded the café tables, some having already had too much to drink, others racing to catch up. Most waved. We waved back.

"You'd think," someone said, "they'd have taken this up before the thing was built."

Yesses all around.

Who would pay the cost of its removal, Jacky wondered. The café? The city? Those who'd started the motion against it in the first place? We sputtered past, Gijs, dark-eyed and tan and holding a glass of Beaujolais in one hand, steering the boat around the bend and out onto the river, then turning west toward the Red Light District, which, he assured us, is "extraordinary" from the water.

Whores in windows, Amsterdam accepted with contentment. Cafés on the Amstel were something altogether else. Hence a referendum had been called—at what cost, I do not know—to determine the fate of Café de Jaren.

"People have to understand," said Jacky the art historian, who was clearly not taking sides in this debate, "that what they decide about de Jaren, they decide about the future architecture of this city. And if they call a referendum over architects, what next? Will the entire country vote on every museum acquisition?" For my part, though I didn't say so, secretly I was thrilled by the whole thing: A referendum! To ask the people what they think about a café! To choose so democratically! What glory this country was.

We will have aesthetics by majority rule, somebody suggested.

But the truth was it wasn't very likely. At a time when the postal service ran a department of aesthetics whose role it was to commission artists for the design of phone booths and postage stamps—true, all ratified by consensus, but with an eye toward stimulating, not repressing, experimentation in design—consensual art was not exactly looming on the horizon.

We steered the boat along the Prinsengracht, into the shadow of the Westerkerk, and kept on.

* * *

If a referendum to decide the fate of a café seemed to me progressive, other aspects of life in the Netherlands at the time were not. What they were, however, were equally basic, honest, filled with common sense. In those days, you could not buy furniture cleaner in spray bottles: you used soap and water and a bucket and a sponge. Toilet paper was gray and harsh, and there was no such thing as "instant rice." Broccoli was something exotic, peculiar, new. You bought pantry goods at the supermarket, like coffee, tea, and mayonnaise, and cheese at the cheese store and bread at the baker and fruit at the fruit market. When you did buy produce from the grocer, you weighed it out on scales that issued a sticker with the price long before you reached the checkout line. I mention this because it implied a trust, an honor system in which one would never even think to weigh three apples in a bag, price it, and then add another one "for the road."

No one uses this system anymore.

It is important to understand all this: here was a country planted firmly in the West, the paragon of democracy and model for the modern world. And yet, it was in so many ways riveted to the past, skittish about progress, innovation, change.

When a friend in the United States investigated the possibility of introducing a new, less-costly way to ship flowers to and from the Dutch flower auctions—the center of the world floral market—another friend in Holland cautioned me that he'd have trouble finding takers. "Generally speaking," my Dutch friend said, "people take things like this skeptically. They assume that if it's not being done already, there's a reason—and if it were a good idea, someone would have thought of it already." Even Ab (Albert) Heijn, heir to the Albert Heijn grocery chain and director of its international holding company, Royal Ahold— a firm with assets in the $25 billion range—told an interviewer in 2007, "I am no fan of big steps." And echoing a popular expression in the Netherlands, he added, "*Doe maar gewoon, dan doe je al gek genoeg*": Be normal; that's acting crazy enough. Even the Dutch government resisted advances in technology and culture: it took the privatization of the telecommunications system in 1989 and deregulation of the industry in the late 1990s[1] to get call-waiting introduced—a technology long in place in the United States. Holland's leaders had rejected it: they feared (and rightly so) that it would speed things up too much, increase the pace of daily life.

And even television felt antiquated then: With only three TV channels, the Dutch often tuned in to Belgian stations and the BBC—and on occasion, to the newly-invented CNN. We watched *Dallas* reruns and *The Golden Girls*, and last year's season of *Oprah*, which aired twice a day in Holland and in Belgium every night. We watched a popular Australian soap opera titled *Neighbors*, two-year-old episodes of *The Bold and the Beautiful*, and a Dutch show called *Good Times, Bad Times* with some of the worst acting I have ever seen.

It was all so *gezellig*.

* * *

Amsterdam is a young city, being a college town and a haven for young tourists from abroad intrigued by the so-called "coffeeshops" where it is legal to buy—and smoke—hash and marijuana. In the 1990s, while "yuppies" took the front seats in the U.S., generous government subsidies for students and for artists kept Holland in the throes of a hippie culture, where more books were read per capita than anywhere else in the world, and artists squatted houses throughout the city while the government, for the most part, looked away.

The apartment I lived in then was a sublet, found through a family friend, facing a canal with balconies both front and back. It was an idyllic first apartment for an American in Amsterdam; and in truth, I was lucky to have found anywhere to live at all. ("Don't worry about work," friends told me when I announced my plans to move there. "Find a place to live.") Housing in Amsterdam was—and remains—competitive and scarce, most of it incorporated into what was then a government system through which—unlike such arrangements in the rest of the world—low-cost housing was available to those of all income brackets. It was therefore possible to earn the equivalent of $50,000 a year and pay $100 a month for an apartment, while next door, someone earning $25,000 might pay as much as $500 for a home virtually indistinguishable from the first. In addition, the government regulated rents outside the housing system, and laws almost uniformly favored tenants, not landlords: evicting tenants was, for the most part, virtually impossible. (In fact, though I didn't know it at the time, I could have taken over the apartment simply by dint of the fact that I had lived there. I had only to refuse to leave: finders, keepers.)

In a country already overcrowded—Holland boasts more people per square meter than any other country in the world[2]—housing shortages inevitably resulted, especially in the more desirable areas—like Amsterdam's center, or "Centrum." Waiting lists for subsidized housing in my neighborhood stretched to more than five years. Consequently, despite the country's growing Muslim population, most residents of Amsterdam's Jordaan were native Dutch.

Exacerbating the situation, the intricacies of a complicated housing system even now gives priority to those who have already lived for a period of time in social housing (as any houses not on the free market are called) seeking to relocate. A woman who has lived alone for 10 years in a social housing flat and then marries, for instance, may apply for a larger apartment. Those who have lived in social housing for longer than 10 years and who are also seeking more space will be offered the better apartments first, leaving her the lesser choices—and so, most likely, a continued wait.

Consequently, while social housing was indeed available in the best neighborhoods, such homes largely were reserved only for the Dutch; immigrants, unless they could afford open market rates, were forced to settle in outlying areas and less attractive portions of the city. And there they stayed.

There were also other reasons for this. When the first immigrants arrived in the 1960s from Turkey and Morocco, they were not expected to remain: they came as guest workers, and as such, were provided basic accommodations to suit their needs.

But they did stay. And over the years, halal food shops opened selling imported foods from their homelands and homemade baklava, dolmas, and bread; boutiques sold headscarves and long dresses appropriate for Muslim women. By the time a Muslim family was likely to be registered for social housing and to be eligible for an apartment in an area like the Jordaan, moving would seem almost like relocating to another city—even another land: in a kind of vicious circle, few Muslims in the Centrum meant little need for Islamic shops, and the lack of such shops made the area unappealing to Muslim immigrants. Moreover, commercial rents were high in Amsterdam's center. The Jordaan hosts mostly restaurants, cafés, and chic design boutiques. From the houseboats along the banks of its canals to the tobacco-stained brown bars that faced them, Amsterdam had, in any number of ways, little changed since the days when Rembrandt and the philosopher Baruch Spinoza walked its streets.

This began to change when I arrived in 1990.

In 1989, a number of revisions in economic policy aimed at relieving a growing national debt had begun a privatization of the housing sector, along with cutbacks in rent subsidies provided to families unable

to afford even government housing prices. As better housing com-
manded higher rents (as much as 10,000 guilders per month or more
on the so-called Golden Bend of the canal belt, or about $5,000 at the
time), people who could do so began buying homes. The result? More
stratification. In the nearly two years I lived in the Jordaan, I did not
meet a single Muslim, and in fact, only encountered the occasional
Moroccan or Egyptian man outside the newly built Fatih mosque on
the Rozengracht. Rather, in my apartment on the Egelantiersgracht, I
lived among artists and families with small blond children. (Though,
granted, family reunification programs and high birthrates further
made the small apartments of Amsterdam's center unsuitable to Muslim immigrant families, anyway: there simply was almost nothing large
enough to house them.)

This, however, would change in the later part of the decade, as a
result in large part of the tremendous growth in the Muslim population
nationwide—from just over 400,000 in 1990 to 800,000 by 2000, reaching
nearly 6 percent of the population by 2004.[3] And with that migration,
tensions would mount accordingly.

But in 1990, things had not yet come that far.

* * *

What did begin to change as early as the fall of 1990—before the
Gulf War, before CNN had brought the images of life under Saddam
Hussein into our living rooms—was the coming of the mosques.

Though an estimated 300 mosques already served the Muslim population in major Dutch cities, most were too small, or were ad hoc praying rooms set up in schools, offices, even churches. Plans to replace
them with new buildings spun through parliamentary proceedings and
city planning groups, who must account for the traffic caused by the
arrival, every Friday afternoon, of hundreds of Muslims into the areas.
Sites had to be designated and buildings designed to allow the faithful
to face toward Mecca—a feat not always feasible in the makeshift
spaces. In a 1991 article in the *NRC Handelsblad*,[4] art critic Bianca Stigter
cited plans for five new, large mosques in Rotterdam, aimed at replacing the 30 small ones scattered in abandoned buildings and shops
throughout the city. One of these would later become the center of long
political battles: the Moroccan Essalam Mosque, designed to be one of
the largest in all of Europe—much to the horror of the native Dutch,
who found it inappropriate that the largest religious building in the
country would be Islamic, not Christian. Not only that, but with 50-
meter-high minarets, the building would be the tallest in the city, domi-
nating a town with a strong international reputation for its architecture
and its status as "the port of Europe."

What the new mosques pointed to, of course, was the growth and establishment of the Muslim community, its official participation in the life of the Netherlands, and its increasingly apparent permanence. It is one thing to have Muslim immigrants renting apartments in the next neighborhood. It is something else again entirely when they start building new—and costly—houses of worship down the street. What would that mean for Christians? How big a role would Islam have—not just Muslims, but the religion itself—in Dutch life? Would we soon be hearing prayer calls at dawn?

Only a few steps separated the Fatih mosque on the Rozengracht from the crown of the Westerkerk and the ringing of its bells. The truth was, it wasn't just the fact that the cityscape would look different. Something about it was starting to *feel* different, too.

* * *

It was a ritual as common to Amsterdammers as stealing hotel ashtrays, or buying "Louis Vuitton" pocketbooks in New York City's Chinatown: the buying, stealing, and repurchasing of bikes. Bicycles remain the preferred form of transportation for the Dutch: city streets include bicycle lanes, and sidewalks are often crowded by stalls in which to park them. The bicycles themselves one bought used on Dam Square for 10 guilders each: it was the lock you spent your money on, though even the most expensive was rarely good enough. Inevitably, the evening would come that you left a restaurant having had a bit too much to drink, giddy from the company of friends, only to have your joy shattered by the realization that your bicycle was no longer there. Sometimes the chain would still remain, loosely waving, its links brushing against the metal pole to which you'd locked it, sounding lost and empty across the blackness of the canals.

But within a day or two, you'd head over to the Dam again, where a junky, usually a foreigner from England or from France, would offer you another. And so the cycle of the bicycle in Amsterdam continued.

To Dutch officials, bicycle theft constituted part of Holland's criminal activity. Statistical reports came prefaced with cautions about the rising crime rates in the cities, in which bicycle theft—and the stealing of radios from cars—prevailed. Methadone and needle exchange programs in Holland kept the rate for break-ins, violent crime, and major household theft reasonably in check. And while in New York City the murder rate for 1990 reached an all-time high of about 2,260, or 25 per hundred thousand, in the Netherlands entire the official murder count per hundred thousand people that year—also a historic high—came in at 1.2.[5]

But in the neighborhoods outside the center, this, too, began to change.

In 1988, a report on criminality among Moroccan youth in Amsterdam leaked to the press and was reproduced in its entirely in the daily broadsheet *Het Parool*. Crime rates had been rising throughout the 1980s all over Europe; now the Dutch had somebody to blame—and not without reason. Thirty-two thousand Moroccans lived in the city in 1989, 3,500 of them between the ages of 13 and 25. By 1989, newer press reports noted that 33 percent of those youth had had contact with the police.[6] Any unspoken resentments, the frustrations of those Dutch families who had seen their neighborhoods change with the coming of Muslim immigrants—those in the Pijp, or in Amsterdam Oost, the Eastern section of the city, and in the outlying, mostly working class areas—could now be said aloud. It was in the newspapers, after all. There had been research.

The Netherlands often boasts of its "openness" to foreigners, the arrival of Portuguese Jews in the late 16th century being a particularly popular example. But the country has never had to absorb an immigrant population quite as large—and as different—as this one. They had known the Jews were staying, and planned for it. The gradual rootings of the Muslims into their society, by contrast, took them by surprise. Moreover, the Portuguese Jews had been relatively financially independent, becoming moneylenders, merchants, patrons of the arts. Muslims, however, have lived largely on the generosity of the Dutch welfare system. Most of the women who arrive here do not speak the language and are barred from taking jobs by their religiously conservative husbands—even if they wanted to. And how does one form neighborly relations with neighbors with whom one cannot converse? And then there were the children who immigrated here, children who fell behind in school (and still do), deterred by social and language barriers, and lacking the support of parents who could guide them either through daily life in Western Europe, or the homework that they struggled with each night. Many dropped out. That they became involved in drugs (particularly through the active hash trade with Morocco) and crime should have been entirely predictable.

And yet, somehow, it wasn't.

For various reasons, too, the problem centered around the Moroccan population in particular. Handfuls of researchers have proposed reasons for the fact that, by and large, Turkish immigrants to the Netherlands have assimilated better than their Moroccan counterparts (though this trend may be reversing). But what few have ever been willing to acknowledge are the fundamental differences in the cultural norms of their respective homelands—and not just those between their homelands and the West—differences that go beyond religion-based oppression of women, persecution of homosexuals, barbaric doctrines of sharia law that call for such things as the death by stoning of women suspected of adultery, or chopping off the hands of thieves. A friend of mine at the time worked as a criminal attorney, and he had studied

Dutch Moroccan criminality at university. Once, as we drove together to visit a mutual friend in Arnhem, he explained to me his findings: Moroccans, he said, come from a more heated, violent culture than ours.

"If you are in a movie line," he suggested, "and someone cuts in front of you, what do you do? You might ignore him. Or you maybe tap him on the shoulder and say something like, 'excuse me, the line actually goes to there' and point to the end of the line. And probably he will say 'oh, sorry,' but okay, let's say he doesn't. Let's say he says, 'yeah, and?'

Well, you might say something sharper to him. And then he would say something and you would say something.

But with a Moroccan, in their culture, if someone steps in front of you in line, you push him. And then he turns around and pushes you. And then a fight starts.

But we haven't been prepared for that," he said, "and we also haven't taught them that it doesn't work that way here."

These words have stayed with me all these years. And yet I've never once heard anyone else express a similar observation.

I have always wondered why.

* * *

In January 1991, I returned to New York City to visit family and friends. On the night of the 16th, my friend Robert, an art critic and Moroccan Jew who had come as a small boy with his family to the United States, invited me to a press preview of a new Japanese film, attended by minor celebrities like Mathilde Cuomo, wife of the then-Governor of New York. Just before the film was about to start, a man appeared at center stage.

"For those who have not heard," he announced, "we want to inform you that hostilities have begun in the Persian Gulf."

Robert gasped. We sat together, clutching one another, silent. The film was about Samurai warfare. No one could bear to watch it.

Afterwards, we walked on Second Avenue, feeling the chill of a damp and frightened night. Police blockaded the UN, with ambulances at the ready. The homeless lay on the rain-soaked sidewalk, blankets pulled up over their heads, searching in the dark for sleep. On 42nd Street, peace demonstrators had already begun: one man tossed a garbage bag into the street, another returned it to the sidewalk, and one called out to us, "it's your conscience." On the subway, men sat with grim faces and with furrowed brows. No one spoke a single word.

Days later, I returned again to Amsterdam, noting in my journal as I waited for departure from JFK: "Security is high; guards check passports regularly at doorways. Another checks passport photos against faces at the boarding gate. A salesgirl at the Duty Free tells me a bomb was found earlier at Pan Am.

It's a different world, now."

The canals all froze that winter, and we walked on them, as far as to the Rembrandtplein, and back again.

CHAPTER 3

Nineteen ninety-one was all about Rembrandt. Vincent van Gogh perfumes and coffee mugs vanished from the stores, replaced quickly with dish towels bearing Rembrandt self-portraits, books about the Old Master's life, and pencils emblazoned with his signature. The Rembrandt Research Project (RRP), the official body responsible for authenticating the painter's oeuvre, released an updated volume of its findings, which were in turn hotly contested by American Rembrandt scholar Gary Schwartz, who argued that even from a mathematical perspective, the RRP's findings made no sense. For Schwartz, who has lived in Holland since the 1960s, the project's conclusions suggested that Rembrandt had produced very few works in his lifetime, when in fact he was known to have been quite prolific. Even had he painted slowly, given the duration of his life, Schwartz argued, the RRP conclusions would mean that some 600 Rembrandt paintings had never been discovered.[1] Where were they? And this wasn't even to mention the flaws he found in the researchers' scholarly analyses of the works.

One expert after another argued the issue in the newspapers, in public symposia, and on TV. All of it brought hordes of visitors—Dutch and foreign—streaming into the Rijksmuseum, Holland's national museum of art, where two major exhibits of Rembrandt's paintings and drawings adorned the galleries. If Vincent van Gogh was the Dutch darling of the world, Rembrandt was Holland's hero. And it wasn't just about his painting. Many simply enjoyed the stories of his philandering, his bohemian existence. For some, the tragedy of his demise—he died a pauper—makes him, like Van Gogh, a romantic figure. And much has been made of the fact that he long lived in what was then Amsterdam's Jewish quarter, and that Portuguese Jews, then recently settled in the city, counted among his biggest patrons. (Over the years, some have even tried to contend that Rembrandt himself, in fact, was Jewish, an argument that experts, especially Schwartz, have repeatedly and quite thoroughly debunked.)

This, too, is one of Holland's prides: the haven the Dutch gave to Jews fleeing Portugal after the 1536 Inquisition. Though officially denied full rights as citizens, the Jews of Amsterdam were able to practice their religion so long as they did so privately—one of history's first examples of the trait some Dutch now proudly call their "tolerance" and others angrily describe as a coldhearted standoffishness: "Do whatever you want," the attitude seems to say, "just don't bother *me*." For some, this way of thinking, which characterizes the Dutch way in many areas of life, constitutes moral relativism at its finest: nonjudgmental, undemanding. To others, it forms the core of what is wrong with Dutch culture, and the source of the sociopolitical conflicts Holland—and in turn, all of Europe—now faces: a nonchalance and neutrality, a refusal to be bothered by the behavior of others that, these days, allows even the most inhumane and uncivilized behaviors (like honor killings and wife beatings) to flourish while those who could be intervening look away. (Some, in fact, might argue that it explains the ease with which so many Dutch Jews were murdered during the occupation: the Dutch, you might say, tend to have something of a reality problem.)

But for the Jews of the 17th century, this attitude was nothing if not a blessing. Forced from their homelands, not just Portuguese but soon after, also Eastern European, or Ashkenazi Jews, began coming to the Netherlands, where they flourished as merchants, publishers, bankers, and in the diamond trade. (The word "Mokum," a nickname for Amsterdam still commonly in use, is actually the Hebrew word for "place.") Only centuries later, with the establishment of another major immigrant group—this time, from the Middle East—would that viewpoint eventually be challenged.

And it was, in fact, at around the same time of the Rembrandt celebrations, in 1991, when the challenge began, as Dutch intelligence, following the fall of the Berlin Wall and the end of the cold war, began re-examining state security. According to a report by the ELISE Consortium at the Centre for European Policy Studies in Brussels, "Already before the beginning of the Gulf War, the Minister of Interior Affairs, [Catharina] Dales, stated that the communist threat which had disappeared after the collapse of the Berlin Wall was replaced by the special attention for a terrorist threat."[2]

By taking an active role in Operation Desert Storm (Holland, unlike most of Europe, supported U.S. actions and offered its fleet to U.S.

military command), the country was forced to confront the possibility of domestic retaliatory attacks that might be perpetrated by Muslims living within the Dutch borders. Noted the ELISE report:

Once the war had begun, the Minister stated that this new threat was linked with the Gulf War. However, this general threat would not require more measures than already had been taken. The Secret Intelligence Service (BVD) expected special threats, such as sabotage and terrorist activities from activist and Muslim communities, who were—according to the BCD—called by Baghdad and groups affiliated to commit such crimes in the countries of the allied forces. [. . .] In an overview report of the BVD and its functioning, the unpredictability of international terrorist violence and the undemocratic activities against and between minorities in the Netherlands were also mentioned as developments which could constitute a threat to the democratic legal order.[3]

In addition, noted the ELISE analysis,

The 1991 yearly report of the Intelligence Service reported that during the Gulf War, the Turkish left wing revolutionary movement, Devrimci Sol, attacked repeatedly organizations, government, and NATO representatives in Turkey. After the Dutch army had put several Dutch air defense units on Turkish soil, the Intelligence Service claimed to be aware of the possible danger of attacks in the Netherlands. However, they were not prevented. In July 1991, the Dutch affiliation of the group ignited several firebombs in Rotterdam and Amsterdam in various Turkish offices.[4]

But this wasn't all. Dutch intelligence also feared radicalization of the Muslim community through migration, particularly via family reunification programs that sought, on humanitarian grounds, to bring family members still based in the country of origin to join with family members now living in Holland—men who had followed the European call for guest workers from the 1960s to 1980s. Often, these family members would have had minimal contact during the time they were separated, during which those in the homelands may have become—and occasionally were—involved with local politics, and political and ethnic rebel groups. In addition, one study found that the separation between fathers in the Netherlands and their families in Turkey and Morocco had created discipline problems among the children—particularly sons, who, scornful of their mothers and without the authoritarian guidance of their fathers to control them, became violent and prone to involvement in street crime. When reunited with their fathers in the West, these youths, unaccustomed to—and resentful of—parental discipline, and feeling alienated from their new society by language and cultural barriers, became ripe for the picking by budding radical groups and were easily taken in by fundamentalist imams at the growing number of Dutch mosques.

It hadn't started that way. My friend Esther grew up in Limburgh, in the southern part of Holland, where, as she says, "things come a little late." Born in 1968, she recalls the first arrivals of immigrants from the Mediterranean—Italians, Spaniards, followed by Greeks and Moroccans—as a time marked by interest and gratitude. "They were exotic," she tells me as we sit outside the Hotel des Indes in The Hague. One of Holland's top luxury hotels, the Des Indes stands at the top of the Lange Voorhout, within a brief walk to the Parliament and the Palace, around the corner from the Mauritshuis museum, resplendent with its paintings by Rembrandt and Vermeer. It is the area of town where the embassies are gathered, the international quarter, and it is among the most elegant neighborhoods in the country. There are no headscarves here. The only Muslims you will find are dignitaries and their assistants. It is Holland as it used to be.

"We were happy they had come," says Esther. Her husband, fifteen years her elder, nods in agreement. "They took jobs that needed to be done. They were quiet. Of course, when there are new people, you look at one another a bit askance, but there was no enmity at all on either side."

Such was the experience through most of Holland, where the Dutch recognized the sacrifices these men—and it was only men at first—had made in leaving their families behind. Even if their stay here was temporary, the Dutch took measures to make it comfortable: some immigrants still tell stories of receiving "a free round" at cafés from time to time, and Muslims were freely given spaces for prayer in the factories where they worked. For the most part, the Dutch knew nothing about Islam, nothing about the countries these men had come from. A colonist country with a long history both of trade with and rule over African nations and with Turkey, Holland approached its Turkish and Moroccan newcomers almost as if they were museum exhibitions: from a slight distance, but eager to know more.

But these guests were not from the intelligentsia. These were not university professors prepared to explain the tenets of Islam or the cultural traditions of their people. Many were, in fact, illiterate. Dialogue often proved impossible. As each culture watched the behaviors of the other, puzzled by their unexpected differences, unable to ask for explanations or to give them, wariness and suspicion grew—and with them, resentment. When psychiatrist Salah Sidali described his experiences during the early years of Muslim immigration for a broadcast on VPRO, he remembered frequently being told he had to adjust, to adapt. It made him, he says, feel inferior: *their* way ruled, not his. *They* set the standard, not he. It was to the immigrants to meet the expectations and demands of their hosts, and be judged by how well they did so.[5]

They were right. But the dictum "when in Rome" was not one, it seemed, they were all prepared to live by. Esther, my friend, says things changed for her mostly when the family reunification began, and Muslim boys appeared on the streets of her small town. "Suddenly, you would walk along the way you always had, and they would be looking at you. It was an odd look, like you were a whore, both disapproving and lustful." She shudders. "You thought, 'why are they looking at me this way? What am I doing wrong? Is it me?' And you were only doing what was normal in your own culture, living the way you were accustomed to. So you felt these strangers were making *you* feel strange."

At first, the Dutch responded to this awkwardness with their new national guests as they would to an annoying guest in their own home, the one who doesn't make his bed or help to do the dishes, or shut the lights out when he leaves a room. With such guests, you say nothing; you grit your teeth, focus on your enjoyment of their company, and remind yourself that they'll be leaving shortly, anyway.

But imagine that instead of leaving, your guest invites his wife to join you, too, and she, in turn, her sister. The house grows cramped. They speak together in a language you can't understand, and they can't understand you. There are secrets. Sometimes you think you know what they are, but you say nothing. These are, after all, your guests. They have their privacy, their ways. And anyway, you don't know for certain. You only know that while you continue living in the same house together, you become more and more like strangers.

This is what happened in the Netherlands as the Muslim immigrant population expanded during the late 1970s and early 1980s. While men continued to mingle—at least in the workplace—with Dutch society, women were often kept, as they traditionally had been in Turkey and Morocco, at home. Few learned the language, making it impossible for them to have made friends among the Dutch, even had they wanted to, and certainly unable to avail themselves of social services. In keeping with the traditions of their own culture, men presided over these homes, imposing the same oppressive rule over their wives and daughters as their fathers had before them. Not for their wives and daughters the miniskirts favored by long-legged, blonde Dutch women.

But the children themselves—then as now—faced the conflicting messages of their families and the world around them with confusion. Dutch girls had playdates. Muslim girls may not. Dutch teenage boys had girlfriends, went to parties, drank beer. Muslim boys may not. Sometimes they went anyway, returning home to beatings from their fathers; behind many of the closed doors in the closed communities of Muslim immigrants, the screams and scars and tears of family violence were as commonplace as breakfast.

The effects on children of domestic violence are by now, for Westerners, well-known: violence breeds violence. But for uneducated families from a culture where such behavior was the norm, these consequences were of no concern. That their sons then, in turn, got into street fights, or that their daughters forfeited any hopes of emancipation, that their children dropped out of school because of an inability to socialize, or because their parents were often neither willing nor able to assist them with their schoolwork—these they took in stride. It was the Dutch who noticed, and primarily the government and its institutions, who watched the statistics every year: unemployment among Turkish and Moroccan immigrants and their children rose to four or five times that of the native population. Disproportionate amounts of criminal activity came from the *allochtone*—immigrant—communities.

And yet, despite a great deal of clucking and debate, little was actually done. Sidali's observation—that he was expected to adjust to the status quo—could not have been more on-target, both for the immigrants and for the Europeans. At a conference in 1991 about the fall of the Soviet Union, Dutch Minister Frits Bolkestein asked, "If integration is officially declared government policy, which cultural values must prevail: those of the non-Muslim majority, or those of the Muslim minority?"[6] (What he failed to ask, but might have wondered, too, was: What happens when, as some predict, the Muslim minority of Europe becomes the majority?)

Throughout Europe, this was—and remains—precisely the problem. Don't Western women, after all, don headscarves in countries that require them?

Bolkestein's very question recalls an era of colonialism, of Europeans who aimed to "civilize" Native Americans, for instance. Underneath the resentments, the confusion, the anger, that Europe now faces, I wonder: is there not a similar battle taking place?

The situation in the early 1990s wasn't helped, either, by the establishment, in 1992, of the first all-Muslim schools—though that wasn't how J. De Jonge, an Amsterdam politician who oversaw the project, perceived it; to him, it was glorious, an example of the way Muslims were integrating by following the previous example of the Catholic schools. "There will be about 100 Islamic primary schools, ten for higher education, and a university," he boasted in the *NRC*. "Wonderful, no, that in this little spot of tolerance in the world, everyone finds his place?"[7]

With little contact left between them, both Europeans and immigrants (and their children) were now forced largely to rely on what they saw, and on the media—and here, too, segregation played a role: the Dutch read the national papers, watched local news and the BBC or CNN; the immigrants relied largely on state-provided (read: propagandistic and censored) information they received from their homelands and from Saudi Arabia via satellite TV. With antipathy between the Arab world and the

West going from bad to worse—exacerbated by such events as the Iranian hostage crisis of 1979-1981; the Hezbollah attack on a Marks & Spencer shop in Paris in 1983; the hijacking, in 1984, of the Italian cruise ship, the *Achille Lauro*; and attacks on Vienna International Airport and Rome's Leonardo da Vinci-Fiumicino Airport by the Abu Nidal Organization, a militant Palestinian group—it is safe to assume that neither the Muslim immigrants nor the Europeans were being fed the most favorable (or even objective) impressions of one another. With the publication in 1990 of Salman Rushdie's *Satanic Verses* and the subsequent uproar that it caused in England and across the Continent (not to mention the bombing of the book's publisher, Riverdale Press, in New York), it became clear to both sides that their differences were real and, quite possibly, irreconcilable. They were strangers to one another in the same land, and strangers they chose, then, to remain.

CHAPTER 4

"Going down, 1862, going down, going down, copied, going down."

It had been a warm, autumn Sunday in Holland on the fourth of October, 1992. Families made late-season visits to the beach, boats sailed the Amsterdam canals, girls drew chalk figures on the sidewalks or joined their brothers playing soccer in local parks.

And then, just before sundown, as if from nowhere, flames and metal roared out of the sky and crashed, exploding, into an apartment complex in Amsterdam Zuid-Oost. "A strike, an explosion, a wave of shock, a sea of fire. It was sudden, immense, and total"—so was the event described later in a government report that attempted to analyze the crash of the El Al 747 jet into buildings that housed mostly Surinamese and Antillean immigrants, leaving, according to many, a toxic chemical cloud behind. Stunned residents scrambled desperately to safety, rushing past the flaming ruins of what had been their homes. Some jumped from windows. Others ran up the stairs of the nine-story buildings to rescue family members before rushing down again, usually alone, defeated by the flames. In a small-scale preview of what would take place in September 2001, in New York City, an airplane and a building collided, and everything began to change.

From the beginning, conspiracy theories flew as fast as rumors of the numbers killed—first estimated at 200, then at 70, and ultimately settled, even now, at a vague "we'll never know." Traveling from New York to Tel Aviv, Flight 1862 had off-loaded some of its cargo at Schiphol airport just before it crashed; unlike most other airports,

Holland's main hub often turns a blind eye to shipments that skirt international regulations. Surely, many thought, an El Al jet would have been carrying munitions. And equally certain, too, they thought, the fact that the plane crashed into a largely-Muslim neighborhood was no coincidence. Were the Dutch aware? Were they, in fact, involved? What was the plane actually carrying anyway?

Stories emerged of strange rescue workers in white hazmat suits appearing days later on the scene. At first, officials claimed the cargo contained only perfume and toiletries. Later, Israel admitted the plane had been carrying 240 kilos of DMMP, a chemical used in the manufacture of sarin nerve gas. And to this day, the cockpit voice recorder has never been recovered. Worries and allegations whirled through the news and enclaves of the Dutch community for years; and even after parliamentary inquiries determined they were baseless, the theories have never entirely been stilled.

But there was another aspect of the story that would have lasting impact on the Dutch; for revealed, too, in the destruction of so many homes and families, was the fact that quite a few of those families were larger than anyone had realized, and the homes housed several hundred more people than officials had been (or admitted being) aware. What exploded on October 4 was not just a 747 cargo jet, but the hidden problem of illegal immigrants in the Netherlands.

For the public, this revelation tied all too closely with another: that while the victims of the crash lay burning and others lost everything they owned, while police and emergency service teams rushed to save what lives and property they could, immigrant youth took advantage of the distraction to loot neighboring stores and shopping malls. Until now, the Bijlmermeer flats—located, as they were, on the southeast fringes of the city—had gone largely unnoticed by the rest of Holland's population. Now the question came: Who were these people living there, and what was to be done about them?

Some responded to the reports of plundering with immediate sympathy for the plight of an immigrant underclass; others reacted with anger at the disrespect and unappreciation "foreigners" had shown to the country that had so generously taken them in. And as the investigation into the crash dragged on, immigrant Bijlmermeer residents argued that Dutch officials simply didn't care—that had the crash occurred in a neighborhood of "blond Jans and Jannekes," far more would have been accomplished.

The outrage was beginning.

In The Hague, the Parliament debated a slightly different problem. How had the population of illegal immigrants grown so large, and why had no one noticed? More important, what was to be done? Should the illegal immigrants whose lives had just been torn apart in the Bijlmermeer be deported, or allowed, in a one-time pardon issued under extraordinary circumstances, to remain? And if pardoned, since their names and even numbers were unknown, how could the government protect itself from other illegal immigrants claiming falsely that they, too, qualified as residents of the Bijlmermeer apartments? Once pardoned, how was Holland to accommodate them all? Where would they live? At whose cost? Many already had jobs, earning cash in restaurants and construction. These could be made legitimate. But what about the rest?

And how was future illegal immigration to be curbed—especially now, with the eradication of borders between countries of the European Union?

Forgotten these days by the Dutch are the words spoken by more than a handful of parliamentarians and ministers in the weeks after the crash: "Holland is not an immigration country, and that is how it will stay." In that phrase, first coined at the beginning of the guest workers program, ferments the germ that caused the current virus of cultural bafflement and unrest.

In the face of the Bijlmermeer episode, arguments about immigration and asylum rose to the top of the political agenda, and splashed across the press. Not only conservatives but even social democrats argued that, while outright deportation was undesirable, illegal immigrants should be nudged to return home, and called for crackdowns on those who hired illegal immigrants as a first measure.

"Police state!" exclaimed their opponents, accusingly, in response. And why should the Dutch be penalized when it was the immigrants who had committed the actual crime?

Others suggested an alternative: legal immigrants would be given national ID cards to be presented to authorities on request. No ID, you took the next flight out.

But, argued minority groups and Muslim organizations, this provided an open invitation to police to harass non-whites, as they were clearly likely to be immigrants—even when they were not. The potential for racial discrimination and abuse loomed too large.

In its place, Dutch officials created the *Koppelingswet*, or Linking Act, which would essentially require all citizens applying for health insurance, welfare, and other services to identify themselves by SOFI number, the Dutch equivalent of a U.S. social security number. Until 1991, anyone who asked for a SOFI number could get one, legal or not; but in November of that year, SOFI numbers became restricted to Dutch nationals and to legal immigrants, who received their numbers in conjunction with their residency permits.

On its face, the system differed little from that of the United States; but private enterprises found ways of using it to weed out clients and beneficiaries of their services: I recall the initiation of an air miles program in which the fine print across the bottom of the application form announced that the information therein would be subject to the Act. Not legal, no miles. Simple.

More ominous, though, was what this said—and continues to say—about privacy in the Netherlands. By connecting to the Koppelingswet, the air miles program—through which consumers rack up mileage points by shopping at certain supermarkets, using certain bank services, and so on—essentially gives the government a window into the consumer behaviors of every one of the program's several million members. It is not for nothing that the reality TV show *Big Brother* originated in the Netherlands.

The days of anonymity and a carefree life were over.

* * *

The racism began within weeks of the Bijlmermeer disaster. In November 1993, the Amsterdam broadsheet *Het Parool* documented the racist incidents reported in the previous 12 months, counting over 120 documented attacks on foreigners—mostly Muslims—and Jews. "From 1 January 1992 to July [1993]," the paper reported, "the Central Research Information Service noted 337 calls to police regarding actions against Muslims." The report totaled 17 cases of arson, four bomb threats, 95 incidents of graffiti, 59 threatening letters, and 67 occasions involving pamphlets and stickers.

* * *

"My name," the dark woman said in a voice that was practically a whisper, "is Ayaan Hirsi . . . Ali."

It was not in fact her real name. But "Ali" was as anonymous a name as she could think of, and the man at the immigration desk for asylum seekers seemed sympathetic enough. She did not think that he would question her or the fact that the name she spoke differed from the name her travel documents contained. She had arrived on impulse, really, bolting as she was set to fly from her uncle's house in Germany to the home of her new husband in Canada. Her Somali father, Hirsi Magan Isse (in accordance with Somali tradition, Ayaan's real last name was Magan), had arranged this marriage; she herself wanted to have no part of it, and when her husband mentioned his hope that she would bear him "at least six sons" she knew she needed, somehow, to escape.

This had been in Nairobi, where they'd wed; Somali by birth, Ayaan had moved to Kenya with her family as a young girl. Now her

husband had returned to Canada, and she, once her visa and immigration papers were put in order, was to follow. It was sheer luck that
these papers were easier to obtain in Germany, and that transfer to
Germany from Kenya was easier to arrange than from Kenya to Canada, that she had an aunt and uncle who would take her in while she
was, as it were, in transit, and so it all had fallen into place.

Until, at the last minute, she ran.

Now she had arrived, on her own for the first time in her life at the
age of 22, a refugee in the Netherlands. It was July 24, 1992.

Hirsi Ali's transformation from shy, devout Muslim to outspoken,
secular, Westernized activist portrays, in many respects, the complete
antithesis of what has happened to other Muslim women—and men—
in the Netherlands since the time of her arrival. As she gradually grew
more Westernized—riding a bicycle, allowing her headscarf to slip
from her hair and eventually even removing it completely, and then,
after 9/11, renouncing Islam completely—Dutch-born Muslims, by contrast, grew more and more conscious of their non-Western identity,
and in many cases, began taking Islam seriously only after the attacks
of September 11. It would not be overstating things to say that the core
of the cyclone that has hit the Netherlands since the early 1990s
springs, finally, and revolves around, the person and the story that is
Ayaan.

* * *

The summer Ayaan Hirsi Ali arrived, I was living on the Jan
Luykenstraat, considered by many to be the most exclusive address in
Amsterdam. My apartment there was indeed magnificent, with marble
bath and enormous rooms—a rarity in Amsterdam—and a view onto
the gardens and mosaic-covered walls of the Rijksmuseum, Holland's
national museum of art. It is here that Rembrandt's greatest works re-
side: the *Jewish Bride*, the *Night Watch*, the *Anatomy Lesson*, and hundreds of his drawings. Here, too, hang portraits by Frans Hals, church
interiors by Pieter Saenredam, landscapes by Jan Lievens, and the intimate, often humorous household scenes painted by Jan Steen. Outside
my living room windows, gold leaf accents in the mosaics of the museum façade shimmered under floodlights through the long, dark winter nights, and in the spring, roses and cherry blossoms filled the
Rijksmuseum gardens.

Designed in 1876 by Petrus Josephus Hubertus Cuypers and opened
in 1885, the Rijskmuseum stands as a lavish and ornate monument, a
cathedral, as it were, not to the immortality of gods but rather to the
immortality of art. Typically, Dutch architecture is, as they themselves
say, "sober." It is an architecture made for a land with little sun and

so, with few shadows to be cast: not for Holland the Baroque carvings that typify Parisian buildings, or the sculptural friezes that adorn the architecture of the Mediterranean. The 17th-century row houses for which Amsterdam, in particular, is famous, bend their plain brick faces toward the water, built at a slight angle to facilitate the raising and lowering of cargo from hooks driven just below the eaves—a necessity during the mercantile Golden Age (and a convenience now for hoisting one's belongings in and out when moving to a new home—so much so that even contemporary Amsterdam buildings almost always include the bar-and-hook detail). Function, practicality, and modesty were then and remain the keywords of Dutch aesthetics. Ornamental gables serve less for aesthetic purposes as practical ones: once, in a time before buildings were numbered and postal codes put in place, such gables served to identify each home. True, in the southern regions of the country, 19th-century buildings have incorporated the Jugendstil influences of the Flemish—especially in cities like Maastricht and The Hague; but the Dutch standard remains understated, with adornment often so smoothly integrated into the structural design it simply holds its presence, rather than announcing it.

This is especially true of Dutch Amsterdam School design, which reached its height at the turn of the 20th century, and in which colored bricks lend pattern to the facades and inner walls of landmark buildings like the Beurs (Stock Exchange) by Hendrikus Berlage (the master of the Amsterdam School movement), and the American Hotel; and geometric forms, sculpted in the laying of the bricks, thrust out into the open spaces surrounding social housing projects and union headquarters throughout the country.

In all of this, the splendor of the Rijksmuseum stands regal and romantic, with its neo-Gothic turrets, its archways, and golden towers glinting in the sun like the castles of age-old fairy tales.

The idea of a national collection dates from the reign of Napoleon's brother Lodewijk in the early 19th century. The museum now contains not only paintings, but other treasures of decorative art, particularly 17th-century Delftware, the blue-and-white earthenware for which the Netherlands has, over the centuries, become renowned.

And indeed, this is what the Rijksmuseum has become: a monument to the past, to the best that Holland ever was. It preserves a history that has remained the Dutch mystique and magic a half millennium beyond its time, a history that confirms what Dutchness is: stately, sober, secular, passionless, Calvinist, precise. Only in the faces of the figures in Jan Steen's witty genre paintings and the later portraits by Frans Hals does laughter seem permitted. The starched lace collars of aristocratic couples, the wooden shoes of townsmen and of peasants, the endless, wide expanse of sky, the small brick houses and canals of Amsterdam—this is what everyone the world over associates with the Dutch, and remains the country's self-image, even now, and its pride.

And why not? For the streets of Amsterdam—and Delft, and Haarlem, and Utrecht, among others—still look much the same today. Step into the Rijksmuseum and then step out again, and one becomes confused for a moment about how long ago the past was, and how contemporary, now, the present. What you see in the paintings of 500 years ago is what you see in the lives of Holland's cities, still, today.

This, too, points to a particularity of the Dutch and Holland's—Europe's—current problems. For Americans, no matter where they or their parents come from, the Statue of Liberty, the Lincoln Memorial—these are part of what it is to be American, and U.S. immigrants embrace them. And for centuries, being Dutch meant having a heritage that included Rembrandt and Erasmus and Spinoza. But for nearly a million Hollanders now, these artists and their legacies are *not* their heritage. They inspire no sense of national or historical pride. So what does it mean, in this new millennium, this changed society, to be Dutch? Has the culture failed to inspire nationalism, Dutch identity, in its immigrant youth? Should children be force-fed a Dutchness into which they born?

Does Rembrandt even matter, anymore?

* * *

Still, one thing you have to love about the Dutch is how much they love their art. I noticed it my first visit here, on the train from Amsterdam to Maastricht, where small reproductions of paintings by the Masters hung in the spaces where, in the U.S., advertisements for MCI and the *Wall Street Journal* would have been. Debates about museums and their directors were, in those days, a national sport in the Netherlands, with battle lines drawn as vividly as those between Yankee versus Mets fans, and arguments as passionate as Americans' tend to be about certain presidents. The new Groningen museum, with its experimental architecture including a wing designed by American artist Frank Stella, was either a "garish" and "egocentric vanity" of its director, Frans Haks, or the most innovative thing to happen to museums in the history of art. Stedelijk Amsterdam director Wim Beeren, who throughout the 1980s staged exhibitions of graffiti artists (Keith Haring, Kenny Scharf) and their compatriots (Jeff Koons), was either an idiot who knew nothing about art, or a man with his finger on the pulse of the avant-garde (though in fact, it was Haks who was once heard to proclaim himself "the only one in this country of my generation who actually understands the real nature of the *Zeitgeist*").

Then there was Rudi Fuchs.

Rudi Fuchs is a portly, angel-faced man with blond curls slowly turning white and a wardrobe of three-piece suits and fountain pens. Once, he was named Holland's Sexiest Man, a title that has been conferred on no one else before or since. It is not a title one would usually associate with a museum director; but Rudi Fuchs has a quality rarely found in the moderate, easygoing landscape of the Netherlands: charisma. Always prepared to rock the boat, he earned recognition early in his career for directing the 1982 Documenta 7, an international art exhibition held every four years and considered, like the Venice Biennale, the plume in any curator's cap, the Nobel Prize of the museum world, the Oscar of the Visual Arts. Being selected to do the Documenta is A Very Big Deal, and anything that constitutes A Very Big Deal becomes, in this small country, Bigger.

It was Fuchs, not a politician or soccer star, for instance, who garnered front-page headlines for much of the 1990s, during which time he also penned a biweekly column for the *NRC*, held a weekly radio show, wrote a book (I was the co-author), and was regularly the target of gossip, rumors, and what, in the Netherlands, passes for "paparazzi." Like Haks (or the Yankees), one either loved him or hated him. Like Van Gogh, he had opinions, and was not shy of speaking them. (Speaking to a reporter for *Het Parool,* he once noted, "Culture is under pressure . . ., I find that dangerous. How long will it be until there are but a few people left who are still able to look at a painting?") And it was Fuchs who, years later, would in fact take on the challenge of teaching Dutch-Moroccan students about Rembrandt.

But while Fuchs was a somewhat extreme example, generally speaking, whatever happens in Holland's museums happens in Holland's brown cafés, in Holland's living rooms, and above all, in Holland's newspapers, which seem to delight in any scandal the art world can conjure up.

Take, for instance, the Goldreyer case, which enjoyed the particular distinction of extending across the reign of two Stedelijk Amsterdam directors, gentlemen who would have had enough trouble getting along on the basis of their aesthetics were not political rivalry added to the pot.

But first, about the Dutch and art: When in 1997, the Russian art duo Komar and Melamid created a "work" consisting of the polled results from the citizens of various countries when asked to describe the "perfect" work of art, Dutch preferences proved to be distinctly different from the ones found everywhere else. Whereas people from other countries have shown preference for realist work (such as a couple in a landscape with animals and blue sky), in Holland, abstraction beat out the figurative hands down: the ideal painting in the polder is abstract and blue. (The least desired painting in Holland is an interior, like someone's living room, with a portrait of Bill Clinton hanging on the wall.)

I point this out because it explains, at least in part, why a nearly-monochrome canvas by Barnett Newman became, in essence, a national hero for the Dutch, why one painting's plight so stirred not just the art elite, but the waitresses and taxi drivers and train conductors of the Netherlands.

"Red," is what Rudi Fuchs, Beeren's successor at the Stedelijk, recalls thinking the first time he saw the work, an 8–by–18-foot canvas titled *Who's Afraid of Red, Yellow and Blue III.* It is, in fact, extremely red, lots of red, interrupted by a vertical line of yellow on one side and a vertical blue one on the other. It is a painting that speaks of the inter-relationships and nuances between "vibrant" and "vibrating." It is huge. It is abstract. It is red.

And in some inexplicable way, perhaps as a red cape raises the ire of a bull, the Newman taunted a Dutch self-proclaimed artist by the name of Gerard Jan van Bladeren. In March 1986, he entered the museum with a box cutter, found his way to the gallery where *Who's Afraid* was hanging, and sliced a gash straight across the canvas, practically from end to end.

But that's not what the controversy was about. The controversy centered around the restoration of the painting, performed by one Daniel Goldreyer of Brooklyn, New York, at a cost of 800,000 guilders, or nearly half a million dollars. Years passed—four, in fact—and then Goldreyer shipped the restored Barnett Newman back to Amsterdam.

But something seemed wrong. Newman painted with a brush, the presence of an artist's hand visible in the painting, and, said some dismayed curators and critics, vital to the work. Where were those brush-strokes now?

Investigations were ordered. Experts were called in. Chemical tests were conducted. The findings: Goldreyer had restored the work by first repairing the gash, and then repainting the canvas using a roller and ordinary house paint.

Conflicting opinions were questioned. Explanations were demanded. Fingers were pointed: at the painting, at the restorer, at the Stedelijk's Wim Beeren who had ordered the restoration in the first place. Additional experts were brought in from abroad. Politicians argued in the Parliament: had Beeren given Goldreyer adequate instructions? Had half a million dollars of Dutch taxpayer money been wasted? Worse, was one of the country's great art treasures now damaged beyond repair?

The story hit *Time* magazine and the *Wall Street Journal* in articles rife with accusations. Goldreyer hit back with defamation lawsuits: $15 million against *Journal*, a similar amount against Time, Inc., and 25 million guilders against the Stedelijk. In total, Goldreyer's lawsuits against individuals and the press mounted to 200 million guilders—or by then, about $150 million. In a handwritten letter to Beeren replicated in the Amsterdam press, Goldreyer demanded a copy of the Dutch lab report, and denied the results that had been made public. "We have been accused in the press of terrible acts," Goldreyer wrote. "Why are you doing this terrible thing? If not you, who?"

Cabinet members began demanding Beeren's resignation, while one Amsterdam *wethouder*, Marja Baak, who had defended Beeren as being the "dupe" of Goldreyer's misdeeds, was forced from office. "She reminds me of an unemancipated housewife," quipped one of Baak's colleagues, "who puts a rotten meal on the table and then, when the whole family gets sick, doesn't understand why they blame her."

Understand here: This is about a painting. And what a painting: This was, after all, not a Rembrandt or Van Gogh. The artist wasn't even Dutch. It bore no recognizable image, like a cow, for instance, or a bowl of fruit. But from Maastricht up to Groningen, everybody knew the work, and suddenly, everybody loved it. They debated in the cafés and in taxicabs. Who was right? Who was wrong? Why did the museum send the painting to the United States to be repaired? (One consultant to the Stedelijk griped in Amsterdam's daily *Het Parool* that Americans only know about commercialization anyway. "They're businessmen, he said. "But tradition and expertise don't come from money.") Was the painting worth keeping? Barflies became philosophers: The painting is still a Newman, some said, because it's his creative force. The painting is a Goldreyer, said others, because that's who applied the paint. But what, then, the first would argue, of all the Rembrandt paintings worked on by his students?

And so on.

Eventually, the hubbub dimmed. The court cases, costing over $1 million for the Stedelijk, were dismissed. Beeren, who would be 65 soon anyway, announced that he intended to retire.

But if Beeren was out—who was in?

And the conversations started up again: Who should run the Stedelijk? In a decision that had shocked the art world—not just in Holland, but internationally—Fuchs himself had been beaten out for the post by Beeren seven years prior. "I will not," he said, "offer my name in application again." And speaking to me on the phone from his office at the Gemeentemuseum in The Hague, he promised: "I will consider the position only if they come to me on bended knee."

Two months later, Bill Clinton became president of the United States, and Fuchs was named director of the Stedelijk.

CHAPTER 5

I visited Theo van Gogh a couple of times during those years. He lived in an apartment not far from me on the Noorderstraat with his magnificently beautiful and long-legged girlfriend, Heleen Hartmans. He had trouble figuring me out: Why would a New Yorker come to Amsterdam to live?

"I just want to live in America," he said.

I had come at the suggestion of Christopher Dickey, an editor at *Newsweek*, to conduct a background interview: *Newsweek* ran profiles at the time, and the editor thought Theo might make a good subject. (In the end, the article never happened. Theo wasn't quite interesting enough just yet.)

It was early summer and unusually warm. Theo sat on a couch in his small and sparsely-furnished living room, his belly seated in his lap, and ranted about the inadequacy and inauthenticity of Holland, its smallness, that it was too uptight. He spoke rapidly, pausing only to light another cigarette, as if relishing the chance finally to say so much he hadn't said—or, that is, at least not to anyone who would listen.

I left there struck dizzy by the contrasts in our perceptions of our respective homelands. How could they be so different—and why?

I called Chris at *Newsweek*. "I don't know," I said. "He's a bit nuts."

Soon after, Heleen left Theo, moving out with their infant son, Lieuwe. Theo was used to fights, and he was gracious, if contemptuous, when he lost them. But not this one. Everyone noticed Theo's *vermagering*, his rapid weight loss in the months following the split. On TV, where he appeared regularly with his talk show, *Een Prettig*

Gesprek, he grew handsomer, and yet at the same time, more and more ordinary looking, like far too many other attractive, blond Dutchmen one encountered anywhere in town. Perhaps I was alone in this, but I found it disillusioning. There was much to be said for a fitter, good-looking Theo. But it wasn't really Theo anymore. In an interview published in the *Filmkrant* in February 1993, however, he reassured, "raising a child doesn't go well with drinking. It's that simple. For the moment I'm dry. The drinking will come again." [1]

It was during this time that Van Gogh faced yet another court battle over a statement he had made in one of his columns some years earlier in response to what he considered melodramatic chest-beating on the part of Leon de Winter, a popular Jewish writer. "My, but it smells of caramel," Van Gogh had written. "They must be burning the diabetic Jews today." Accused of anti-Semitism (he contended the comment was a personal one, aimed specifically only at de Winter), he faced a fine of 2,000 guilders (roughly $1,250) and the threat of imprisonment were he to print the piece again. (It had already reappeared in his book, *The Weldoener* [*The Benefactor*]). To the *Filmkrant*'s Jos van der Berg, he challenged, "If they threaten me with a one-month sentence, then I'll immediately reprint it, so that they have to arrest me. I hope they do; my heart is pounding with the anticipation. Do they think they can scare me so easily? And in jail, I'll write articles with twice the power."

In the end, Van Gogh never received his jail term, much as he welcomed it. He did, however, pen an apology at the demand of the court, which he delivered dryly: "Whoever read it, and was upset by it, I offer my apology. The dead can no longer respond to me, even if they should be gently massaged by a third-rate writer such as Leon de Winter." As for his future, he stood resolute: "I do not believe," he said, "that the court can determine what I may or may not write. I also don't particularly think the column is insulting. I fully intend to go on, precisely because I will be condemned."

And he did.

*   *   *

On Tuesday nights during these years, my friend Claudia hosted what she called a "naches," a café night for second-generation Holocaust survivors and the children of the hidden children—sons and daughters of Jewish parents who sent them off to be raised in Catholic families either as foster children or—more often—grateful but indentured servants. The children of these children, she tells me, are united by parents who were filled with secrets, with guilt, with identities lost and found again. To be a hidden child during the war meant changing everything: your name, your religion, who you said your parents were, whether you had siblings and what their names were, too. It meant leaving behind friendships, landmarks, bedrooms, schools, the rituals of your life. For the years that you were sheltered, you were someone you didn't even know, with a history you made up as you went along, or else no history, no tales told of "when I first learned to ride a bicycle." And then the war was over, and suddenly this family that had been your family (if you had been sheltered by a family and not an orphanage or church) wasn't yours anymore, nor was this name you'd come to think of as your name. Some chose to become Christians, grateful for the generosity and courage of the families and the organizations who protected them. Others tiptoed back to being Jews. But they would not be the same again.

The children of survivors and of the hidden children, Claudia says, grew up with mysteries, with rooms full of Things That Could Not Be Said. On Tuesday nights, they come together now as adults, some with children of their own, and say them.

Claudia tells me the Jewish community in Amsterdam is small. Arranging these nights wasn't difficult to do; word gets around quickly.

And so I come with her one week, in part to meet a man she wants to introduce me to, in part because I want to understand what it is these people share and I am not, cannot, even as a Jew, be part of. They have rented the Arena, a club in the south of Amsterdam. We park her car on an asphalt lot and walk across the grass. Peering through the darkness and the rain, a few people recognize Claudia by the wildness of her thick black curls and wave as we approach. But she is looking concerned, her head moving quickly as she surveys the grounds outside the club. Two guards stand at the door.

"Are they always here?" I ask her.

"Always," says Claudia. "Whenever Jews congregate in groups for these kinds of events, we always have our own guards." Despite the risks faced by the Jewish community in Holland, the government provides no protection of its own.

It is 1992, nearly 50 years after the Third Reich fell, and still, they are afraid. I ask her if this isn't paranoia. This is Holland, after all, where tolerance reigns, where they tried so hard to save the Jews.

Claudia looks at me, her hazel eyes reflecting the lights in the disco's chandeliers, her black curls falling across her forehead. She pushes them back as if annoyed. "This is a myth," she tells me. "The Dutch have been selling that story like herring for decades, but it isn't true. Don't let the reputation fool you."

What is true: During the occupation, they say here, the Dutch would perform a test, luring strangers to say specific words, like "Scheveningen," or even entire phrases: "acht-en-tachtig prachtig grachten in de stad van

Amsterdam" ("eighty-eight beautiful canals in the city of Amsterdam"). If the person got the guttural *"ch"* and *"g"* right, the legend goes, one knew that it was safe.

But it was never safe. Of some 170,000 Jews living in the Netherlands before the war, 30,000 survived—and only 10,000 returned. Like Anne Frank, the rest were rounded up and sent to Westerbork, a camp near the Dutch-German border known as "the portal to Auschwitz." One hears stories sometimes of people like Loet Velmans, who, on May 14, 1940, was alerted that the Dutch were preparing to capitulate to Hitler. Grabbing his bicycle, the 17-year-old Loet, along with his cousin Dick, headed south, where the Dutch army was still engaged in battle. Not gone far, according to Velmans' wife, Edith—herself a hidden child during the occupation— when a group of four students on their way to Scheveningen harbor intercepted them. "Come with us," they urged. The plan was to board a boat and sail across to England. The cousins hardly needed to be convinced.

But Scheveningen, they soon discovered, was mobbed, as others with similar hopes of fleeing desperately struggled to board any boat they could, Edith Velmans says, "but no fisherman dared to take them." Undaunted, the young men kept searching until they found an unmanned coast guard boat; but no sooner had they stepped foot toward it than the captain suddenly appeared. Thinking fast, the boys explained their plight. They were lucky; the captain let them go.

Loet scribbled a note to his family explaining where he was and handed it to a young boy. "Take this to my parents," he said, and gave the boy his address, "and you may keep the bicycle."

Word of the departing boat spread across the docks. As fast as they could, others seeking to escape crowded toward them, scrambling aboard until finally the boys announced that the boat could take no more; 40 people were aboard, and 40 it would stay.

At home, Loet's family was gathered tensely around the radio, listening for updates when the young boy arrived on Loet's bicycle and handed Mrs. Velmans the message he had brought. Loet's mother read the note, rose to her feet and, announcing to her family, "where my son goes I go," called a taxi. The entire family tumbled in with her, leaving everything they owned, exactly as it was, behind them. At the harbor, still swarming with people desperate to escape, Loet looked up just to see their taxi pulling in. "That's my parents!" he called out to his mates.

The voyage, with 47 people on board, took about 24 hours. Midway to the British coast, the boat was picked up by a British destroyer and ushered on to Dover. It was one of few boats that made it.[2]

* * *

"Come," Claudia says, and leads me to a table. A tall man, even by Dutch standards, in a soft brown suede bomber jacket nurses a cocktail.

He is handsome—Dutch-looking, with high cheekbones and a strong chin—and prematurely gray. I am wearing a short black leather skirt and suddenly feel misplaced. She introduces him to me as Michael and tells him I believe the Dutch are liberal in the way they treat the Jews.

"Why do you think that?" Michael asks me.

"I used to live in Switzerland," I tell him. "In Switzerland, they only knew me as 'the Jew.' I've never felt that here."

"So, compared to Switzerland," Michael says.

"So," I say, "I guess compared to Switzerland."

His eyes match the color of his jacket. He looks at me intently.

"You're American," he says.

"From New York."

"Ah," he says. "That is not America."

It is something many people say.

He asks me what I'm doing here in Amsterdam, and I explain to him that I am writing about art, that I do some art dealing on the side, and he runs through a list of names of artists he admires, and the conversation turns. As I peruse the room, it occurs to me that all the people here are Jewish. For two years, I have been practically alone, afraid at times to tell, amused by taxi drivers and other strangers who ask if I am from Greece or Spain. Here, we are all Jews, and it matters because had the Nazis not come to Holland in the first place, this party would not be taking place, and yet it doesn't because no one here is pointing fingers and asking. We are just people, without religion or nationality, at least for right now.

We don't need, after all, to speak about the Jews, or being Jewish, or about anti-Semitism and the Dutch.

We need only the chance to speak.

* * *

It was around this time that I moved from the Jan Luykenstraat to Amsterdam's Nieuwe Zuid, or New South, where Claudia had taken me for "Naches." Created originally by Henrikus Berlag, who designed the area on commission from the city in 1914 and built it between 1917 and 1925, the Nieuwe Zuid quickly became one of Amsterdam's chicest shopping districts, and remains so nearly 100 years later. It was here, amongst the wide streets and abundance of new, available apartments, that German Jews, fleeing their homeland in the 1920s and 1930s, gathered. Some 15,000 German Jews found refuge—however temporary—in Amsterdam on the eve of World War II, and in shops along the Beethovenstraat, they bought groceries from German-Jewish grocers, and they argued politics at German-Jewish owned cafés.

And then the Nazis came.

It cannot have been a coincidence that the occupation operated largely out of two buildings in the Nieuwe Zuid, or that these were the centers from which many Jews were deported to the camps.

The apartment I rented faced a church in the front. In the rear, a balcony overlooked the splendid gardens of my downstairs neighbors, an elderly couple—call them Mr. and Mrs. L—who, in proper Dutch form, took drinks outdoors in good weather promptly at half past five and dined equally promptly at six. I'd been told in advance by my friend Gijs, from whom I sublet the apartment, that they were not an easy couple to live with, often prissy and prone to ridiculous complaints. And indeed, I was struck by Mrs. L's pronouncement when we first moved in that she was "allergic to footsteps," and to her husband's boast on our first meeting, over a neighborly glass of sauvignon blanc in the shade of Mrs. L's fragrant jasmine trees, that he had been "the first white child born in Indonesia." As such, and having spent much of his childhood in the former colony, he now collected Indonesian art, and he pointed out a few extraordinary items placed throughout their home. Whatever else could be said of them, they had exquisite taste, and Mrs. L was a talented gardener, a fact that I particularly appreciated in early spring, when climbing roses made their perfumed way in through my bedroom window.

It was on such an evening in early spring that I received a call from Gijs. It was the first night of Passover, and though I neither held nor considered even attending a seder, I had earlier in the evening paged through a copy of a Haggadah my sister had given to me months before.

I live, by any standard, a quiet life. Although by that time I'd acquired a stereo system, I never used it. If I watched TV at all, it was to follow the O. J. Simpson trial highlights and other news at six on CNN. I do not wear shoes indoors. My boyfriend at the time—now my husband—had a two-year-old son who visited only on rare occasions, obeyed when told not to run around, and never threw a tantrum. What I did do, however, was work out, doing aerobics for about an hour every day.

It drove Mrs. L positively insane.

And so, on this particular Passover night, Gijs phoned as I was sitting on my bed, as I had been most of the evening, reading. When I answered, he didn't even say hello.

"It's war," he announced.

Alarmed, I sat up. War? Again?

"Mr. L phoned just now," he continued. "He said, 'Get the Jewess out.'"

I had never even heard the word "Jewess" before.

For years, when I related this tale to others, they shook their heads in disbelief. "A Dutch man?" they would say. "That's not normal."

Now, they only nod their heads, knowingly. They've heard more stories like this since.

I didn't let it end there. Once having secured another apartment, I began making real noise, jumping from my bed in the morning, turning up the volume on the TV. I even hooked up my stereo one sunny afternoon and stuck in a tape of Mozart string quartets before opening the balcony doors wide. As I sat sunning myself, Mr. L looked up from his garden chair.

"Could you turn the music down?" he asked me in Dutch.

"No," I answered, also in Dutch and loud enough for other neighbors to hear clearly, "not for an anti-Semite."

"Anti-Semite?" he answered, as if surprised. I told him I'd been informed of his comment about the Jewess.

Mrs. L grew pale.

"How could I be an anti-Semite?" she asked me, even as she was not the one I had accused. "I'm from Breda."

To this day, I have found no one who can explain to me what she may have meant by this. True, many families in Breda sheltered "hidden children." But even those families were few and far between, the more so given the large-scale occupation of German forces there.

I turned away and left the music on.

The following day, a note appeared under my front door.

"Speak that way again," it read, "and we will have you deported. Foreigners like you are not welcome in the Netherlands."

A month later, I moved out.

CHAPTER 6

I was visiting my boyfriend's family in California when Muslims bombed the World Trade Center. Clinton was our newly-elected president. We were barely down from the post-election high of seeing a baby-boomer Democrat take the country back from the Reagan-Bush regime with a message—later adopted by the next post-Bush president, Barack Obama—that promised and inspired hope. On the television screen in the corner of the living room in a resort community in Palm Springs, the World Trade Center looked suddenly very small, the bombing bizarrely unimportant. Few were injured. Dusty faces with breathless voices spoke haltingly to reporters from CNN. In high school during the 1970s, we often had bomb scares in the middle of the day, forcing an evacuation of the school, and we stood outside clutching our three-ring binders until police had arrived, inspected, and given an "all clear." Most of these scares took place during finals. None of them ever had anything to do with actual bombs. Only one person ever got caught.

Watching the figures walking through the exits of the Twin Towers to the plaza at their base felt very much the same. By the time I flew back to New York five days later, no one even talked about it anymore.

Looking back now, the 1993 World Trade Center bombing provides a near-perfect metaphor for what was happening simultaneously in Holland: we confronted the future, and refused to look it in the eye. Or perhaps better said: we simply didn't get it.

In fairness, this is somewhat understandable. The clash between Islam and the West on Western soil is unlike anything we've ever seen before, making it—as we learned in September of 2001—beyond anything we could possibly have imagined or believed, and even now, difficult to fathom. What European governments may have known about the underbelly of their Muslim populations clashed so vigorously with the cultures in which they existed as to be almost inconceivable. It was a matter of cognitive dissonance at the highest level. Indeed, when Muslims rioted in Paris in 1991, the Dutch blamed it on the French, insisting with a smugness they would repeat a decade later, "it won't happen here."

Seven years later, it did.

Afshin Ellian, an Iranian dissident who now teaches in the Department of Social Cohesion, Citizenship, and Multiculturalism at the University of Leiden School of Law and Jurisprudence and writes a daily blog for the Web site of Dutch weekly newsmagazine *Elsevier*, arrived in Holland as a refugee in 1989. A warm, baby-faced man with a gentle voice and a sharp pen, he greets me in his office at the university with coffee and a slice of cherry pie—as Dutch a welcome as they come—and a friendly handshake before he takes my coat. It is a synchronicity of ironies: the man who, raised in a Shiite family during the Iranian revolution, extends his hand to a woman, the Iranian who welcomes the American—a Jew, at that—with a gesture that binds them together through a culture that belongs to neither of them, but in which they've made their lives.

It is spring of 2008. I have come to talk to Ellian about an Iranian artist now living in the Netherlands whose work has been removed from a museum exhibition out of a concern that "it will be too offensive to Muslims"—a decision made only after Moroccan groups threatened the museum and issued death threats both in public and in private against the artist. By 2008, this kind of censorship has become routine—memories of Theo notwithstanding.

But our conversation soon turns to larger issues. Why, I ask him, didn't we see any of this coming? Was it just not there?

Ellian laughs. "I had come from Tora Bora. You had come from Reagan's Christian right-wing America, which was, in a way, practically the same thing. All you and I saw here was the freedom."

This is true. I was enraptured by the art, the ease, the fact that female naval officers who had stood naked on a ship at sea had their bare-breasted photographs plastered on the newspapers' front pages.

But things *were* easier, back then. The larger problem came, in the earliest years of the 1990s, from the Antillean community, which kept largely to themselves.

Then things changed.

"When we left the asylum center," Ellian recalls, "we moved into a house with a Turkish family on one side, a woman with a rottweiler on the other, and a Moroccan family across the way. I drank coffee with poets. The Moroccan children played with my daughter."

One afternoon, the Moroccan mother came to visit Ellian's wife, complaining about Dutch culture, which she called "filthy." Ellian, when he heard this, burst out laughing. "Why?" he'd said. "Hash? Whores? There's none of this in Morocco?"

But like everyone else, he missed the signal. Suddenly, his daughter was no longer welcome in the house across the street. "The mother says she saw you with a beer," Mrs. Ellian told her husband.

"This," thought Ellian at the time, "is not normal."

He began to pay attention. The father, he realized, regularly beat his wife. Neither the parents nor the children socialized with the Dutch. Even Ellian's own son became something of a pariah, having been taught only to speak Dutch at home, not Persian. "But if I had taught him Persian," Ellian explains, "I'd have had to give him my tradition, and I didn't want to. Whatever my tragedies, my son deserves a good life."

Here, in that one detail, lay the difference between Ellian and his neighbors—and between his phenomenal professional and social success in the West, and their failures. For most immigrant Muslim families in Europe, the language and culture of their host countries is an outside interference, and learning it is something to be done only because, as the Dutch say, *het moet*—one must. Unlike Ellian, these parents want their children to carry their traditions—a noble endeavor in itself, but where it goes wrong here is in wanting the children to supplant the traditions and beliefs of the culture in which they live with those their parents left behind. To other Muslim children, Ellian tells me, his son is more than just "too Western"; he's a "traitor."

And yet even as he began to recognize the goings-on around him, Ellian turned away. "I was afraid," he admits now. "I thought that if I saw it, I'd have to have an answer. And I had none."

In fact, no one did.

In 1992, the Dutch government approved the creation of Islamic schools for Muslim children—an effort to provide the population with the comforts of home, without recognizing that "home" was here, not there, and that further segregation could only breed contempt. What they also overlooked was the fact that the quality of education in these schools, where teachers were immigrants themselves and lacked fluency in Dutch, never mind Western history and culture, would inevitably prove inferior to that offered by "regular," established schools. For many Muslim parents, of course, this was no concern: they didn't want their children learning about Western mores and a history that wasn't their own, anyway, and they certainly didn't care about the language: after all, they frequently couldn't speak it themselves. What mattered was that their sons and daughters, surrounded by this "filthy" and corrupt society, still grow up to be good Muslims, carrying exactly those traditions from which Afshin Ellian so carefully protected his own son.

But with inferior education comes, inevitably, an inferior future. Kids attending Muslim schools rarely went on to university, or obtained desirable positions in the workplace. I have never been entirely certain whether or not the Dutch, in allowing these schools to operate, knew that they were creating an entrenched underclass, and did so, deliberately, anyway.

What they certainly did not realize was the influence Salafists from abroad would wield in Islamic classrooms and after-school events.

Saudi-backed Salafist missionary works are nothing new, but their presence in the West increased significantly during the 1990s, extending to orthodox mosques, bookstores for the sale and promotion of Salafist material, and, now, schools. According to Dutch intelligence, such aid was particularly strong in Holland between 1997 and 2000.

Salafism, also referred to as Wahhabism, is the so-called "pure" form of Islam advocated by the Saudi government and practiced (as is Takfiri Islam) by extremists in the Muslim community, who reject all other forms of Islam—including Sunni and Shia beliefs. As defined by the AIVD in a March 2005 report, "Saudi Influences in the Netherlands: Links between the Salafist Mission, Radicalisation Processes and Islamic Terrorism":

In today's Salafism, two main trends can be distinguished. On the one hand, there is the *salafiyya ilmiyya,* a broad movement that recognizes the power of the *ulema* (theological mullahs) related to the Saudi Royal family. On the other hand, there is the *salafiyya jihadiyya,* which does not recognize this power and propagates the worldwide jihad against both the Western world and the Saudi Royal family. The rejection of violence by the Salafism that is loyal to the Saudi Royal family, however, does not mean that this movement is in general less vehement in its repudiation of the Western world. Several spiritual leaders in this pro-government form of Salafism state that the way in which society is given shape in the Western world (in, for example, democracy, equal rights for men and women, freedom of expression, et cetera) is un-Islamic and they question the desirability of integration of Muslims in Western society.

The report continues:

For a long time, the Salafist and a number of other ultra-orthodox mosques in the Netherlands actively propagated unrestrained radical, extreme, and isolationist views. Very plain messages were propagated, such as sermons in which "seculars, socialists, or democrats" were compared with the "allies of Satan" or which claimed that each law that goes against Islamic law should not be complied with. The congregation were [sic] also told that lapidation was a justified remedy against adultery. Also obtainable in these mosques was (and is, as was recently shown [through the uncovering in 2003 of a popular pamphlet titled "The Way of Islam"]) literature which fulminates against homosexuality or incites to female circumcision.

But some young Europeans went further, discovering, by way of Salafism and its outreach, the ideas of Takfiri-wal Hjra, an Islamic sect especially popular in Algiers, but which is spreading not only within Africa, but among North African immigrant groups in Europe. (A 1995 attack on the Paris Metro has been linked to Algerian Takfiri groups, as were plans to kidnap members of the French national soccer team and to fly a hijacked plane into the Eiffel Tower. Takfiris are also believed to have been behind the assassination of Egyptian President Anwar Sadat in 1981.) A branch of the militant Islamic Brotherhood, Takfiris may adopt many Western behaviors—they are often unbearded, may drink and party, much of which is aimed at "blending in" to Western society in their efforts to defeat it.

As for the Salifists, Takfiris reject democratic, secular law, acknowledging only Islamic law (sharia). One may not speak to or associate with non-Muslims, or with Muslims who have adapted to Western culture. Takfiris view these as apostates, and as investigative reporter Siem Eikelenboom notes in his *Jihad in de Polder*, an apostate must be put to death.

In the Netherlands, according to Eikelenboom, many Takfiri adherents are illegal, living in the major cities; of approximately 800-1000 in Holland, about ten percent are believed to be involved in criminal activity, especially any that would assist in the creation of false identities and travel documents, facilitating international travel by fundamentalist members.[1]

Afshin Ellian's story puts these developments immediately into perspective. For the mid- to late 1990s marked, too, the coming of age of second- and third-generation Muslims in Europe—exactly those children who increasingly alienated Ellian's young son. These attitudes came largely not from their parents, but from the mosques that they attended and from literature that circulated among students at the Islamic schools. Some of this material arrived there via the students themselves, those who attended some of the more extremist (Saudi-backed) mosques and simply passed the materials they received there on to fellow students. But some of it, too, arrived through teachers and was distributed in "Islam" classes, somewhat akin to American Sunday schools, held in the school buildings on weekends and after hours. For these children, already isolated from their Dutch peers through a segregated educational model, the materials and lectures worked like a drug, seducing them into new perspectives, new ways of life, and above all, the kind of structured identity young teens of all stripes and colors yearn for. Some become the cool kids, the tough ones, the ones others often may look up to as much as fear. But contemplative, studious types can often be swept in as well, saturating themselves in Koranic literature and Salafist or Takfiri ideas. Not all will become violent, of course; but they have found a philosophical direction and an identity that in every way run counter to the democracies in which they live. And with missionary zeal, they spread the word and—worse—practice what they preach.

However unintended, much of this was the fault of the Dutch themselves, and, ironically, of their democratic commitment to the separation of church and state, which had prevented the government from providing funding for the building of the mosques. In their place, other governments eagerly stepped up to the plate—Libya, for instance, and Saudi Arabia—that then filled their new houses of worship with the imams and visions of their choosing. Some have said, too, that in their naïveté, the Dutch had failed to understand that Islam also has a political side, and that those politics—or rather, that political Islam, equally sponsored by the regimes of the Middle East—were being sent their way, as well. In 1995, after numerous Algerian, Moroccan, and Tunisian immigrants had been arrested in France for their participation in a plan to blow up the Paris Metro, Yussef Ibrahim, a journalist for the *New York Times*, reported on the extent to which political Islam had already taken root in Europe. "Over the last year," he wrote, "France, Germany, and Belgium have arrested or expelled close to 200 Islamic militants on charges of subversion and arms trafficking."[2]

In the small Dutch town of Heerlen, Ibrahim met a Moroccan immigrant, Sheik Ahmed Ali Saroukh, who "fidgeted with a cup of tea in a grimy factory that was transformed seven years ago into Masjid Al Nour, the Mosque of Light, as he pondered how to turn the town into a center of Islam." According to Ibrahim, Ali Saroukh wanted "to put up a minaret on the building, topped by a loudspeaker to broadcast the call to prayer five times a day, starting at dawn. He advocates that Dutch women who are teachers in Heerlen wear a veil in schools when teaching Muslim children, and that boys be segregated from girls."

Another Muslim in Heerlen, the Palestinian Khalil Shahine, however, voiced his disagreement. "Before conquering Europe for Islam, which is a hope" he told Ibrahim, "we should concentrate on building up our weak, illiterate societies, our people, with education and knowledge."

* * *

Throughout Europe in the 1990s, Muslim families shattered. If the wayward youth who had earlier joined their parents in family unification

programs had proved difficult to manage, these kids were often
worse. They spoke a language their immigrant parents—especially their
mothers—did not understand, giving them not only access to secret lives,
but a position of power within the family structure. It was—and still is—
they who read the bills and letters that arrived in the daily mail,
they who negotiated with government officials who supervised youth
recreation programs or welfare checks or immigration and residency
permits.

Mohammed Bouyeri was one of them. Born March 8, 1978, he was
the older son among six children born to his Moroccan immigrant
parents, a quiet child and a responsible, if not particularly remarkable
or exceptional, student.

What is known publicly about Bouyeri comes largely from a deeply-
reported story published in the *NRC Handelsblad* on July 9, 2005, and
paraphrased in translation by Ian Buruma in his *Murder in Amsterdam*—
a book that, while receiving accolades in the United States, was
panned in Holland, where a newspaper reporter counted 150 factual
errors on its 260 pages. (I have since pinpointed more.) However,
because the *NRC* remains the primary and most reliable source, I, like
Buruma, have pulled much of my knowledge of Bouyeri from its
columns.

As the older of two sons, Mohammed was always his mother's favorite, but he was doted on as well by his father, who boasted of his
son's accomplishments as related to him by Mohammed himself—
some, but hardly all of which were what they were said to be. At the
age of 12, Mohammed bicycled daily from the Marius Bauer basis
school on the August Allebéplein—later a center of Moroccan immigrant unrest—to Koran lessons, where he paid little attention: the
classes were held in Arabic, while Bouyeri's parents were Berbers, and
so Arabic was to him a foreign tongue. On the streets and with his
teachers, he spoke Dutch; with his parents, brother, and four sisters, he
spoke Berber. Here alone, the schism between Dutch and Muslim
worlds, inner and exterior, us and them, became a part of his very
characterological makeup from the start; and while he may not have
understood Arabic, he identified it as a part of the Muslim, ancestral
aspect of his being. Language, the spiritual, ancestry, heritage—all
these were bound up in one another weighing one side of the scale, as
it were; Dutchness, nation, law, and a sense of alienation, of being different, tipped the other.

"He was a warm, kind person," recalls Fatimazohra Hadjar, a coun-
selor for troubled youth who worked with Mohammed Bouyeri briefly
as he began to grow increasingly violent in the late 1990s and early
2000, "until he became unsatisfied." (Bouyeri was arrested five times
between 1997 and 2004, all for violent behavior.)

The difference between cultures must have been apparent to Mohammed early on: In 1990, when he transferred to the Mondriaan Lyceum middle school, according to the *NRC*, 40 percent of the students were *allochtoon,* or Muslim foreigners, though these students took part in most of the activities Dutch students did. (Five years later, things had changed; former teacher Cor Meijer told the *NRC*, "Moroccan children only watched satellite TV, they didn't read. We couldn't take class trips for longer than a day, because the girls weren't allowed to stay overnight. The school became totally black, while the teachers were white. I didn't particularly like the school anymore.")

At home, meanwhile, Mohammed increasingly took over the authoritarian role: his father worked days at Schiphol airport and, according to the *NRC*, ran errands for the family on weekends, leaving childrearing responsibilities to his wife—who, in turn, would have relied on "Mo," her oldest son. My own guess is that the power he enjoyed there, in contrast with his comparative secondary status in the Dutch milieu, helped cinch his identity as a Muslim in a world where, increasingly, one had to choose between the two. Indeed, while some have pinpointed the start of Bouyeri's radicalization at the time of his mother's death, it had in fact by then already begun—linked in no small measure to his role within the family. Again according to the *NRC*, when his sister Wardia was 17, the then 22-year-old Mohammed learned she had been dating a neighborhood boy, 18-year-old Abdu. Furious, he confronted his father, demanding he put a stop to the relationship: In Islam, the proper conduct would have required Abdu to ask Bouyeri *pere* for Wardia's hand before they even began to date.

"I've talked to her," Mohammed's father said, "But she won't listen. What else should I do?"

Mohammed immediately took control: Wardia may no longer leave the house, and Abdu was not to visit.

This was in 2000, when—unbeknownst to most Dutch—such situations were taking place with growing frequency in immigrant neighborhoods around the country. Wardia, in a moment of clarity—or perhaps it was desperation—called the police, claiming she was being held hostage.

The two worlds—modern, liberal, European and traditional, conservative Islam—had come crashing through the walls of the Bouyeri home.

* * *

But even as this transition played itself out, a similar situation was taking place across Europe within its indigenous population, set off, however silently, by the 1992 signing of the Maastricht Treaty and the formal establishment of the European Union (EU).

Like most of Europe, the Dutch regarded the whole EU business warily. They welcomed the dissolution of national borders, but eyed cautiously plans for a single currency and, even more, community-wide laws imposed by countries far more conservative than their own. And not without reason.

That same year, an organization called the Consumentenbond voor Cannabisliefhebbers (Consumer Organization for Cannabis Lovers) organized, in conjunction with the Dutch government, what they called a *hasjkeurmerk*, a kind of "Good Housekeeping Seal of Approval" for cannabis and hash sold freely over the counter at Dutch "coffeeshops." The seal assured buyers that the products were pure and untainted, of good quality, and above all, safe (as such things can be said to be "safe" at all). Many heralded the move as a gesture that even more firmly established the fabled Dutch liberalism, grounding a Dutch identity distinct from the rest of the world and one of which every Dutchman was rightly proud. (What many ignored, however, and still do, is the amount of hash sold in the Netherlands by Moroccans who use the money in part to finance jihadist organizations and activities, both in Europe and in the Middle East.)

The Dutch drug laws were, in fact—and still are—remarkable for their uniqueness and overall effectiveness. Begun in 1976, the legally approved sale of soft drugs in so-called coffeeshops, where hash and marijuana are sold by the gram in limited quantities, has allowed the country to enjoy one of the lowest rates of hard-drug use in the world. In addition, free methadone and clean needle programs, begun in 1984 (the first in the world)[3], have kept the addict population largely AIDS-free, while keeping incidents of drug-related crime and theft far lower than is found elsewhere in Europe: after all, if addicts can get their fix for free, they don't need to break into people's homes to get the money they would otherwise need to buy them.

But with a pan-European legal system on the horizon, all of this came under threat, and most vociferously from the French, who demanded both programs be shut down. With open borders, they argued, what was to keep trafficking in soft drugs out of *their* country, or keep their citizens from coming to Holland to buy (as if they didn't already)?

Holland fired back: because France had, in fact, failed to provide needle programs to its own addict population, many had come to Holland for its free drugs, bringing their HIV infections with them. Indeed, the highest HIV-positive rate in Holland was among French drug users, not Dutch gays or prostitutes or addicts. If France wanted to keep their drug users home, they were welcome to come and get them.

But they were certainly not welcome to impose their medieval laws and morals on the Dutch.

The battle lines were drawn. Since the end of World War II, no one had been more hated in the Netherlands than Germans; when I first arrived, it was not uncommon for bar fights to break out between drunken Dutchmen and German tourists, simply because the latter had made the tactical error of letting their nationality be known (say, by conversing among themselves in their own language). So bad had the situation become, in fact, that by 1991, schools had begun offering German culture classes to teach Dutch children that there was more to Germany than Nazis. But the ideological battle with the French proved an even better antidote. Attentions turned. Now there was someone new to hate, instead.

The thing was, it wasn't really about the French; it was about being Dutch, about Dutchness as distinct from anything else, a new nationalism taking hold. In the art world, tax structures were altered to make works by Dutch artists more appealing: these would be taxed at six percent, versus eighteen-and-a-half percent for everything else. Newly-appointed at the Stedelijk, Fuchs began an exhibition program that reflected his tastes and attitudes toward modern art, showing largely artists from Italy, Germany, and the U.S.A. But the Stedelijk is a government-run museum, and the government was not pleased.

"You need to show more Dutch artists," he was told.

"There aren't enough good ones," Fuchs retorted.

"Show them anyway," they said, and so mediocre Dutch art supplanted greater international paintings and sculpture in the country's most prestigious modern art museum. (Tired of the fight, Fuchs resigned in 2002. The museum has never recovered.)

It was a new time. It was a new mood. In 1994, a new government took office in the Netherlands, steered largely by the outspoken leader of the Volkspartij voor Vrijheid en Democratie (VVD), Holland's Liberal (Libertarian) Party, Frits Bolkestein. The multiculturalism debate was poised, now, to begin.

CHAPTER 7

Gay rights. Women's rights. MTV. New mosques interrupt the rhythms of Rembrandt's city skyline. Islamic schools, Islamic grocers, open along the streets. The irony of segregation is that as two cultures grow apart, they become more apparent to one another—and more at odds within themselves. Imagine a 15-year-old second-generation Muslim boy—whose religion and culture have trained his intellect to see scantily-clad blonde girls as disgusting, filthy whores, but whose instincts tell him something else completely—faced, now, with Christina Aguilera and with Britney Spears wannabes in his classroom. How does a young girl, urged in magazines and movies to pursue her own career, reconcile her longings with the domestic and subservient role been told her entire life is "right"?

As Holland grew more open, tackling gay marriage and the rise of women in the workplace, the shock became more than the Muslim community could bear; and the more distant and disparaging they became, the more the Dutch in turn grew distant and disparaging of them.

By the mid-1990s, there was no longer any question—integration didn't work. And things were getting worse. The unspeakable had happened: "Holland," Minister Rogier Boxtel finally concluded in 1998, five years after the Bijlmermeer disaster, "is an immigration country."

And the immigrant population was indeed growing. In 1990, the Muslim population of the Netherlands was estimated at about 400,000; in 1995, it had reached nearly 700,000.[1] (By 1996, 12 percent of these minority families included more than five children, versus 1.5 percent of Dutch.[2]) And within these Muslim families, 12 percent of those children were born to teen mothers, while only one percent of Dutch mothers were under the age of 20—a statistic that would later cry out to Ayaan Hirsi Ali.

"At a very young age," she said to me the first time that we spoke, Muslim girls in Holland "are forced to share their lives with someone they've never met. And from the perspective of that young man, he, too, is forced to sacrifice his life, and at a time that he himself hasn't chosen, when he is not ready to commit, to start a life with someone— a complete stranger. These people are forced upon one another, and at the worst time ever that this can happen—just after the end of secondary school, when it should be an opportunity for them to go on to higher education or to learn a career, or become independent and make their own lives." Within a year of marriage, the first child is born. "And the question no one ever asks," Ayaan continued, breathless in her efforts to say so much in just a few hours of our time together, "is, 'are these kids even wanted?' Is a woman who gets raped by a strange man just because everybody has declared 'this is your wedding night' and gets pregnant, is that child born of love? There are numerous ethical and moral questions that are never, ever asked that we run away from. And it is in this environment of desperation, as I call it, that these kids grow up."

Often, Hirsi Ali also told me, those infants are born to children who were themselves beaten in their homes—a tradition they continue in the raising of their own families. It is all they know. "The kids are in filthy clothes. At school on parents' evenings, the parents don't show up. So you have neighborhoods where these children are already signaled from age three, four, five, six—they're on the streets, completely neglected, but no one says anything. The complaining starts only when they turn nine or ten or eleven and resort to vandalism, to beating other kids in the neighborhood. No one probes into the upbringing of these boys—where do they come from? Why are they doing this?"

Intertwined as much with the upbringing of second- and third-generation Muslims as with the growth of the Dutch-Muslim population overall were the forced marriages, orchestrated by first-generation parents who coupled their children with "proper Muslims" from back home. And all too frequently, such marriages involved the very teenagers who would soon be counted among teen mothers—girls as young as 15 have been known to be forced into marriage with distant—or even not-so-distant—cousins from the villages of their parents' birth.

Compounding the problem was the culture these newly-arrived immigrants brought with them: non-Western, often conservatively Islamic in both tradition and religion, the new family members served only to accentuate the rift between the Muslim and Western worlds that ripped through thousands of Dutch-Moroccan and Dutch-Turkish homes. Women brought in from abroad were neither interested in becoming a part of Dutch society nor, in most cases, encouraged to do so (in fact, this is why they had been chosen as wives in the first place). Often illiterate, an "import-bride" would not have immigrated so much as been transplanted, re-located from her familiar land and customs to a strange home with a strange family, a husband she may have never met before who spoke, at least to others, in a language she did not understand. She would have had no friends, no place to turn for support or information, no knowing, even, what resources were available should she want them—or how to find them if she did. She kept to her husband, her children—and she would have them quickly—and her mosque. (It is among the most heartbreaking and incomprehensible aspects of Dutch politics and culture that this situation has, by and large, not changed, even now.)

And so the community of Muslims grew even tighter, more insular, more cut off from the Dutch, and at the same time, larger, more visible—and more demanding. The guests who had tiptoed around the house, in effect, were settling comfortably in the living room, ignoring those whose home it was as they consulted over fabric swatches and made plans for reupholstering the chairs.

Unsurprisingly, none of this served to make them any more welcome to their hosts. By the end of 1997, a full 30 percent of EU citizens admitted to being "racist" in an EU-wide survey. Reported the *NRC Handelsblad*, "Although Dutch citizens scored below the European average for racism, 60 percent feel there is no more room for foreigners [in their country]. . . . In the entire Union, 10 percent of Europeans questioned said that immigrants should return to their land of origin, and 48 percent that their country would be better off without immigrants from outside the EU." [3]

Frits Bolkestein had already warned of this, breaking the taboos and silence in a column he wrote for the *Volkskrant* on September 12, 1991. That same day, the *NRC* also published an interview with him, in which he pointed to a lack of schooling among Muslim girls (20 percent of whom did not attend school at all) and (mostly Moroccan) boys, many of whom missed months on end while visiting family in Morocco, as indicators that integration had indisputably failed—and that it was the Dutch who had the most to fear as a result.

By this time—three years after the publication of Salman Rushdie's *Satanic Verses*—the Italian translator of the book had been stabbed and the Norwegian publisher shot (both survived); and two Muslim leaders in Belgium who had opposed the death penalty for Rushdie had been murdered. Now Bolkestein was hearing murmurs of similar intentions and ideas in his own country: in 1990, an imam on the Turkse Omroep Stichting (Turkish broadcasting station) in Amsterdam summoned his followers to murder all unbelievers ("by hanging, slaughter, or exile"). "I've seen Muslims actually demonstrating, calling for Rushdie's murder," he told the *NRC*'s Derk-Jan Eppink. "I cannot accept this." Unlike others in the political sphere at the time, Bolkestein refused to bend to the relativistic perspective of equality that had brought Holland to that point. "We criticize the caste system in India and apartheid in South Africa," he told Eppink. "Both are legitimized on the basis of religion. But we can't say "oh, apartheid comes from the culture of their society, so we can't criticize it. Freedom of speech, non-discrimination and tolerance are universal values. We cannot simply say in Holland: these values apply to 95 percent of the people, and the five percent who come from other cultures don't have to bother with them. That's unthinkable."[4]

Unsurprisingly, under Bolkestein's leadership, the taboo began to break. It was Rogier Van Boxtel who said it first, using the word again for the first time: If Holland was now an "immigratieland" in which integration had so far failed, he stated in a presentation to the Parliament in 1998, then clearly it was the responsibility of the government to make sure it succeeded. For the media, too, this breaking of taboos and of the accompanying silence meant a whole new realm reporters could investigate—and the more they investigated, the more disturbing were their findings. By the end of 1995, it was, for instance, apparent that despite a booming economy, accompanied by large investments in education for immigrant groups and a kind of "affirmative-action" program in which corporations were required to maintain a certain quota of immigrant workers, unemployment levels among the Turkish and Moroccan Dutch had barely budged, hovering at 20 percent. Some argued that corporations were dodging the law, hiring "whites" almost exclusively. Others maintained that the high drop-out levels in the Muslim community made it impossible for many to find adequate jobs. Both, in fact, probably were true. None of it may well have been known at all had Bolkestein not insisted on raising the issue in public.

* * *

It is difficult for a non-Dutchman to understand just how remarkable Bolkestein's audacity to speak out actually was. Holland's famed and nationally-treasured *poldermodel* has, for centuries, made such dissidence rare; as author Herman Pleij has written, "The Netherlands owes its existence to the democracy of wet feet"[5]—which is to say, the Dutch will do whatever it takes to keep their land above water, be it in terms of maintaining internal consensus and peace, or cooperation with foreign lands. In a country ruled by a coalition government for decades and in which Calvinistic sobriety and propriety oversee parliamentary debates (if you can call such polite, civil discussion "debates" at all), outbursts such as Bolkestein's are rare and usually frowned upon.

But not this time. Although many spoke against him—some even indulging in the melodrama of calling him a "Dutch Hitler"—it is probably no coincidence that the elections of 1994, taking place in the midst of his service as leader of the VVD, also marked the first government since World War I (except during 1940-1945) in which the Christian Democrats had not been part of the coalition. By the time Bolkestein stepped down from office in 1998, it was to leave the Netherlands a very changed place.

* * *

In 1998, the year that Bill Clinton was impeached and the film *Titanic* won 11 Oscars, the year Osama bin Laden bombed U.S. embassies in Kenya and Tanzania and Bill Clinton bombed Iraq, the year that Frank Sinatra died and a Van Gogh self-portrait sold for $71 million, the year that Holland legalized gay marriage, the riots that "would never happen here" broke out in Amsterdam.

"Wijkagent Jerry," they called him—neighborhood agent Jerry—or "Jerry Springer," sometimes, to taunt him. If you were to ask the Moroccan kids who lived in Overtoomse Veld what really caused the conflicts that began on April 23, they'd tell you it was all Jerry's fault. Jerry, they'd tell you, thought he was a supercop. Jerry didn't try to understand them—he persecuted them, instead. But if you'd asked their parents and the Dutch neighbors also living there, you'd hear a very different story.

This is how it always is, of course. But more than ten years later, the fingers continue pointing to one another.

Here's what nobody disputes: a fire started in a trash can on the August Allebéplein, the same city plaza where Mohammed Bouyeri had attended primary school. By nightfall, 150 Moroccan boys had taken to the street, hurling rocks at shop windows, buses, and the police. What happened in between, and why, has never been made quite clear.

What the boys themselves declared to journalists, in courtrooms, and in pamphlets that circulated in the days after the rioting had settled was that two kids, ages nine and 11, set the fire and ran off. Someone called the fire department, who must have alerted the police. By the time the police arrived, two other boys, slightly older, were seated near the flames. The police harassed them, shouted epithets, and eventually smacked the 12-year-old in the head. Fighting erupted as the cops knocked the boys nearly senseless. And that, they say, is when all hell broke out.

Others tell a different story: of kids who had terrorized the neighborhood with truancy and petty crimes, who hung around the plaza and called the white girls "whores," who revved the engines of their stolen motor scooters and frightened the elderly residents of the block. Before Jerry came along, another agent had acted amiably, chatting with the guys, acting as sometime social worker. But the mood changed with Jerry's zero-tolerance approach. For the Moroccan boys in Amsterdam West, "zero tolerance" was an invitation to act out. "Zero tolerance = maximum arrogance," they said. In response, the city circulated pamphlets describing behaviors that would not be tolerated and the punishments for each, including, according to one local youth worker, an eighty-guilder fine for leaning against a window. Boys were not to hang out in groups of more than four. "If you read these rules," the youth worker said to a journalist at the time, "you'd never believe they came from Amsterdam. But there they are, on paper."

By the time April 23, 1998, rolled around, everyone had had enough.

When I read accounts of the Mercatorplein and August Allebéplein riots, I can't help but pity the journalists and youth workers who wrote them, forced, as they were, into the position of disciplinary parent, confronted by siblings who all scream at once, "he started it!"—as if identifying the instigator would somehow solve the problem, as if they hadn't *all* been behaving badly, as if this was all anyone had to know so they could go back to playing with one another nicely again.

Less than half a year before the riots, in December 1997, a study counted 9,000 residents in Overtoomse Veld, 1,500 of whom were Moroccan (first- or second-generation), 400 Turkish, and 34 percent of those under the age of 65 unemployed. The neighborhood had declined economically in recent years. A local Moroccan businessman complained in the NRC that he himself no longer felt comfortable there. "Everyone talks about a multicultural society," he said. "But I don't see any of that here. Only Moroccans." [6]

Four days later, it happened again. School windows shattered. Police rallied. "Jerry's fault," the boys declared. Jerry was the problem.

But the problem, of course, was not a person. It was not going to be settled by determining who had started what. The problem was a rage that brewed in all the Netherlands, born of a clash of cultures who now barely spoke to one another. Five million people in the Netherlands in 1998 were below the age of 25, and ten percent of these, some 500,000, were considered "problem youth." One hundred seventy-five thousand of them had been in trouble with the law in the past year, and most of these from Turkish, Antillean, and Moroccan families. [7]

The problem rose up in schoolrooms as "white flight" transformed more and more schools into "black" or "white" institutions, and no one thought to consider the American success with busing and enforced integration, preferring, as the Dutch do, to let people essentially do anything they want. Occasionally, Moroccan and Turkish parents grew exasperated, too, and began driving their kids to schools in distant, "whiter" neighborhoods, where, they hoped, the children would learn what Dutch children learned, where schoolyard games were played in Dutch, not Turkish or in Berber, and where Western norms were emphasized and expected.

But such parents were sadly few and far between. Worse, when enough of them had brought their children to a single school, the whites began, again, to leave.

And the problem, as Hirsi Ali had said, lay, too, with the parents themselves, parents too young to be made parents, and with a government that didn't care enough to help with anything but handouts, as if money was all they needed. It was as if Holland's history of global trade had led its leaders to believe that even cultural values, even democracy and equality, could be bought.

And the problem, most of all, came from what a man by the name of Amin Elmouaden so eloquently said in the days after the riots of Amsterdam West had settled: "Geen Mohammed, maar ook geen Willem"—to be "not Mohammed, but also not Willem."[8] "People need to ask themselves what it means to be born and raised in the Netherlands," he told an interviewer at the time, "but to be treated by your parents, for twenty years, as if you live in Marrakesh." Generation gaps, he observed, could be found in any family. "But in a Dutch family, the norms and values of the parents and children are pretty much the same. With Moroccans, there is also a cultural gap." These parents do not understand, he said, a young girl who wants to go to a disco. "Even watching TV isn't simple in a Moroccan family: the one wants to watch MTV, listen to music, while the other wants to watch Arab stations in their own language."

The problem lay in Gordian knots too complex to untie, too easy to ignore.

A year later, Jerry had been replaced.

Everything else in Overtoomse Veld remained the same.

CHAPTER 8

It was my friend Christopher who told me.

I had spent the summer with my family, staying with my parents in New York City, and would be leaving in two days. I phoned him quickly, while I packed, to say good-bye.

"Honey!" he shrieked into the receiver. "My God, are you okay?!"

The sun shone across the city. The air was warm. The winds were still. It was 9:02 A.M.

I was fine.

"Where are you?" he bellowed.

"Home."

He kept yelling in my ear. "Turn on your TV!" he cried. "Turn on your TV! A plane just crashed into the World Trade Center! Turn on your TV!"

Chris is well known to his friends as an incorrigible practical joker, and I suspected he was up to something yet again. Still, I did as he asked.

The image came up just in time to see the second plane hit. "Oh, my God," I said, and I don't remember if I moaned it or screamed. My mother said, "What?" My father said, "What?" I said, "A plane just flew into the Twin Towers. Two planes."

I said something else to Chris and he said something else and then we hung up and I stood with my mother and my father and 20 million others across the United States and watched the fire spew from these two great symbols of the free world, and then they hit the Pentagon. Reporters said people were jumping but I didn't believe it. I wanted to see this; I wanted the camera to film the people they said were jumping from the windows at the rate of seven a minute because it could not possibly be true.

There were sirens and there was silence.

Any minute now, my father said, Orson Welles will come on and admit this isn't real.

I squeezed my mother's hand as we watched the director of St. Vincent's Hospital talk about being prepared for the incoming wounded.

And then it collapsed, even as we watched, like a house of cards, tumbling in, tumbling down, and people were running and we were helplessly watching and the streets were silent and the sky was blue and crystal clear.

My two best friends were traders at the time. Bill had moved to London a year or so before. Steven was working at the American Stock Exchange. He lived, with his wife and newborn son, on Liberty Street. Unable to reach Lower Manhattan, I phoned London. No; no word from Steve. I hung up. London called back. Bill's brother-in-law was downtown. He needs help, Bill said. He says limbs were flying past his head.

If he can find his way to me, I said, he can stay here.

The sirens had stopped.

There were no more firemen to send.

And all of this came, a barrage of events, of phone calls (still can't reach Steven), of moments remembered: Steven and Bill taking me to Windows on the World to convince me not to marry the man I planned to elope with two days later; walking, the day before the unthinkable happened, only a block from the Towers and not even thinking—innocent that I was—of the World Trade Center or terrorists or being hit out of nowhere by suicide hijackers trying to destroy us; a succession of *scenes* devoid of all other sense and of sense, thinking over and over "*this is not real*," because not only could the attack on the Twin Towers not be real, or an attack on the Pentagon, or the thousands on thousands of injured and killed, but what could not be real, what simply could *not* be real, was what it would mean if the rest *were* real.

But it was real. And what was left to us then, and still, was the making sense of the rest of it—of the firefighters with dust on their uniforms and blood on their cheeks, of the photographs of the missing strung like rosary beads throughout the city, of the flowers, of the mourning, of the fear. What we then did not realize, though, was this: that what we had the most to fear, in ways Roosevelt could not imagine when he uttered these words the first time, was fear itself.

* * *

In Europe, they watched, too, from offices and cafés, or listened to the news on radios where they could. Friends sent e-mails, unable to penetrate phone lines into the United States. Yes, I was home. Yes, I was fine. We held one another's hands across oceans and wept. In Amsterdam, Tobe Robinson, an Australian who worked for an American finance company at the time, recalled that his boss advised the company of the attack. "Everyone in the area where we were was Muslim," Robinson told me later, "and he said, 'we're an American company. We could also be a target.'" The office closed early. Robinson sat in a sports bar and watched with various other foreigners as CNN broadcast the events live. "All the speculation was about how and why and what reason and who did it. How could it happen—that was the biggest question—how could that occur?" he said. "Such a country that is so big on defense and armies—the NYPD was bigger than the Australian army when I was a kid. It seemed so bizarre. There was a feeling of uncertainty. Insecurity. A sense of dire catastrophe pending in the immediate future."

But as the day wore on, another image appeared on television screens across the West: Palestinians, dancing in the streets, aging women with lined faces and gnarled hands and jubilation in their eyes.

What we did not know yet in the United States was that these celebrations were not limited to the Middle East. In Holland, parties broke out in villages like Ede, with its population of some 7,000 *allochtonen*.[1] "Should we not be happy," wrote an anonymous user on an Internet chat room, "that there finally is someone who could make America small, so they can feel what the Palestinians have felt for years?"

In Belgium, Lebanon-born Dyab Abou Jahjah, who would soon come to dominate (however briefly) Muslim politics in the Benelux as founder of the Arab European League (AEL), heard the news in passing. Years later, he recalled he'd been on his way to visit his friend Souad at her new apartment on a September afternoon, when he passed a few friends sitting at a café.

In the café, the TV was on, and I saw a building in flames, the WTC in New York. I asked the owner what had happened and he said that there had been an accident, in which a plane had crashed into the building. I took in the information and continued on my way. When I arrived at Souad's place, she met me at the door with a huge smile on her face. I asked her why she was so happy, and she told me that a second plane had hit the building. At first, I found it hard to believe, but realized then that it must be an attack. Souad, who had just moved in, did not yet have a TV, and so we sat as if hypnotized by the radio and heard that another plane was missing, maybe two. And that the Pentagon had been hit. We couldn't hold our joy, and laughed together. She had tears in her eyes and said: 'There is a time for revenge; those who have killed us are now also being killed.' My telephone rang constantly. People called from everywhere and everyone had but one feeling: thank God that we could live to see the day of America's humiliation.[2]

* * *

Over the next days, I wandered the streets of the Upper East Side alone, dazed, as everybody else was dazed, unsure, as everybody was unsure. I took photographs: a sign at Barnes & Noble on Lexington and Eighty-Seventh Street declaring "Closed, due to act of war"; the first few of what would soon be several thousand colored sheets of paper, marked with photographs of the "missing," now known dead; impromptu shrines on the doorsteps of brownstones and apartment buildings, and waves of flowers at the doorway of Engine 22, our local firehouse on Eighty-fifth Street and Third Avenue. Smoke and stench and death rose up and over New York City in the wind.

On September 18, exactly one week after the attacks, I returned to Amsterdam.

Everything had changed.

Suddenly now I had become a curiosity, someone to whom no one knew quite what to say, but everyone—whether they asked them aloud or not—had questions they wished to ask, and everyone, whether they spoke them or not, had opinions they ached to give. In place of the sense of intimate connection I had felt in New York City, I confronted now an odd detachment, an alienation: there were those of us who had been there, and those of them who had not. We could not quite understand one another the same way anymore.

And as I walked this city, a city whose very gentleness now felt practically obscene (leaving New York had felt obscene, like having walked out in the middle of a funeral for a business meeting), where the sun slid into the gardens and over the balconies, where the smell of the smoke and the sorrow and the dead did not roll along the streets and into our lungs, I struggled to feel what I felt as I still walked the earth of New York City and held the hands of strangers with whom I would be forever extraordinarily, if inexplicably, bound. And I realized then just how far away from a new United States I was. No American flags waved along the street. No one else wore ribbons for the dead. I was alone in my fury, my bewilderment, my anger, alone in my sorrow, in my indignation, in my defiance. Leaving had robbed me of the chance to share all that filled this moment.

I was alone in Holland, too, or nearly so, in my fear: a scant thirty-three percent of the Dutch said they feel less safe now than they did before September 11. I counted myself among them. With the passing of every plane—and there are many over Amsterdam, and they fly low—my blood chilled, my pulse quickened, my heart pounded. I followed the sound until it was safely beyond hearing. I waited for the sirens. None came.

In Amsterdam, I found a world where one could express sympathy and horror, say a prayer, light a candle; a world where one could read the papers and watch the news and feel one's throat tighten at the images, and then still return the paper to the table, turn the station, leave the candle burning, and walk out into the sunlight to play.

We could not do that in New York City.

In New York, in Manhattan, it was everywhere: in dust, in the wind, in stores that did not reopen, in the piles of newspapers outside a neighbor's apartment that announced that he was not home and most likely was not coming home again. It was in the eyes and questioning voices of those who asked if you were okay—and everybody asked: the drugstore cashiers, the postal clerks, the doormen of nearby buildings with whom for years you had shared only silent nods as you passed. "Are you all right? Is everyone you know?" One did not see a woman wearing black without wondering if it was fashion, shul, or a funeral that had dressed her.

In Amsterdam, there was only wariness, a kind of gentle, if often ubiquitously polite sympathy, and silence.

Or mostly. In the first few days of my return, I wore a ribbon on my lapel, just as others had done in New York, only in place of the red, white, and blue, which I thought would be too obvious, I wore white— a symbol, someone had told me, of universal peace. As I walked along the Van Woustraat by my home one afternoon, a man in a white djellaba approached me in the street. Within seconds he had planted himself directly in front of me, blocking my movement, staring straight into my eyes. He stood there just a few seconds—perhaps a half minute, no longer—and then went on his way.

When I got home, I took the ribbon off and laid it on my desk. I never wore it publicly again.

I mention this because it happened, because it is a part of the story of the Netherlands in the weeks after 9/11. But it was an exception. In all my other encounters with Muslims in Amsterdam then, we approached one another in a way reminiscent of a junior high school dance, where the groups of girls and boys stand and stare from opposite sides of the room with curiosity, interest, eagerness, and fear, each hesitating to be the first to cross the floor. There was, for instance, the shoemaker, on the corner of my street, whom I visited within days of my return.

He spoke no English.

I spoke no Turkish.

Still, often, we'd talk.

Ever since I'd moved to this street five years earlier, any time I brought a pair of shoes in to be repaired, I'd end up staying in his

shop for 20 minutes or more. Sometimes there would be other neighbors there as well, drinking tea with his wife behind the counter. He
wears Western clothes, but she does not. He appears to be much older
than she is. They have been in love since they were children, they told
me once. They came here to Holland in 1979.

So we'd talk.

In the beginning, it was about little things: the shoes he hand-makes
for the handicapped, for people with prosthetic legs or clubfeet or legs
of uneven length. His Dutch is better than mine, but his accent is
thicker. Scrub-faced, pretty, his wife, working alongside him, speaks it
charmingly. "*Charmante,*" the Dutch say, like the French.

Then once he asked about my last name. I said my grandfather had
come to the United States from Lithuania, but that there were, I had
discovered, a great many Esmans in Holland. "Lithuania," he said.
"Lithuania and Turkey have a history together. You are Jewish?" And
he began to trace for me the history of war and friendship between
Turkey and Russia, between Turkey and Austro-Hungary, between
Turkey and the Jews. His wife said, "He's always reading about history. At night, I can't get his head out of the books. Other women's
husbands watch TV. All he ever does is read." She threw her hands in
the air in mock frustration, but he smiled at me and winked, and I
smiled back. We had come from two such different worlds, and yet
perhaps from the same history.

Our neighborhood then was small and compact: A Dutch supermarket on the corner, a flower stall run by a laughing Dutch woman with
dyed strawberry-blonde hair and her amiable husband; a video rental
whose doors I never saw a single person enter; a café run by an Irish-
woman who served English breakfasts and bagels with smoked salmon
and cream cheese; an Indian grocer, presided over by a tall woman
with large eyes and high cheekbones who rarely smiled; a Turkish bakery, also owner-managed by a couple and their children, who sold
what were said to be the best croissants in Amsterdam and some of
the best shoarmas; and a flourishing Turkish grocer, this too, family-
owned.

At the Dutch store, the shoppers were mostly women, tall and
blonde, with children who pointed and questioned and demanded, or
with the men they'd just moved in with, men in suede bomber jackets
who sidled up to them with one or another bottle or jar and asked,
"what do you think of this?" as if they'd discovered a new form of
reptile in the sand. The counter by the window at Mary's Irish Café
held the coffee cups usually of men, many of them with long gray hair
below their shoulders and denim shirts that had seen better, cleaner,
days. Past them both and past the flower stall between them, the Muslim women walked, their bodies draped in shapeless coatdresses, their

hair carefully covered by scarves, their faces cleanly scrubbed, most often alone. Sometimes I ran into the shoemaker's wife as we each made our rounds of all the shops; she always stopped to smile and say hello.

On an October afternoon in her husband's shop, she offers me a pastry. "From Turkey," she says, and so I take one. I am expecting something sweet, but when I bite down, I taste savory: cheese. It is delicate and hearty, at once. My mouth still caressing that first bite, I point to her and then to the plate. She understands. No, she smiles, she did not make them. They are from the bakery next door. "We eat these all the time," she says, "in Turkey, where I'm from."

Growing up in New York City, I had a next-door neighbor whose mother was Swedish and father, Danish. They spoke English, Swedish, and Danish at home. It was as if they had secret languages, special words and communications that bound them together, and I envied that. But they were family. It was different. We are strangers. We are from, if not warring countries, warring religions. When I returned to Amsterdam after September 11, they were the first people I saw. I confess, I was afraid. Would they talk to me, still? What would I say to them—or they to me?

As it turned out, what they said was what anyone would say: that they were shocked by what had happened, saddened. He told me he thought it was all about oil—a theory that at that point, September 18, had not had much play yet, if any. I suspect this was his own deduction. But I admit I smiled a little too hard at him. I tried a little too hard. I was saying: I really do not hate you. Really. As if I needed to say it at all.

These kinds of things happen often when one lives in a foreign country, but we don't think of them when they occur around us in our own. How often have I entered coffee shops in New York City to find a Greek waiter taking an order from a Frenchwoman, or—what always makes me laugh—walked into a bagel joint to find a Chinese deli man wrapping a bagel with nova for a Puerto Rican guy and his Ecuadorian girlfriend, or an old Jewish butcher packing chopped liver onto rye bread for a Pakistani cabdriver—all of them speaking to one another in English? I never much pay attention to it there; but living here, I have found that conversations in Dutch with other non-native Dutch-speakers brings me close to them in a way I am not when I speak in Dutch to the Dutch. There is no power playing out here. What we are saying to each other is: I am not Dutch. You are not Dutch. Isn't it wonderful that we are both here, speaking Dutch? Is it not miraculous that this language and this place we share bring us together?

As he stood on his side of the counter and I on the other, I would show him my broken shoes. His hands followed mine along the lines of the sole, the curves of the leather. We held them together. I'd pass the shoes to him, and know that he would fix them well, and he would pass them back to me, he on his side of the counter, me on mine, the shoes, our hands, the words we'd speak, meeting in the middle.[3]

* * *

But what I couldn't help but notice was that once the requisite sympathies had been expressed, the mandated moments of silence across the continent performed, a certain smugness settled over European lips. While those who baldly went so far as to state publicly we'd "had it coming" were quickly shamed and scolded, far too many made it clear, nonetheless, that they sort of thought so, too. Certainly they remained convinced that the acts of 9/11 had been politically inspired, having nothing whatever to do with Islam or religion, except insofar, perhaps, with U.S. support of Israel and the thriving Jewish culture on its own shores and cities. Europe, which had rid itself of most of its Jewish population years before, had, most seemed to agree, little to worry about.

As an American and a Jew, this was where I felt my love affair with Holland coming to an end. As an American and a Jew, I felt Holland's ranks start closing in. It became quite quickly clear: it wasn't just the Muslims. None of us were wanted here anymore. More than once, I thought of my former neighbor, Mr. L. There seemed to be a lot of him around.

Oddly, behind the scenes, European intelligence officials took a completely different view. Shaken by the discovery that Mohammed Atta and several others of the nineteen September 11 hijackers had lived previously in Hamburg, Germany, European counterterrorism officials began focusing on radical groups at home. In Hamburg, Atta and his henchmen had frequented the Al Quds mosque, where an imam known as al-Fazai preached hatred of the United States and called for the slaughter of Christians and Jews around the world. Even before the attacks, the *New York Times* announced on September 23, 2001, militants had been arrested in Spain, Italy, Germany, Britain, and France, some said to have had plans to bomb the European parliament in Strasbourg and to supply weaponry to other militant groups in Germany, Belgium, and the UK.[4]

In Holland, the uncertainty and unrest played out, polder-style, in public lectures and debates. Paul Scheffer, a member of the social-democratic labor party (Partij van de Arbied, or PvdA) and author of a highly controversial statement published a year earlier, "The Multicultural Drama," stood at the forefront. "By 2015," he had warned, "about half the population of our largest cities will be *allochtone*"—a word which originally meant non-Dutch-native, but which, after the 1970s, increasingly came to replace the term "non-Western," a polite idiom used to cover what was really meant: "Muslim." These *allochtonen*, declared Scheffer—rightly—form an ethnic underclass; and if they make up half the population, we're in trouble.

Scheffer's statement, brazen when it first appeared, began to take on new dimensions after 9/11. His argument—that Holland had tried too hard to pacify its Muslim immigrants rather than stimulate them to join Dutch—Western—culture, had done too much to ease their lives and not enough to encourage them to build their own, had ignored entirely a generation of hateful antipathy in the name of "tolerance"— burst forth with new popular support.

"What it mostly is about," he wrote, "is that the separation between state and church is not effectively followed in the Islamic community. Now and then we see what imams preach, and we hear examples of hate-filled expressions against the culture in which they are expected to participate. This was why, during the time that Ed van Thijn was mayor of Amsterdam, the observation was made that Muslims would no longer have to follow the laws of a city that was run by a Jew." Fear of Muslim—especially Moroccan—youth, he noted, had now become palpable in Amsterdam and other major cities.

These and other examples led Scheffer to conclude:

And so the house of cards of the multicultural society collapses. All unspoken expectations, as if integration were essentially a question of time, are unre- warded. Under the surface of public life lies a sea of stories about the confronta- tion between cultures that are almost never heard. We sit now with the third generation of these immigrants, and the problems have only grown larger.

Scheffer did not stop there. Every aspect of Dutch culture, he noted, had ignored the problems and the changes that filled the country's spi- rit and its streets. "We live next to each other," he wrote, "each with his own café, his own school, his own idols, his own music, his own belief, his own butcher, and soon, his own street or neighborhood. The reality is that old and new Netherlanders know little or nothing about one another."

"The conclusion," he continued, "is clear: Integration is now more an exception than the rule." Calling for a parliamentary investigation in immigration and integration ("because at the moment, entire generations are been written off in the name of 'tolerance'"), he noted: "Tolerance groans, crumbles, under our lack of attention and of care. The multicul- tural drama that results is the largest threat to the peace of our society."

That Muslim students were failing in schools, falling behind profes- sionally—and economically—was already clear by the time Scheffer published his observations. What is puzzling is that no one else had seemed to notice the impact this would inevitably have on attitude—resentment and anger among the immigrants for being, as they claimed, discriminated against in the workplace, and equal resentment among Dutch taxpayers who perceived their immigrant neighbors as parasites living on welfare programs, loitering on street corners, harassing women where they could.

In the last months of 2001, followers of Scheffer's manifesto had now been split in two: those who supported easing barriers for immigrant youth, lowering standards for their academic successes, providing more government services to support them; and those who argued that this was only more of the same, a way of throwing good money after bad, and that what was needed now were harsher measures, higher demands, more rigorous limitations, and, if necessary, forced integration into Western ways.

In November 2001, I attended a panel discussion at the American Book Center in Amsterdam—where such events frequently take place—at the invitation of Jay Rosen, chairman of the Department of Journalism at New York University, who was among the panelists. Jay, like me, had been in New York City the day of the World Trade Center attacks. In fact, at the time, he'd been downtown, where he lives and works.

Speaking at the event, too, was Dutch journalist Joeri Boom, who had spent that same day seated at his desk in the offices of *de Groene Amsterdammer* [*The Green Amsterdammer*], an alternative weekly newspaper with a leftist, Green Party perspective. Fré Meijer came along with me, as did my now-husband; a standing-room-only audience filled the hall, divided rather equally between Americans and other ex-pats, and Dutch. Whether it was out of fear of reprisal or disinterest, I don't know, but there was not a single Muslim in the room.

"I remember that day," Joeri Boom began. "I stared at the TV in shock all afternoon and wondered how I was ever going to write this story. I had a deadline to meet, but I didn't know what to say. All I felt was shock and horror and disbelief.

"And then," Joeri Boom continued, "I realized: It was about America, not Holland. I realized it had nothing to do with me."

These words still echo in my mind from time to time, bringing with them all the hot blood and anger I felt when I first heard them, and all the incredulity at the arrogance, the ignorance, the blindness that they represent. At the time, I only stood up from my seat and argued back at him: It was about humanity. It had everything to do with you. Several people approached me after the debate to shake my hand and thank me for speaking up. I was grateful, and still am, but I had seen something in that moment I had never seen before: this indifference that masks itself as tolerance in the Netherlands, and the unwillingness to confront the possibility and magnitude of a loss of equilibrium. It was why so many Dutch Jews perished in the Holocaust. The encomium, generally quoted as "You are free to do whatever you want to do, as long as it doesn't hurt me," was not, as it turned out, about liberalism and openness, but rather a selfish lack of empathy or concern. For Muslims to beat and kill their daughters in their homes was one thing; for them to pinch a Dutch girl's derriere and call her a whore was something else entirely. And this, they would *not* tolerate.

As long as the attacks took place in America, it had nothing whatever to do with them.

"Do you really think," I asked Mr. Boom in an e-mail some days later, "that if Al Qaeda actually succeeded in conquering America, that this would be enough? Do you really think your own life would not be affected, too?"

But it wasn't Joeri Boom who had drawn these lines between us: they had been put in place already in a system that essayed to value Dutch art above all other, a nation that refused to call itself a land of immigration, or to bend to suit the needs of one when that fact—that it was an immigration country, after all—could no longer be denied; by a people who, however unaware of it, had divided themselves into a world of "us"es and of "them"s. Integration had, as Scheffer had pronounced, failed entirely; but it wasn't just the Muslims' fault. It was Holland's, too. And it was getting worse.

By this time, I'd learned Dutch well enough to understand pretty much everything that anybody said. After 9/11, I came to understand, too, the words they didn't speak.

CHAPTER 9

On November 13, 2001, a group of panelists sat before an audience of several hundred at Amsterdam's De Balie, a forum for debate and popular events on the Leidseplein, the social center of the city. The subject: "Who Needs a Voltaire?" The real question: Should Muslims be re-examining their culture? Or is it the West who has a problem, the West which literally billions of people deem "decadent"?

Six speakers discussed the issue: Four Dutch men, one Dutch-Turkish woman, and one Iranian—Afshin Ellian. As usual, Ellian was the lone dissident: he alone declared that self-examination was long overdue amongst the Muslim cultures of the world.

As the conversation heightened, one woman in the room raised her hand. "I'm sorry," she said, her voice soft but determined. "I'm really sorry, but you must allow us to have our *own* Voltaire. All of you in this discussion, Muslims and Westerners, are all criticizing the West. So apparently when it comes to self-criticism, the West is really good at it. But why doesn't one Muslim come out and say, 'maybe, just maybe, the Islamic culture has a few disadvantages'?"

Heads turned. The woman sat back down. Voices murmured.

Ayaan Hirsi Ali had spoken out for the first time.

In retrospect, the entire premise of the event was pretty stupid, and it typified the Dutch proclivity for discussion in place of action, its Calvinistic self-recrimination, and above all, its politicians' tremendous talent for distraction. The West, after all, had *had* its Voltaire already, along with its Sigmund Freud, its Karl Marx, even its L. Ron Hubbard and Ayn Rand. The West, with its churches full of confessionals and billion-dollar industry in self-help books, was plenty good at examining itself. Hadn't it done little else since 9/11, asking, in magazines and newspapers and interviews with "experts" on TV, over and over again, the same question, "Why do they hate us, so?"

Nonetheless, Ayaan's outburst caught the attention, not only of her fellow audience at De Balie, but of two reporters from the national broadsheet, *Trouw*, who approached her with a request to write an article for their paper. Ever eager for a platform, she agreed.

Ayaan had shed her headscarf years earlier, but it was not until 9/11 that she freed herself entirely from her religion. "If this is what Islam is," she determined that historic afternoon, "then I am not a Muslim."

But what, then, was she? Where did she fit in?

Looking back, I think this is the question Ayaan Hirsi Ali has been seeking to answer ever since, and, even now, has yet fully to resolve.

That crisis of identity, of belonging, has not been hers alone. After September 11, Afshin Ellian tells me, Korans flew out of bookstores and mosques across all of Europe at an unprecedented rate. "Jami became a democrat," he points out, speaking of his fellow Dutch-Iranian, former Muslim Ehsan Jami, who, like Ayaan and Afshin, is forced to live under security protection as a result of statements he has made in public, "and Bouyeri became a terrorist." On both sides of the coin, the focus was the same, says Ellian: look what 19 good Muslim boys could do. Just *look at what they could do.* Whether one stood awed and admiring, or horrified and repelled, this was what it was really all about.

One hardly needed a Voltaire for that.

Nonetheless, the question hung there, palpable in the damp Holland air: if what had happened in the U.S. was the fault of the Americans, whose fault would it be if it should happen here?

"Holland's," said Ayaan Hirsi Ali.

"Holland's," said Mohamed Bouyeri.

But for very different reasons.

In that search for understanding, the media took the lead, more so in the Netherlands than anywhere—certainly than in the United States, where anthrax scares muted all the newsrooms and political correctness washed over the pages of the press. True, it was easier here in Holland; radical Islam had been allowed to flourish unhindered, as politicians turned their heads and failed to absorb responsibility. The mosques and religious schools the state had refused to fund had found eager sponsors in Saudi Wahabbist leaders, who often sent their own imams to run them. Journalists made their way in to them and reported, in a press eager for sensation and not yet intimidated by reprisals, what they found.

And so the U.S. invaded Afghanistan.

Daniel Pearl was killed.

Kabul fell.

The Prospect, which I picked up while visiting my friend Bill in London, sold its November 2001 issue with a CD of the Koran attached to its inside cover.

Around the globe, eyes focused on the Muslim world and Islam. For the United States, at least outside of New York City, it was about somewhere far away. For most of Europe, it was only down the street.

But no one came closer to the truth than Hirsi Ali did in writing her first article for the *Trouw*, making clear what others, for the most part, had only dared surmise; and as a Muslim (or former Muslim) herself, her words carried more weight. Islam, she explained, insists on a hierarchical structure: man above woman, god above man, religious law over civil law, Islam above all other religions and Allah, of course, above all other gods. With insight few others could have brought to the situation, she wrote: "Man stands above the woman, and children must obey their parents. People who do not follow these rules are to be killed in the name of God."

Explaining further, she went on:

"[For Muslims], life here is temporary and the best that believers can do to show their fear of god is to keep closely to his demands and laws and so earn a place in heaven. Unbelievers are only on this earth to act as an example to believers of how they should not be. . . . Sharia— Islamic law—stands above all laws created by man. It is the duty of every Muslim to live as purely as possible according to Sharia. Fundamentalists take it so far as to say that the lives of moderate Muslims do not comply with Islamic rules.

This we Muslims learn as young as possible from our parents, from Koran school, and in the mosques."

Prone as Hirsi Ali may be to melodrama and exaggeration, in this she could not have been more spot-on. The conflicts she described in *Trouw* were—and remain—real ones, the center force behind the "clash of civilizations" growing fiercer by the day across both the Western and Islamic cultures of the world. The resulting confusion, particularly for young immigrant Muslim men (and increasingly, for Muslim women) now living in the West, had been mounting for decades. Now, with the population of youth in their teens and early twenties growing rapidly (and with all the identity crises that accompany the age), it was seizing hold of much of Europe, regardless of the events of 9/11. September 11, in other words, did not cause them; it only forced more Westerners to pay attention.

And pay attention they did. Dutch officials produced reams of reports in the years between 2002 and 2005 (particularly after Van Gogh's murder), each showing a rise in radical Islam among the country's Muslim youth. As early as September 2002, the Ministry of Justice pronounced, "Radical Islam is a political force that mobilizes masses and indoctrinates them on the bases of an all-embracing view of the world. Political action is flanked by terror and violence; opponents and enemies are eliminated by death." Fundamentalists account for only five percent of all Muslims, according to an article in *Trouw* describing the report, "but they are wealthier and better organized, they have a clear strategy and compelling leaders." (Oddly, the article failed to note that five percent of 1.2 billion Muslims is nothing to sneeze at.) "Modern, liberal, and progressive Muslims, the report stated, "are powerless against the force of Muslim fundamentalists."[1]

But for Dutch Intelligence, or AIVD (Algemene Inlichting En Veiligheids Dienst), this was already old news. As early as April, police had stormed five homes across the country—in Amsterdam, Eindhoven, Bergen op Zoom, and Groningen—seeking computers, books, videos, and other items belonging to a group of suspected extremists. Similar raids also took place in August in Rotterdam, The Hague, Eindhoven, and elsewhere. For it all, the police were amply rewarded: as Siem Eikelenboom describes it, the findings included 256 audio tapes about jihad in general, 157 audio tapes about jihad in Algeria, 12 audio tapes about jihad in Bosnia, and 11 audio tapes about the conflicts in Chechnya.[2]

Others, notes Eikelenboom, included Salafistic speeches and bore titles like "the danger of the Jews" and "Caravan of Martyrs," or the "Testament of a Martyr" by Ayman al Zawahiri, an al Qaeda leader.

But here the law ran into trouble: ownership of such items, in itself, is not a crime. Were these simply devout Muslims, targeted by an overzealous police force, the victims of a growing racism? Muslim community leaders declared they were. The rest of the country sat divided. And the media, hungry here as everywhere for a good and controversial story, pressed it for all they could.

In this, they found a treasure trove in Ayaan Hirsi Ali, whose articles began appearing with increasing frequency and passion. Over and over, she repeated her conviction: integration hadn't worked, a crisis had been brewing throughout the European Union now for years, and no one had either dared or cared to see it—only to make it worse.

"Most of the Muslims who came to Holland didn't choose this country specifically," she wrote in the *NRC Handelsblad*[3], "but came of necessity. This migrant comes from rural areas, where tribal traditions are strongest. In his repertoire of knowledge, symbols, norms, rules of behavior—culture—he travels still in a pre-modern time."

If Muslims found such words insulting, the Dutch found them educational, even—for many—a relief: suddenly, the differences were starting to make sense. There were reasons. Hirsi Ali explained, "Take the example of a dysfunctional authoritative way of thinking in the workplace. When a Moroccan manger of a supermarket [in Holland] leads his personnel with intimidation and verbal abuse, he is following the established norms of his culture. He is trying to establish his authority and protect his honor: guiding workers with clear explanations would be a sign of weakness. A request beginning, 'if you please,' is, in his culture, what a person lower in the hierarchy would say to one above him, not vice versa. From the reference point of his Dutch colleagues, the Moroccan's behavior is unworkable and unacceptable.

And if the Moroccan doesn't adjust his ways, if he doesn't put his old manners aside and take on those of his Dutch fellow workers, he loses. He becomes unemployed. These situations emerge every day. They lead to misunderstanding and mistrust on both sides, in which Muslims complain of 'discrimination' and employers determine to employ 'no more Moroccans.'"

Such observations sparked debate, of course, with some arguing that the Dutch need to understand better the original cultures of their Muslim population and take such standards into consideration, and others insisting that the norms of Moroccan and Turkish cultures should not be held as standard-bearers in the Netherlands, cultural relativism be damned. But such statements—and others like them—did not win Hirsi Ali much popularity in Muslim circles. Finally, on a television show that aired on March 8, 2002, she went too far: "Islam," she declared, "is a backward culture."

One week later, besieged with death threats too serious to ignore, Ayaan Hirsi Ali fled the country.

But in fact, Ayaan had not been the first to say these words. Months before this, they had been the words of politician Pim Fortuyn.

Murdered by an animal rights activist on May 6, 2002, Fortuyn rose from being a little-known professor of sociology to a candidate for prime minister in the course of merely months, riding largely on his single assertion, the one that Hirsi Ali only echoed: that Islam was a backward culture, and could no longer be tolerated in the Netherlands. "The Netherlands is full," he declared of the immigration country that still struggled with the term. "It is time to close our borders down."

There was much un-Dutch about Fortuyn: his elegant Italian suits, his elaborate, palatial home (which he named Casa di Pietro), and above all, his outspoken frankness; but Dutch he was at his core, a proud nationalist who bemoaned the "Islamization of our culture," as he put it in a book published in 1997. A flamboyant, shaven-headed homosexual, he hired a butler to care for him at home and rode in a chauffeur-driven Daimler. Though gay marriage had been legal in the Netherlands since 2000, Pim Fortuyn stayed single, sharing his home only with his two Cavalier King Charles spaniels, Kenneth and Carla;

and despite his anti-immigration stance, once remarked, "I have nothing against Moroccans: I have them often in my bed." It was a consciously inflammatory remark, of course, given the Muslim stance on homosexuality (which it considers sinful depravity, punishable by death); Fortuyn lived for such outbursts, and they were the source of much of his popularity. "He says what people think but do not dare to say out loud," his supporters often said of him, admiringly. "I say what I think," said Pim Fortuyn himself, "and I do what I say." The phrase became his slogan, Holland's pre-Obama version of "Yes, we can."

Fortuyn rose to power as the selected leader of Leefbaar Nederland, or "Livable Netherlands," a party founded in 1999 following the success of two regional groups, Leefbaar Utrecht and Leefbaar Hilversum. (Ironically, it was in Hilversum that the party was born, and in Hilversum where Pim Fortuyn was murdered.) Elected to serve as leader of Leefbaar Rotterdam in March 2002, where his party won a third of the city's votes, he expected an equivalent response in the national elections come May.[4]

Rotterdam in 2002 was a broken city: crime was up, tolerance was down. Fully 45 percent of the population was "allochtone," coming largely from Suriname, Turkey, and Morocco. Fortuyn promised a crackdown on crime, improved schools, and resistance against Islam ("a cold war against Islam," he called it in an interview in *Rotterdams Dagblad*[5]), and it paid off.

But his brazenness was too much for a national campaign. Many who had selected him to lead Leefbaar Nederland recoiled, especially from remarks he made in a February 9 interview in the *Volkskrant*.

"You've said," noted interviewers Frank Poorthuis and Hans Wansink, "that foreigners snatch all our blonde women, and then turn around and call them 'whores.'"

"No," Fortuyn corrected calmly. "I said Islamic men do that. That's quite different, sir, than 'foreigners.' I stand behind what Voltaire said: I may object to your opinion, but I will defend your right to speak it. I'm therefore also for abolishing that ridiculous legal article, 'thou shalt not discriminate.' Lovely. But if that means people can't make discriminatory remarks—and one makes them pretty quickly in this country—then I say, 'that's not right.' Let people say what they have to say. There is one limit, and this I find extremely important: you may never resort to physical violence. No democracy can permit this. But if an imam says my way of life is contemptible and lower than a pig, well, okay, let him say it."[6]

Then why, the *Volkskrant* asked, in what would become the defining moment of Pim Fortuyn's political career, and perhaps, of his entire life, "why the hate toward Islam?"

Fortuyn's answer was collected and considered. "I don't hate Islam," he said. "I find it a backward culture. I've traveled a great deal in the world; and wherever Islam rules, it's appalling. It's like the old reformed Catholics. They lie all the time. Why? Because they create norms and values that are so high, no human being can achieve them. It's the same in Muslim culture. Look at Holland. In which country could a candidate with support as significant as mine be openly gay? It's fantastic! You should be proud of it. And I'd like to keep it that way."

But not everyone, apparently, agreed; by Monday morning, February 11, 2002, Leefbaar Nederland had sacked its leader outright. The *Volkskrant* led with the story splashed across its front page. "With his statements that Holland is full, that the borders should be closed to Muslims, and that the laws against discrimination should be scrapped," the paper reported, "he has, according to the leaders of his party, this time gone too far."

This last—the scrapping of anti-discrimination laws—was, unsurprisingly, the most shocking, not only to Leefbaar Nederland but to the Dutch general public. But it was not, in fact, what Fortuyn had actually said. His emphasis had been on his right—on anyone's right—to criticize imams who called homosexuals "lower than pigs," and similarly, on the right of those imams to protest in return. For Fortuyn, the issue was clear: neither he nor the imams should be stopped from saying what they believe, and neither should have the right to prosecute the other for doing so. Free speech should rule above the rest. It was, again, about Voltaire.

Interestingly, it was also about democracy as it is practiced and defended in the United States (and not coincidentally, the reason Theo van Gogh cherished the U.S. as strongly as he did). But it was not the democracy of a post-Holocaust Holland. And no issue would cause greater battles in the Netherlands in the years ahead than this.

Fortuyn formed his own party, the Lijst Pim Fortuyn, within hours, bringing countless fans along with him—including an estimated fifty percent of those aged 18 to 30—supporters who felt, as he did, that the rising Muslim population was putting pressure on essential Dutch principles and freedoms. It was a perspective that had gained increasing currency in the months after 9/11, less because of the World Trade Center attacks themselves than because of the media attention those attacks had brought to the Muslim community in the Netherlands—and the insights Hirsi Ali had brought by now into the public sphere.

Others, of course, felt differently, especially the foreign press, who, in attempting to describe the "phenomenon Fortuyn" to their readers, called him a "racist" and likened him to Austria's Jorg Haider and France's Jean-Marie le Pen—comparisons Fortuyn vigorously rejected. Born to a staunchly Catholic family, a reformed Communist and activist for women's rights, legalized marijuana and above all, the rights of homosexuals, he could perhaps—with the exception of his pro-abortion stance—more accurately be compared to American Libertarian Ron Paul.

And then there were those—and I was one of them—who thought Fortuyn was little more than a pretender, a narcissist with a big mouth and glib tongue who would quickly be exposed and then forgotten.

We were the most wrong of all.

* * *

Pim Fortuyn's murder, like Theo van Gogh's, took place in broad daylight, in public, committed by a man motivated entirely by politics, a follower of ideologies millions would describe as "peaceful." Shot as he left a radio station in Hilversum, where he had just finished giving an interview to Ruud de Wild of Radio 3FM, Fortuyn died immediately from his wounds. His chauffeur, who witnessed the shooting, chased after the attacker, who was arrested by the police within hours. The killer's name, to the surprise of everyone, was not "Ahmed" or "Mohammed," but Volker van der Graaf—a 32-year-old white, leftist Dutchman, an animal rights activist who later confessed openly to the murder, saying killed the 54-year-old candidate "to protect the vulnerable—animals and Muslims" from Fortuyn's destructive politics.

Nearly a decade later, it astounds me that no one, particularly no Muslim leader, has ever expressed distaste for Van der Graff's position, the equation implied in his phrase "animals and Muslims"—nor, for that matter, have Muslim groups protested even once the assumption that they are helpless, so much so that they needed a white man—a Dutchman—to kill in their defense. The outrage simply isn't there.

But outrage there was, at least among the Dutch, who had not experienced a political assassination since the lynching of the DeWitt brothers in 1672. Hordes of people flooded the Rotterdam suburb where Pim Fortuyn had lived to pay respects; one supporter expressed his fury and admiration to a reporter from the *Independent*, "He had the guts to kick the government in the ass."[7]

Perhaps it was such admiration, powered by that fury, which led to the LPF's sweeping victory in the elections held just nine days layer. (Dutch law made it impossible to remove Fortuyn's name from the ballot.) Of 150 seats in the Parliament, the LPF took 26—making it the second most powerful in the country.

CHAPTER 10

I read an article in the *Volkskrant* about a woman who is, they say, sparring with Islam. A photograph of a young black woman standing too close to the camera stares back at me. I clip the page and file it away.

Months later, I come upon her name again: Ayaan Hirsi Ali.

I decide I want to write about her work.

Even though she is under 24-hour guard and presumably not speaking to the press, I e-mail her through an address I find online. A few months earlier, I had won an award from the *Economist* for an essay about terrorism and domestic abuse, and in the hope that this will make my request stand out from others, I mention it in my note; three days later, she e-mails me back. "You *won?*" she says, incredulous. "I was going to enter that competition, but I didn't have the time." She asks me to phone her, which I do, and we agree to meet the following week in Amsterdam at the Rode Hoed, yet another of the many places that is often hired out for lectures and panel discussions, where she will be attending yet another of those discussions about multiculturalism. I tell her I am petite and have long hair.

"Okay," she says, and adds, "and I'm black." I laugh.

She arrives late at the event, the last one to enter the room, flanked by enormous bodyguards on either side. "Look," someone whispers as she makes her way into the hall, "there's Ayaan." She takes her place in the seat just in front of mine. Ahead of her, seated at a table facing the audience, Paul Scheffer and Arie van der Zwaan, author of *Uitdaging van Het Populisme*, begin exchanging words about the problems of the multicultural experiment and its failure. Here and there, I pick up pieces of the conversation, but mostly I am watching Hirsi Ali, who wriggles impatiently in her seat, scowls, smiles, pulls on a stray hair that has popped out on her chin, nibbles on the cap of her Bic ballpoint pen, shifts her head, listens. Before she was a politician, she was a student, and the student still takes notes, tries harder than the rest of us to understand what is being said, most of which strikes me as useless, theoretical political nonsense. She is tiny, delicate-boned, and slim in a brown leather jacket belted at the waist, small silver hoop earrings, and jeans.

After the discussion, I tap her lightly on the shoulder.

"Long hair," I say, and show her my long braid.

We chat a bit, and she begins introducing me around along with Fré, who has come with me to the event. There are many hugs and photographs and greetings, mostly with her former colleagues in the PvdA, or social-democratic labor party, where she was working as a researcher at the time of her debut. "That's why they call us the social democrats," one of Ayaan's friends whispers to me, jokingly. "We're not always very democratic, but we are extremely social."

Afterwards, we all repair to another room for drinks. Fré and I are among the first to enter; I notice briefcases abandoned here and there throughout the room. I point one out to Fré.

"You would never find that in New York anymore," I say. "They'd all be confiscated and checked for bombs."

"Ach," Fré waves me off, dismissively. "Not here. Not in the Netherlands."

We mingle a bit, then find Ayaan again, who pulls out her agenda.

"Shall we meet for dinner?"

We settle on a date, and agree to arrange a time and place by e-mail. She kisses me good-bye three times, as the Dutch do, and Fré and I head back to the Pieter Aertszstraat once again.

When Ayaan and I meet again, it is late April, when Amsterdam is at its best, with sun-filled sidewalk cafés and days that stretch well past eight o'clock at night. At a table outside restaurant De Walem, her bodyguards positioned at tables near to ours, she talks softly and in a rush of words about her childhood, her philosophies, her life.

Ayaan Hirsi Ali grew up in Africa, the daughter of a Somali rebel, Hirsi Magan Isse. As a child, she endured the ritual of genital cutting at age five, and, she tells me, was for the most part kept indoors and veiled. Outside of school hours (and before she was old enough to attend), she and her sister read and recited the Koran at home in Arabic and went to Koran school on weekends. The West, she was told, was evil, especially the Jews.

"At night," she told me once, "I said my prayers: 'God, please help me with my homework. Please help me to be a good girl. And please destroy the Jews.'"

What "saved" her, she says as she sips a glass of chardonnay in the Amsterdam sunlight, were "the hidden moments," moments she spent reading *Oliver Twist* and *Nancy Drew* hidden in the folds of her Koran. From these secretly borrowed, ragged books, she discovered other cultures and learned to think about and to investigate what is: she learned, she says, to reason. And "that is what I am trying to appeal to," she says now, "because beyond the vicious circle of irrationality and religious extremism [in the Arab world], I *know* there are humans with reason and I *know* reason will prevail." Her voice is soft, poetic, musical, her hands move like wild grasses in the wind. She leans toward me as she speaks, breathless, pleading: "All we have to do is appeal to that, insistently, just as these jihadists appeal to their irrationality."

Her father's political activities required that the family move often, under the safety umbrella of the UN High Commission on Refugees: first to Saudi Arabia, then Ethiopia, and finally, in 1980, to Kenya. It was here that she learned English and read the books tucked into her Koran.

In Kenya, Ayaan's schooling included lessons she never could have learned in Somalia: about evolution, about history, lessons that horrified her mother—and inspired the beliefs that motivate her now. "I read about apartheid, colonization, slavery," she recalls, "that it was white Americans who said 'we don't want slaves anymore.' That generosity made such an impression on me. I grow angry when I see literature now in white countries that says white people are 'bad,' they 'have a debt to pay.' Black people have always been 'victims,' 'enslaved,' 'colonized.' Now they are being 'exploited by rich, industrial multinationals.' And what I want to convince my continent and my people is: we are not victims. We just need to learn the key."

At 22, Hirsi Ali was married off to a cousin living then in Canada. The groom came to Nairobi for the wedding and arrangements made for her to join him in the West. "He wanted six sons," she recalls. "I thought, 'Six sons! No way.'" (From this emerged the title of her book, published in December 2002: *De Zoontjesfabriek—The Son Factory*.) When she had trouble getting a visa from the Canadian Embassy in Nairobi, she traveled to relatives in Germany to obtain one through the Canadian Embassy there. Her husband was to meet two weeks later, and she would return to Canada with him. She stayed two nights. Then, with help from a friend, she fled to Holland.

She still remembers the shock of her arrival in the West: "It was summer. Women were walking around with bare arms, men in short pants. I thought, these people are crazy. How can they walk around like that in public?"

In Holland, she lived first in an asylum-seekers' center, where she devoted herself to learning Dutch. She cleaned homes for Dutch families and volunteered as an interpreter at battered women's shelters and abortion clinics filled with terrified young Muslim girls. The contrasts between the two intrigued her. "I'd come to a rich Europe from a very poor Africa, and the contrast was amazing. Yet when I got to know the [Dutch] people, I found that, in what we want in life, the similarities were more gripping than the differences. I wanted to understand how they managed to live in security and prosperity and peace, whereas where I came from, there was so much violence and misunderstanding, so much killing, disaster, plundering."

The questions led her to the University of Leiden, where, under the tutelage of Paul Cliteur—a colleague of Afshin Ellian—she received her doctorate in political science in 2001. It was here she found her answer: individualism.

"Do you know, there are no psychological studies on Islamic societies," she tells me, "because psychology is the study of the individual mind. And we are just one lump of hysterical humans. We are either Muslims, or we are a tribe, or we are an army, or we are a bunch of women—but we are not individuals."

This, she maintains, is what makes horrors like the Holocaust possible, "marking people as Jews and then systematically destroying them. The Hutus marked the Tutsis as Tutsis and then systematically destroyed them. In Somalia, my clanmates were marked by rote and systematically destroyed. It's about not seeing the individual human being."

In her studies, she had found her answer. Freedom of the individual, and freedom from the tribe, became her raison d'être.

After university, she took a job researching integration issues with the Wiarda-Beckman Stichting, the research arm of the PvdA. It was September 3, 2001. A week later, Osama bin Laden launched his attack against the United States.

It can be fairly said that few lives were changed more by 9/11 than Hirsi Ali's. She renounced Islam entirely. The incident at de Balie and the articles in *Trouw* soon followed, projecting her into the national spotlight. That Islam had missed the Enlightenment became a repeated theme in her writings and increasingly-frequent interviews—and the subject of increasingly hostile messages against her posted on Dutch Muslim communities online: a visit to the Dutch page of Somalinet.com, for instance, produced such messages as "That whore Hirsi Ali must die," and "If I saw her, I would give her the beating of her life."

On March 8, 2002—International Women's Day—Hirsi Ali appeared on a TV talk show about women and Islam. To her amazement, another guest on the program—a Dutch-Moroccan woman—denied that Muslim women were oppressed. It was this remark that pushed a frustrated Hirsi Ali to denounce Islam as "backward."

Uproar ensued. Op-eds by Western and Islamic Dutch alike appeared in all the papers, supporting her right to speak her mind but often condemning her for imposing Dutch mores on non-European cultures. Local Muslims began sending threatening e-mails and letters. At first she ignored them; but by December, when faxes started coming in from Sweden and elsewhere in the West, she went to the police.

"We were very afraid," her friend and publisher, Tilly Hermans, recalled when I interviewed her in the fall of 2003. "She was a rising star. Everyone knew who she was." The government sent police to protect her. Supporters raised additional funds for private guards. Hermans organized a petition, signed by over 100 prominent Dutch authors, supporting not what Hirsi Ali had said, but—in the tradition of Voltaire— her right to say it. The threats continued. There were warnings that she risked a fatwa, and rumors that one already was in place. On September 28, 2002, with financial assistance from the PvdA and others, she fled the country.

It was while she was in hiding that the VVD—or People's Party for Freedom and Democracy—first contacted her. The results of the May 16 election had proved short-lived; battles within the LPF and other parties had led to yet another government collapse, with new elections now scheduled for January, 2003.

Perhaps best compared with the American Libertarians, the VVD praised her for her outspokenness, asserted her right to free speech, and offered her a place in their party, serving in the Parliament. They guaranteed her state-subsidized protection. She said yes.

"Personally," Hermans told me, "I thought she should keep quiet when she came back. But she obviously determined that she couldn't. She sees herself as a voice for women who are kept in their homes by brothers and husbands and can't speak out for themselves."

Quiet, she indeed was not. Shortly before Hirsi Ali was sworn into office, *Trouw* published yet another interview, in which she compared the Prophet Mohammed to Osama bin Laden and Saddam Hussein. "By our Western standards," she said, "Mohammed is a perverse man. A tyrant. If you don't do what he says, you'll pay for it. It reminds me of the megalomaniac powers of the Middle-East: Bin Laden, Khomeini, Saddam."

This time, she had gone too far.

Claiming to represent the 57 countries of the Organization of the Islamic Conference, the Ambassadors of Saudi Arabia, Malaysia, Pakistan, and the Sudan delivered a letter to Gerrit Zalm, chairman of the VVD, demanding that Hirsi Ali be silenced and forced to apologize for her statements. The document bore the signatures of 21 Arab nations, though two—Turkey and Indonesia—later denied that they had signed. Zalm responded diplomatically, but with concern that a foreign alliance had seen fit to interfere in domestic affairs. No actions were taken. Hirsi Ali remained in the Parliament as a member of the VVD, assigned to handle integration.

By now, even Dutch-Muslim leaders who had condemned the earlier threats and acknowledged serious problems in the Muslim community were starting to feel that Hirsi Ali had taken, at best, the wrong approach. Some simply called her crazy and "a danger to herself." Others accused her of feeding anti-Muslim hate.

But when we speak over dinner at Walem, Hirsi Ali makes it clear that she doesn't care. Her mission is far more important. "What I'm trying to appeal to," she says, "is human reason. Beyond all this vicious circle of irrationality and religious defeatism, I *know* there are humans with reason, I *know* humans are reasonable, and I *know* it's going to prevail. All we have to do is just pursue that, insistently, just as these jihadists appeal to the irrationality of humans. There's no competition with them out there. There's no competition!"

So what is it, then, that she wants to say?

The question unleashes a storm of words and passion.

"What I want to say," she begins, "and especially to New Yorkers, who after the eleventh of September feel threatened, is that that threat is real. That that threat is coming from *my* world, my civilization, my people. The first and immediate reaction is an increase in security measures and military means, but for a long-lasting solution, they must look into how we as Muslims are brought into this world, how women are treated by men. And most of all, I would like to say to them, 'please wake up to the fact that all humans are gifted with reason, and start with full energy appealing to the reason of the masses in those countries.' The hearts and minds of Muslims—of 1.2 *billion* Muslims— are now exposed only to extremists, religious extremists, who use religion to cultivate a culture of terror."

The West, she says, must start to consider the hearts and minds of those 1.2 billion people to be a market. "A free market," she calls it. "And right now, the jihadists, the Islamic extremists, have a monopoly on this market, and they're winning. And I'm saying—especially to Americans who understand what freedom is, what reason is, and what responsibility is: start appealing to that market. Don't leave it in the name of culture or tradition or religion. I'm not talking about condoms and all the stuff that development aid is about now. I'm talking about developing our *reason*. Because the Islamists come and appeal to our irrationality. And both of them are in us."

As she talks, I find myself forgetting to take notes, so astonished am I by her passion. Why does this seem so clear to her, while others who share her background, her culture, her upbringing, find these ideas so hateful?

"The books," she tells me. "What helped me in my life were the hidden moments and the books." She and her sister read them, in fact, less because they found them interesting but because they understood them—the books were written in English—while they did not understand Arabic, the language of the Koran. But read them they did. "We read *Nancy Drew* and *The Hardy Boys*. We read the *Famous Five*. We read all the Enid Blyton books, just putting them into the folds of the Koran and pretending we were reading the Koran, and my mother would come and look at me, very pleased, and say 'good girl,' and then she would leave, and she wouldn't know what I was really reading. But it was through the books of Enid Blyton that my sister and I discovered that we were just kids, that kids could play, and have friendships, and it wasn't necessarily a sin." *The Hardy Boys* and *Nancy Drew*, she says, "developed our curiosity. We played detective, too."

Her sister since has died, though the circumstances of her death have never been quite clear. (Hirsi Ali writes about the events in her autobiography, *Infidel*, but the story she tells there is quite different from one that she told to me, and another that she has related yet to others. What is known is that her sister, Haweya, was psychotic by the time of her death in Nairobi in 1998. "She wanted to write Enid Blyton books," says Ayaan. "And I know she would have.") Of her five living siblings—including half-siblings—she shares the same mother and father with only one, her brother, who she describes to me as "brilliant" and "manic-depressive," living in Somalia.

And so she takes what she has learned and tries to bring it to the lives of others—not out of "anti-Muslim hate," but because she feels she has no other choice.

"My mother became pregnant eight times," she tells me, "and now there are only two kids living: one is my brother, the other, me. So if you look at all that and you consider that I am the only one leading the kind of life I lead now, then perhaps you understand why these things just cannot let me go. I am doing it for me, for my family, for my friends, for my classmates, for my countrymates, for my continentmates, for all the Muslims in the world. I am aware every day of how lucky I am. So I can't just ignore them. I cannot live a life like your average 33-year-old European."

But even at this early stage of her career, when we meet, it is already a frustrating struggle to get things done. "I am constantly busy," she says, "trying to figure out how I can ever communicate to the world what I have seen, and what my world is about. My world is affecting this world in a dramatic way, and I want to explain why we have terrorists, why we are poor."

She looks at me. "I'm thinking I want to give up government, do something else." Leaning toward me, she places her hand against my arm. "I have this project I want to do," she confides. "It's very secret, but I have to do it. And if it means my death, then at least I've done something for those people. Maybe you can even help me: it's an art project. I'm calling it *Submission*."

CHAPTER 11

Our dinner lasts until nearly midnight. Ayaan asks her chauffeur to drive me home—a trip, he later informs her, he will not make again. I live in de Pijp, and there are too many Moroccans and Turks living there. Even in her car, the bodyguards do not want her on these streets.

And it is certainly secure, this car, bulletproofed by doors so heavy we—Ayaan and I—are not permitted even to try and open them. That's what these huge men are for.

Along the way, we chat more about *Submission*.

"You should do it in New York," I tell her. "Holland is too small. No one will notice it here except the Dutch."

The next day, Ayaan phones to tell me that British-Pakistani author Tariq Ali will be speaking at De Balie in Amsterdam later in the week. She suggests we attend together, and I, of course, agree.

Ayaan's presence is always evident before you actually see her, the first of her ubiquitous bodyguards arriving a minute or two before she does. I spot them from the entrance of De Balie—men this big are hard to miss—and rush down the stairs to greet her. She tells me she's made plans for us to meet another friend of hers for dinner before the lecture starts, and so we walk together to the restaurant, two bodyguards ahead of us, two behind, and one on either side. It strikes me that one can feel so safe with them so close by, and yet at the same time, forget that they are even there.

The woman we are to meet, Adelheid Roosen, is at the restaurant already, tall and dramatic looking with long, straight, black hair and red lipstick, and dressed in a combination of clothing only a certain, theatrically bohemian kind of woman can wear without looking ridiculous, a kind of East Village chic that suits her perfectly. Adelheid, Ayaan explains to me, performed in the Dutch version of *The Vagina Monologues* and has now written a production of her own, inspired by Eve Ensler's original. Titled *Veiled Monologues* [*Gesluierde Monologen*] Roosen's play is acted entirely by Dutch Muslim women who tell stories based on interviews Roosen conducted with Muslim women around the world. It is to debut in a few weeks, if threats from unhappy Muslim groups do not force it off the stage; in fact, the project is extraordinarily courageous, not only for the women taking part, but for their director, Adelheid. Muslim sexuality was expressly not discussed in early 2003, despite Hirsi Ali's persistent efforts to bring the subject to the public eye, making known the fact that over 60 percent of women in Holland's battered women shelters at the time were Muslim, and well over half of all abortions were performed on Muslim teens, girls who were never told they could get pregnant by having sex, girls who knew their lives would be in danger if anyone found out.

But no one would talk about such things.

Roosen's project would put the subject directly center stage.

And so I ask her about the play, marveling at her manner as we talk, warmed by her unselfconsciousness. Adelheid does not fuss with propriety: she eats her chicken with her fingers, wipes the sauces from her dish with a sliver of potato she pops into her mouth. It is a carefree ease that, I realize suddenly, has vanished from Dutch culture, a style of living I once loved about the Netherlands, a looseness and gaiety that slowly had been crushed into extinction—like an ant, you might say, or, perhaps, a ladybug.

Sadly, one could describe the lives of many of the women portrayed in *De Gesluierde Monologen* the same way: young girls who rush to doctors for hymen restoration procedures, even if they have never had sex; 16-year-olds who are told whom and when they are to marry; young women still traumatized by childhood circumcisions and vaginal mutilation; of bloody sheets, as one reviewer noted, hung "triumphantly" out of windows for any and all to see. More than once, when the show first ran, Muslim families, expecting something entirely of a different nature, walked out on the performance. But the Dutch stayed, shocked by the discovery that this was happening in their own country, their own neighborhoods, and even, sometimes, their own homes.

Other stories also appear in the play, equally surprising: love stories, women who speak of wonderful lovers and romance, of erotic moments and whisperings.

"Still," Ayaan says, "I find it strange. I couldn't talk about these things on stage."

I nod in agreement. I haven't ever wanted to see the Ensler play either. But for Ayaan in particular, it is a culture shock that even ten years in the West have not fully prepared her for. I tuck that thought in with others I have collected in my mind about Muslim immigrants and their descendants in the West, the second-generation who, even having grown up in Europe, struggle to make sense of two often-contradictory sets of values.

And what, anyway, are pan-Western values? Equal rights yes, and free speech yes; but the free sexuality of Northern Europe is not shared by much of my own culture in North America. Holland's attitudes about soft drug use are unique to this country alone. As I write, Americans debate the question of gay marriage. It isn't, it occurs to me, quite so clear-cut as we often make it out to be.

Still the three of us exchange thoughts and, giggling, memories—the Dutch woman, the American, and the Somali immigrant. One of the most difficult things for Ayaan to grow accustomed to at first, she tells us, was not bending her torso into her lap to hide her breasts whenever a man enters the room. She recalls her first visit to a co-ed sauna, where, she laughs, "I had to look. But I couldn't look. But I had to look." I do not tell her that, as an American, my experience—when I, too, was already in my thirties and living in the Netherlands—was the same.

And so we continue on through dinner and dessert until the guards, sitting patiently at the next table and pretending not to listen, remind us that it's time to go. As we leave the restaurant, saying our goodbyes to Adelheid, they surround Ayaan, an impenetrable wall of male bodies, and I follow. On the street, we walk together, she and I, with a guard ahead, one on either side of us and another one behind.

* * *

Born in Pakistan under British rule in 1943, Tariq Ali has made a name for himself as spokesman for the radical Left since the 1960s. Based now in England, where he writes frequently for Britain's Left-leaning *The Guardian*, he is a proud and outspoken critic of the United States and of Israel, and in Amsterdam, he misses few chances for hyperbole: September 11 happened because of hateful U.S. foreign policy and its alliance with Sharon, and so it's the Americans' own fault, and Jewish Americans especially.

"America is to blame," he says, and the audience says, yes. "Britain is to blame," he says, and the audience says, yes. "Holland is to blame," he says, and the audience looks blank.

The audience is comprised mostly of Green-Party types who all applaud and a couple of Moroccans who give him a standing ovation and one lone Mexican who disagrees when question-and-answer time arrives. There are Arabs in the room, and Dutch boys with dyed black hair and t-shirts with the sleeves ripped off and girlfriends with three nose rings, and Christian students nodding eagerly at the Israel hate, and I say nothing. A booming Hans Dulfer, Holland's great sax player, speaks of the indignity of the interrogations now at U.S. immigration the last time he was there to perform. "I'm not going back," he says. I scribble notes with underlines and exclamation points, demanding evidence for Ali's claims, but do not raise my hand to speak and, surprisingly, neither does Ayaan. My notes read things like:

Where is the evidence behind the "information" you present?

The U.S. didn't make Fundamentalist Islam the enemy. They made us the enemy.

Barrage of conspiracy theories.

So the whole thing was the Jews' fault?

"Islam isn't modern because it's ghettoized."

To hold a party line because it is a party line is blind bigotry and hate.

By the time we've filed out of the auditorium, Ayaan and I, all of Ali's books are sold, and he is taking orders. I linger for a moment, watching the last few hangers-on request his autograph, and join Hirsi Ali and her entourage at the lobby café for drinks.

Amsterdam is, for all its status as a European capital, still a small town; one runs into friends and acquaintances at such public gatherings, and eventually I am swept into discussions with people I run into as Ayaan is with friends she finds of hers. I find her again only by coincidence, as I make my way to the ladies' room behind the bar. The guards stand watch, even there.

May I? I ask.

They know me. I may.

And I realize it is even lipstick-wielding women they must protect her from. The jokes about naked men were funny, but there will be no more saunas for her anymore. She's the one who's naked now.

* * *

Late April and early May are festive times in the Netherlands. The country celebrates the birthday of Queen Juliana on the thirtieth of April with parties, festivals, and in Amsterdam, a city-wide flea market-cum-street fair in which live bands perform throughout the city, boats of partiers fill the canals, and the streets are lined with families ridding themselves of *spullen*—junk and bric-a-brac and clothing they no longer wear or need—and millions of shoppers in search of bargains or the buried, unknown Van Gogh original they hope to find in some unsuspecting seller's array of goods.

The next week sees a parade of historical observances from May Day (May 1) to Holocaust Memorial Day (May 4) and Liberation Day (May 5), which marks the anniversary of the end of World War II. These last two could not form a greater contrast to Konninginnedag, the Queen's birthday; somber and sedate, they are marked with two minutes of silence and, on May fourth, the laying of wreaths on monuments across the continent.

But in May 2003, Tariq Ali was not the only one spewing hate against the Zionists and Israel. On May 4, in the Baarsjes section of Amsterdam, Moroccan boys were caught kicking memorial wreaths along the streets and chanting the popular refrain, *"Joden, die moeten we doden"* ("Kill the Jews," or—literally translated—"We *must* kill Jews"). That wasn't all. Newspapers reported that teachers had begun receiving threats when they attempted to teach about the Holocaust. In its 2003 report on anti-Semitism in the schools, the Peace Education Foundation cited a 16-year-old girl who declared confidently that "the six million Jews were needed to create Israel"—a "fact" she'd been taught at Koran school. (That "fact" still appears on Internet chat boards for the Dutch-Moroccan and Dutch-Turk community with disturbing frequency.) In April 2002, anti-Israel demonstrations on Dam Square in Amsterdam were accompanied by cries of "Hamas, Hezbollah, Jihad!" British, American, and Israeli flags were set afire. Overall, the Dutch Center for Information and Documentation on Israel (CIDI) confirmed a 140 percent increase in anti-Semitic incidents in the Netherlands between the last quarter of 2002 and the first quarter of 2003 over the same period a year earlier, most of them committed by Muslim youth.

Such findings were not unique to Holland: In 2004, the European Monitoring Center on Racism and Xenophobia self-censored its own report in which "North-African" Muslim immigrants were found responsible for numerous anti-Semitic acts across Europe, including 91 percent of the 193 violent attacks against schools, kosher shops, rabbis, and cemeteries that took place in France in 2002. Concerned that this information would result in anti-Muslim backlash, however, the agency moderated its findings and published an altered—and misleading—report in its place. (The draft of the censored report was later made public by various other organizations.) In an article about the situation, the British *Telegraph* reported: "But most of the [censored] report focuses on Jew-baiting by Muslim youths. It paints an alarming picture of daily life for France's 600,000 Jews, the EU's biggest community. In schools, Jewish children are beaten with impunity, and teachers dare not talk about the Holocaust for fear of provoking Muslim pupils, it said. Britain," the article continued, "which saw a 75 percent rise in incidents last year, was gently rebuked for hesitating to take 'politically awkward' measures against Islamic radicals. 'The government is very anxious not to upset the Muslim community,' the report said." [1]

It was also around this time that Dyab Abou Jahjah appeared on the public scene, first in his adoptive homeland, Belgium—where he'd arrived as a Lebanese refugee in the early 1990s—and shortly after, in the Netherlands.

Hollywood handsome (think George Clooney meets Robert De Niro) and politically charismatic, the eloquent Abou Jahjah speaks of assimilation as "rape" and "fascism." His aim, rather, is to bring Islamic principles to European law: banning the sale of alcohol in grocery stores, nationalizing Islamic holidays, and introducing the foundations of sharia to form what he calls a "sharocracy"—a notion that is, in fact, a thorough contradiction in terms. On an international level, he advocates destruction of the state of Israel, replacing it with a Palestinian state that would become part of a so-called "pan-Arab Federation."

Born and raised in Hanin, South Lebanon, during the civil wars of the 1970s and the conflicts of the early 1980s, Jahjah grew up amongst the clashes between his homeland and Israel—notably the murders in the camps of Sabra and Shatilla in September 1982. At 19, seeking a better and more comfortable life, he traveled to the West, landing in Belgium where he applied for political asylum, citing persecution by the terrorist group Hezbollah, of which he claimed to be a member. As authorities began questioning his story, he married a Belgian ex-girlfriend. (The couple divorced shortly after his residency papers came through; though he maintains this was a coincidence, his ex-wife subsequently filed charges against him for fraud.) Since then, he has denied involvement with Hezbollah, explaining his earlier misrepresentation to Belgian officials as a "foolish error." Still, he occasionally lays claim to military training, and maintains that, so far as he's concerned, Hezbollah is not a terrorist group anyway.

During his first years in Belgium, he completed a graduate degree in political science, but had difficulty finding work. "Some said I was over-experienced, while others said I hadn't experience enough," he writes in his memoir, *Tussen Twee Werelden* (*Between Two Worlds*). This, he maintains, was a clear sign of racism on the part of the Belgians.[2] In response, he founded the Arab European League (AEL) in 2000.

But Jahjah and his AEL received international attention in November 2002, when Belgian authorities arrested him for "inciting violence and disturbing the public order" as riots erupted in Antwerp in response to the murder of a Muslim immigrant by a deranged, racist Belgian. Jahjah, the police and politicians argued, had encouraged the rioting, when he had been in the best position to call for calm among the country's Muslim youth. Ultimately, however, the arrest—and subsequent publicity—worked entirely to Jahjah's advantage, as Muslims and pro-Palestinian Europeans rallied to his defense.

Part of the incentive for founding the League had been the growth in Belgium of the Vlaamse Blok ("Flemish Block"), the country's Far-Right nationalist party. In a country already divided by centuries-old internal conflicts between its French-speaking Wallonian population and its Dutch-speaking Flemish, the emergence—and growing demands for recognition—of yet another culture was more than many Belgians were prepared to take. True, the country's Orthodox Jews had also created an enclave of their own; but outside the privacy of the their homes and synagogues, and beyond their way of dress, they were fully assimilated into Belgian culture, and—at least as important—stood at the heart of the country's economic strength and much of its international allure: Antwerp's diamond industry.

By contrast, in Belgium—as elsewhere in Europe—immigrant Muslims and their descendants frequently showed no interest in the cultures in which they now lived, watching satellite TV broadcasts from the Middle East and frequenting Arab Web sites and chat rooms. Where the Vlaamse Blok largely supported Belgium's Jews, who were—and are—seen as vital to its economy, it frowned on the Arab immigrants whose high joblessness rates it saw as a parasitic force on taxpayers and Belgium's overall well-being. (The Jews, of course, also benefited from the attitude of "the enemy of my enemy is my friend" that swept much of the west after the events of 9/11.)

In this environment, Jahjah's youth, charisma, and fury, capped by his ethnic background and defense of Islamic culture, swept him to the lead of Belgium's Muslim youth, and his anti-Israel rants became their own. With their support and backing, he then marched his party into Holland, creating its Dutch chapter in the spring of 2003, and a French division shortly after. That summer, the AEL founded its Muslim Democratic Party, aiming to take part in the European parliamentary elections of 2004. In the process, Jahjah encountered a surprising ally in the Netherlands: Gretta Duisenberg, wife of European Bank president Wim Duisenberg. Gretta's anti-Israel campaign had set off firestorms when, in April 2002, she hung a Palestinian flag from the balcony of her home in Amsterdam.

Duisenberg was not alone—as the CIDI reports revealed; and it was this that gave speakers like Tariq Ali and various local imams their popularity. "*Kankerjood*" ("cancer Jew") became a favorite insult among the Dutch Muslim community; in Sweden, a Jewish couple I met told me that Muslims had begun greeting one another with the simple phrase, "Kill Jews" (as in, "Hey, kill Jews. How's it going?"). Dutch and Belgian rap groups recorded "kankerjood" songs with lyrics like "Fuck the Jews, cancer Jews, the *allochtonen* will come and kill you" or the especially popular "Paf-Paf," which, directly translated, ends, in a reference to the events of 9/11:

"And you should know, it does me good
This time blood flows from the other side."

As such songs hit the airwaves—and they did—politicians and civil rights groups immediately cried out for censure. Several sought lawsuits against Gretta Duisenberg, who later took part in anti-Israel demonstrations, walking alongside hundreds of fellow-marchers as they chanted the "Hamas, Hamas, all Jews to the gas" refrain, and some called for her husband's resignation. ("My wife," he said, "is her own person.") Others called for Mrs. Duisenberg to be fined, and for the arrests of the songwriters (one of whom later turned himself voluntarily in to the police). Many of these objections came from Hirsi Ali's party, the VVD, via her colleague Rita Verdonk.

And yet, despicable as they were, were these songs and chants substantively different, really, from Ayaan's own description of the Prophet Mohammed as a pervert? These were only words that people spoke. What had happened to all the talk about Voltaire?

At the same time, the songs pointed to the seriousness of the anti-Semitism problem. Jew-hate in the Muslim community had become virtually the norm—"zelfsprekende," as the Dutch say—self-evident, and expected. On the forums of Morokko.nl, someone calling himself Misstoerkoe expressed his opinion of one song, recorded by the group NAG (Nieuwe Allochtoon Generatie): "At first I thought it wasn't good, but after I read a story or two about what a couple of Jews had done to some Muslims, then I thought, yeah, fuck the Jews."

By November, I find it everywhere, even in the most unexpected of places—painted in graffiti along the streetlights designed by artists Alexander Schabracq and Tom Potma on the Rokin: swastikas where Sotheby's Auction House used to be.

There lies, in fact, a certain symmetry, a sad irony in this, the confluence of Sotheby's, the lampposts, and the swastikas on the Rokin. The lampposts had themselves been commissioned by the Aesthetics Department of Holland's Postal Telegraph and Telephone (PTT)—a branch of the organization considered largely responsible for pioneering the internationally renowned Dutch traditions in graphic and industrial design, and whose very existence delighted me when I first arrived in the Netherlands. Originally named the Dienst Esthetische Vormgeving (Aesthetic Design Services) when it was founded in 1945, and renamed Concernstaf Kunst in 1989 when the PTT privatized and became KPN (Royal Post Nederland), the department commissioned everything from postage stamps and post cards to phone booths, mailboxes, and other so-called "street furniture" from designers and from artists. (It also maintained the country's oldest and largest corporate art collection.)

It was Jean-Francois van Royen who, in 1904—the same year that the art nouveau mansion that would come to house Sotheby's was built on the Rokin—brought his personal passion for art and design to his new job at the PTT. Disgusted by what he called the "ugly, ugly, ugly" design produced by government offices, he set about developing a new typography style and commissioned artists to design postage stamps. By the 1920s, he had partnered with artists on projects ranging from post boxes and delivery trucks to a new complete "house style," all while running a printing and publishing company on the side.

Then the Germans came.

In an effort to counter attempts at forming a German (read: Nazi)-based art organization under the occupation, Van Royen established his own group, the Netherlands Organisatie van Kunstenaars. But the Germans were stronger: all artists, actors, performers, musicians, writers, and composers were soon required to register with their Kultuurkamer, an organization that demanded that the nationalist socialist message be communicated in all works of art. Adhering to these rules was mandatory for all registered artists; and artists who chose not to register were not allowed to work.

In March 1942, German authorities arrested Van Royen, accusing him of inciting resistance to the Kultuurkamer. He died on June 10 in a concentration camp in Amersfoort. Three years later, the PTT formally established its Dienst Esthetische Vormgeving in his honor.

And now, 60 years later, scrawled across the lampposts created from his legacy, was the emblem of the force he'd so bravely fought against, and of the men who had finally killed him.

What's more, the Alexander Schabracq lampposts extended further than the Rokin, on along the Damrak—the street that encircles Dam Square, that center of Amsterdam political activity where the palace stands, where the anti-Israel protests usually take place. It was on Dam Square that the Dutch first celebrated Liberation Day on May 7, 1945. The festivities did not last long: German military opened fire from a building that overlooked the plaza, killing 22 and wounding 120. Largely in their memory, the national Holocaust monument now marks the center of Dam Square, where the Queen places the memorial wreath each year in honor of those who perished.

And now Muslim boys were calling "Death to Jews" on that same day. Soon, thousands would assemble there again in calls for freedom and for peace, and in the memory of one more man who had fought for art, and lost.

CHAPTER 12

The e-mail arrives while I am visiting my family again. "Yipppeee! I'm coming to New York!"

It is May, 2004. Ayaan will arrive, she tells me in her next communiqué, on the thirtieth, staying just three days at a hotel I have found for her a block from my parents' apartment on the East Side. We will talk to my mother about *Submission* and ask her for suggestions: curators to contact, artists who might work with us, anything. I have also had the idea to propose the project to the Museum for African Art. The artist Arman, a good family friend, has long been involved with the museum, and his wife, Corice, with whom I'm particularly close, is a member of the museum board. The Armans have also just recently returned from a visit to Iran. They know the plight of Muslim women. I am certain they will help us.

I am also certain that the project should take place in New York City, and not the Netherlands. There will be more support and fewer protests in the U.S. Security will be tighter. Anyway, there is no more real art scene left in Holland. By the fall of 2002, the new conservative Right government had already begun its cutbacks in the arts. Plans to expand the Stedelijk, a project Fuchs had fostered, nurtured, and nearly brought to fruit, had been put on hold, replaced with a new proposal to open a new museum on the outskirts of the city on the Zuidas, a newly developed business quarter then under construction. The Stedelijk, suggested Amsterdam's new Cultural Alderman, Hannah Belliot, could move there—or if not, then it could be split into two parts, with modern art remaining in the current location beside the Van Gogh and Rijksmuseums, and contemporary art transfer-ring to the Zuidas.

It was a decidedly unpopular proposal. Petitions circulated on the Internet, signed by artists and curators around the world. Meetings and protests and debates filled cultural centers and the newspapers once again. With the future of what had once been one of Europe's leading institutions for 20th-century art now hanging in the balance, an exhausted Rudi Fuchs threw his hands up in despair. In December 2002, he resigned as director of the Stedelijk Museum. Although, in the end, the protests were successful—the Stedelijk would stay where it was, and the expansion would go through as planned (albeit in a dra-matically altered version), the museum has floundered with no artistic direction since, and none, as this book goes to print, in sight ahead.

* * *

It is evening when Ayaan phones me from her hotel. I hurry out to meet her, and we take a brief walk around the neighborhood, Ayaan's dark eyes absorbing the lights and energy around us. We pass the Met-ropolitan Museum and the Eighty-fourth Street entrance to Central Park, and she wants to know if the park is safe during the day. I assure her that it is.

As I leave her at the door to her hotel, she turns to me. "I feel," she says, and her voice is calmer than I have ever heard her, "so wonder-fully anonymous."

In the morning, she is late to breakfast with my parents, arriving, finally, in a breathless rush. She has been on the phone with the NRC, she explains. Her mentor wants her to handle day care issues, and step away from her work with integration. He has refused to accept her efforts to refuse. Ever ready to do battle, Ayaan has now taken the matter to the media, offering an article to the NRC in which she accuses her party of betraying her supporters, those who voted for her with the aim that she would address the integration problem. There will be a firestorm when it appears, I know: in Holland's parliament, one does not speak out publicly against the orders of one's party. One follows along. One is not insubordinate. In many ways, isn't that what the whole multicultural discussion is about?

* * *

I can still picture her now, the member of a European parliament, long and slim and graceful, curled into herself on the dark red Bokhara rug of my parents' dining room in New York City. She is demonstrat-ing to my mother her vision of *Submission*—five women posed across the room, the lashes of a whip visible between words of the Koran written across their backs. My mother, inspired, suggests artists we should talk to: Vanessa Beecroft, John D'Andrea, and directors of museums and art spaces like Exit Art downtown. But Ayaan is only half-listening. The *New York Times* lies open on the table, the photograph of a Palestinian woman who has, the day before, blown herself up for Allah, a beautiful young girl with a determined face and mesmerizing, deep green eyes. Two Jews died in the attack, and one Israeli Arab. Ayaan cannot tear her eyes from the young woman's face. When my parents leave the room a moment, she turns to me. "Ten years ago," she whispers, "that girl could have been me."

She wants to spend the day discovering life in New York City, and she asks me for suggestions.

"Go to the Met," I tell her, "and maybe the Museum of Modern Art if you can handle two museums in a day. I can imagine you may want to see Ground Zero."

Her eyes widen, and she nods.

"But once," I tell her, "at least once while you are here, you have to have a real, New York, Jewish bagel."

Ayaan laughs and kisses me, as the Dutch do, three times on the cheek "goodbye."

* * *

Arman and Corice have agreed to see us the next morning. Corice greets us when we arrive and Arman follows, ill and frail and clearly tired; but as Ayaan speaks and describes the project she has planned, his eyes light up and he begins listening intently.

"Vanessa Beecroft," Corice announces after Ayaan has finished. She picks up the phone and begins dialing as Ayaan and Arman talk further, running through a Rolodex as she leaves messages for artists, photographers, sculptors, the directors of art spaces, one after the other. Within minutes, she's made at least a half a dozen calls on our behalf.

As we talk, Arman stands, silently, walks to the end of the couch, takes a sheet of paper and walks slowly back. Ayaan and I look at one another, wondering. He sits back on the couch again and begins to draw.

"You know," he says, and launches into a tale about his recent visit to Iran—where he is sure democracy is coming soon, where the restlessness and longing for a Western way of life is palpable in the streets, and all the while he is drawing something on the page we cannot see. When he finishes, he shows the sketch to me: a box clad in black on wheels, and labeled: "Proper attire for a Muslim woman."

He turns and looks at Ayaan, who is staring, puzzled, at the figure he has drawn.

"You are very brave," he says.

Our visit over, we take a taxi back uptown and tuck into a restaurant for lunch. A waitress hands us menus and we peruse them quickly.

"Ready to order?" she asks us, pad and pen in hand. I request the Salad Nicoise.

"Miss?" the waitress turns to my companion, who, in turn, looks at me and grins.

"I'd like a real, New York, Jewish bagel," says Ayaan Hirsi Ali, looking most pleased with herself, and proud.

* * *

It was a small piece, just 13 lines, tucked into the inside pages of the *Volkskrant*: a Dutch-Turkish girl from Almelo had been killed by her own father.

Stories like this had appeared, though rarely, in the past. But things were different now in Holland. This time, people paid attention.

Zarife was 17 years old when she died, having gone to Ankara for the summer holidays with her father. How was she to know her father had selected their holiday destination because he knew the murder of his daughter would be prosecuted more lightly there than in the Netherlands? What she did know was only that she'd had problems with him in the past, that he found her behavior far too Westernized, that a neighbor had seen her recently out with friends, no scarf covering her hair—and brought the information to her family.

But nearly as shocking as Zarife's murder was what was uncovered when it finally became known—nearly two months after her death. Zarife's teacher, Jaap Krikke, could not help but notice when the girl failed to return to school at the start of the semester; but it was only when he overheard two Turkish mothers whispering about Zarife's death that he learned why. For weeks, then, the Turkish community in Almelo had known. But nobody had come forward. And if that was so, how many other Zarifes had there been? How many more secrets lurked in Muslim homes that the Dutch did not, could not, know?

Many, as it turned out. A report some 18 months later showed that in the first six months of 2005, 70 women had been victims of honor crimes in The Hague alone—a city housing a total of some 67,800 Muslims at the time. Eleven of those women had been killed—approximately one a month—the others brutally abused.

This was no news to Ayaan Hirsi Ali: hadn't she been warning of it all along? What was needed in Holland, she had told me many times before, was an investigation into all the alleged "suicides" and "accidental deaths" that took place in Muslim families in Europe. But no one, until now, had listened.

Zarife's death broke the silence—in the Netherlands, at least.

It took little time for Zarife's story to become the stuff of headlines and new government reports—despite threats from her brother to take vengeance on Krikke if he took the matter to the press. ("I'm not afraid of these threats," said Krikke later. "A pilot cannot be afraid to fly."[1]) Hirsi Ali, who by now had won her fight to continue to represent integration and not day care, pressed the issue in the media and the Parliament. For too long, she argued over and over again, the Dutch had turned their heads in the name of tolerance. They had insisted Muslim immigrants be left free to follow their religion and their culture as they saw fit to do, whatever this may mean.

No more, Hirsi Ali pleaded. The problems had to be taken head-on now, and stopped.

But the rest of the world, I soon learned, was not yet prepared to face what now confronted them—certainly not the U.S.A. By this time, I'd been assigned to write an article about Ayaan for a major American publication, and it was while I was drafting it that the Zarife story first broke. With Hirsi Ali so much a part of the run of events, and her activities in the Netherlands until then so instrumental to the story coming out at all, I mentioned to my editor that perhaps I should take more time to watch as things played out. American media had not yet reported on Zarife, or on the general trend of honor killings in the West.

"But it already happened," my editor said.

"Yes," I answered, "but no one has reported on it in America just yet. And others are occurring all the time. This is what Hirsi Ali is about. It is the center of her role here."

"But it happened already," the editor said. "So we don't need to mention it."

But the fact was, Ayaan had never been so much a part of the public debate as now. Her cautions, her warnings, her pleas, were finally being heard. More, any article about her importance—and the controversy that she stirred—had to touch on what was taking place and Hirsi Ali's passion for this cause. Without mentioning Zarife, I raised again the matter of honor killings in the Netherlands, and Ayaan's initiative in bringing them to light, when I submitted a draft of the story to the editors for review.

"You can't say this," one of them wrote back in an e-mail. "It's too inflammatory for [us]."

"Too inflammatory."

It was the beginning of what I later understood to be the American media's early capitulation to Western extremist Islam and its threat to

Western culture. Were the editors afraid their offices would be attacked if the information—that honor killings were happening in Europe, too—came to light? Did they fear an anti-Islam backlash would erupt? Or did they, like the Dutch before them, simply prefer to close their eyes?

And it wasn't just this publication: one after another turned stories about Dutch honor killings down.

"We can't print that," they said.

Only one responded, "Can you prove it?"

I could. And the story ran.

But the U.S. still recoils from the issue, even now, even as books about honor killings in the Middle East have become best-sellers. Somehow, this is different.

But if it is different, it is only because when such murders take place in Western cities, it feels worse. We know better. And still, we do not protect these women and the children whose lives are threatened, because we do not want to know, or are afraid to interfere. We become unwitting accomplices in our silence.

And yet Zarife's was not an isolated tale. She was, in fact, the third of Jaap Krikke's students to have been abused in the name of honor. (Zarife herself had twice taken refuge from her father in battered women's shelters before he finally killed her.) Earlier, Krikke had discovered that another Turkish girl was the victim of regular abuse, also by her father. He contacted the girl's doctor. "There's nothing we can do," the doctor had replied, according to an interview with Krikke in *Trouw*. "She's over 18." Months later, the girl committed suicide.[2]

Shortly after Zarife died, a Turkish man in Amsterdam gunned his wife down as she stood at the door of one such shelter, where she and her children had fled from him weeks before. Her own parents congratulated her husband for the crime. When Dutch officials then took the children into hiding, the family threatened to bomb the entire shelter if they were not released into their care.

And more: In Maastricht, an Afghan woman was found murdered in her bed. Officials treated the crime as any other murder; but one journalist went further, visiting the woman's neighbors. She had told her husband she wanted a divorce, the neighbors said. He killed her for honor. "But she knew how Afghan men are," the women shrugged. Many men the reporter spoke to added, "And I would do the same." Explained one, "I didn't bring my wife here for her to divorce me. That's absolutely not the idea." Addressing the man's son, standing with them, the journalist asked, "And what do you think of that?"

"I think it's good," the boy said.[3]

Why was it happening—how could it happen—here?

Reasons vary. For daughters—the children of immigrants—those reasons are often different than they are for wives. A young girl who, like

Zarife, becomes too Westernized, taking off her scarf in public, walking near a boy from school, joining friends for an afternoon of shopping at the mall, may literally be risking her own life—and certainly a beating. And because some of her friends—both "allochtone" and Dutch—are able to enjoy such activities with impunity, the temptation is often more than she is able to resist. Why, after all, *shouldn't* she go out for pizza with her classmates after school? Isn't that, besides, what the Dutch—including its government—is *asking* her to do?

The problem is by no means limited to Holland. Marie Brenner reported extensively on the issue from France for *Vanity Fair* in April 2004,[4] revealing that some 70,000 women in that country were living in oppressive, forced marriages. In deeply personal, intense interviews with a Turkish-Frenchwoman she calls "Yildiz," who was promised off in marriage against her will ("you would sit there and drink tea while the families observed you like an animal," she told Brenner of the process of finding a husband. "Were you tall enough? Were you pretty enough? I was not allowed to say a word.") Brenner exposes the agony that these women endure. In Yildiz's case, her employer offered to shelter her. "The night before she was to leave for Turkey," Brenner writes, "Yildiz quietly packed a bag." Eventually, Yildiz sent her parents a letter to let them know she was okay, arranging to have it sent from Nice, writes Brenner, at which point she "began to get messages on her cell phone: *We are in Nice looking for you. We forgive you. You do not have to get married.* Her boss said, 'Don't be fooled. They will never forgive you, because you have broken the ultimate taboo.'"

When kindness failed, the family resorted instead to threats: *We will kill you if we find you,* they wrote her, says Brenner.

"These girls want nothing more," Hirsi Ali tells me over dinner shortly after Zarife's death becomes known, "than to lead what we in the West call a 'normal' life." But in some families, anything that even evokes the suspicion she may not be a virgin creates a conflict. "And with her," she explains, "the whole family: it's not only her father who is responsible for the act. His whole family is. If Zarife's father had not killed her, he would not have been welcome anywhere, he would have been socially ostracized."

Confronted with the mores of their parents and those of the culture in which they have been raised and that surrounds them, it is no wonder these girls become confused and, not infrequently, rebel.

The impact on the Dutch, in turn, has been palpable. Turkish and Moroccan girls often may not join class excursions, leaving schools and the government with the dilemma of choosing among doing away with such activities entirely; forcing parents to allow their daughters to attend by law—exposing them to the risk of family retribution when they return; or allowing students to be excused for religious or cultural reasons—a solution that only serves to further isolate them from Dutch society and culture, and reward—or anyway, permit—misogynistic values in a country that prides itself on its demand for equal rights.

Married women face another set of problems, especially those forced to wed distant relatives or family friends from "back home"—a trend that, surprisingly, and despite laws that aim to thwart it, seems to be growing over time. Young Dutch-Muslim men find the Muslim women in the Netherlands too Westernized, and they head in search of brides to Turkey and Morocco—while young Dutch-Muslim women consider these boys too radical and conservative, and take, instead, a mate from their parents' homelands who is—or seems to be—more "modern."

That appearance, however, is frequently misleading. Fatimazohra (née Olivia) Hadjar, the Surinamese immigrant who converted to Islam 20 years ago and now works with children and young men and women in the Muslim community in Amsterdam, once married an Egyptian man (from whom she is now divorced) with devastating consequences. He beat her regularly, in one instance inducing a miscarriage; was frequently unemployed; spent much of her money on weddings for his siblings, and ultimately brought her to the brink of bankruptcy.

"Marrying an Arab man is a ticket to hell," she tells me over coffee in The Hague. Fashionably dressed, with long red fingernails, a tight headscarf, and bright red lipstick, she is the very picture of the integrated Muslim woman. "They can't support being with an educated woman. They want someone who can't read or write so they can kick her around." But they hide it at first, she tells me. "They're the nicest people in the world; but what they're really thinking all along is, 'this woman is a ticket to a better life'."

Hadjar is not alone in this view. In a 2004 study titled "*Trouwen Over de Grenz*" [*Marrying Across the Border*], Erna Hooghiemstra found that 70 percent of Dutch-Turkish and -Moroccan youth sought spouses in their lands of origin, but, she noted in a *Volkskrant* interview, "the boys from those countries will act as if they're more modern than they are so they can get to Holland; they only show their real macho nature once they're good and married." On the other hand, she remarked, the Dutch boys frequently find that 'they don't know what to do with these more traditional girls." [5] They grow angry and frustrated, and spend their time with friends—or other women—isolating their new wives or abandoning them completely. A lot of these women get "dumped"—brought back to Turkey or Morocco ostensibly for vacations, whereupon the new husbands take away their passports, making it impossible for them to return to Holland when he does. Even if she is able to secure a replacement, it is rare that a dumped wife can leave a Middle Eastern country without her husband—and he, of course, is no longer there.

In Hadjar's case, things went bad the minute she went with him to spend a couple of years with his family. "It was prison," she says. She tried to leave, sneaking peeks into the phone book whenever she had the chance and finally calling the Dutch Embassy in a free moment. The embassy arranged for her ticket back to Holland—but the authorities wouldn't let her leave. "Not without your husband," they told her.

Eventually, Hadjar returned to Amsterdam—with her husband—and subsequently, as she puts it, "took her liberty." Educated and resourceful, she was luckier than many.

She was also among those who freely chose her husband, having only converted to Islam after they were wed. But she tells me that the arranged marriages she sees in her community are not always as simple as they appear. Sexual abuse is rampant among Dutch-Muslims, she maintains, and girls who become pregnant from a father or an uncle or a cousin leave the family no option: either she dies to save their honor, or she is to be married off to anyone who will have her. And since, generally speaking, no good Muslim boy will wed a non-virgin, the "anyone who will have her" becomes a boy from Turkey or Morocco eager to find prosperity in the West. His character, his education, his ability or willingness to care for his bride or her child are of no importance; and she, because she knows her life depends on it, agrees to be his wife.

"But no one ever, ever talked about any of this," Carla Rus, a psychiatrist based in The Hague, tells me when I go to visit her at her home. Rus, an attractive, strawberry-blonde woman in her mid-fifties, has worked with Muslim families—mostly with young girls—for over 20 years. An invalid herself—she was injured in a car accident and wears a brace around her neck at all times—she holds a unique relationship with her patients, able to empathize directly with their feelings of imprisonment, of limitations imposed against their will. For years, she says, she tried to bring the problem to the politicians, "but they wouldn't listen." The second generation, she tells me, is lost. These girls are five times more likely than native Dutch girls to be suicidal, and twice as many who actually do attempt to kill themselves succeed.

This poses another problem: until the emergence of "hurricane Ayaan," officials failed to understand these suicides or what they represented. More, the numbers were so high that when families reported a daughter's death, "suicide" was often listed as the cause when, in fact, she had been murdered—by a father, a brother, even, in rare cases, her own mother. To protect themselves, Rus explains, some more-Westernized girls will wear a headscarf even when they do not want to: it serves as protection against sexual abuse—a woman in a headscarf be attacked—and familial retribution. It is a lie that thousands of Dutch

Muslim girls live every day, trapped between the demands and longings of two worlds.

But if some girls wear their scarves for protection—or remove them to rebel—others do the opposite. By mid-2004, officials noted a new trend among young women: to veil themselves completely, steeping themselves more deeply into Islam, even as their parents often lived secular lives themselves. Perhaps Ayaan had not sacrificed herself for Allah; but soon enough, other young women in Europe would.

CHAPTER 13

On January 19, 2004, a group of teenaged girls wearing headscarves and boys flaunting the faintest wisps of beard gathered in The Hague, a banner held between them. "We love you, Murat!" the banner read. You would think Murat was a rock star visiting on a tour.

He was not.

Days earlier, on January 13, Murat Demir had entered his high school cafeteria at lunch break and shot the deputy headmaster squarely in the head. The shotgun had been stolen from a nearby police station for him by a friend.

Why?

Simple: honor. Murat, whose parents had come to the Netherlands from Turkey, felt, he said later, trashed by his victim, Hans van Wieren, and by the school Van Wieren supervised. Murat's friends and family members later claimed that Van Wieren had spoken rudely of the boy's father, himself serving a jail sentence at the time.

Debate, of course, ensued: was Murat Demir's ethnicity important? Was this an act perpetrated by a Muslim against a non-Muslim, or by an individual boy against an individual man? Did being Muslim affect Demir's perspective on the problem and shape his efforts at a solution?

Hans Werdmolder, author of the authoritative study of Muslim youth in Holland, *Generatie op Drift* (*A Generation Adrift*), published in 1990, has argued that Turkish and Islamic emphasis on honor had to be considered in understanding what had taken place. "Not for nothing," he wrote in an essay published in newspaper *Trouw*, "did the murder take place in a full cafeteria. Murat's deed became in that way a kind

of public ritual, with students and teachers as his audience. He wanted
to 'show everyone what a man he is.'" [1]

Whether or not Murat's ethnicity inspired his actions, one thing
could not be ignored: the support that he received, which came entirely
from the Muslim community. While the majority of Dutch Muslims
condemned the killing, clearly the overall response within the community reflected a kind disapproval, rather than sheer outrage, as if to
say, "he shouldn't have done it, but I can understand, sort of, why he
did." In one interview, friends of Murat's father blamed the Dutch: the
teachers and the schools and whoever sold Murat the gun—these were
the real culprits. "Teachers should never yell at their students. Turkish
and Moroccan kids take it especially hard when they're reprimanded
among their friends," said one. "At least take them aside." Another
blamed Holland and its openness to Eastern European immigrants,
calling it a country full of Bulgarians and Yugoslavs who smuggle
drugs "and where there are drugs, there are weapons." [2] That gun
ownership is illegal in the Netherlands and yet handgun use common
in the Turkish community was, for him, irrelevant. "With a weapon,
people respect you," another man told the *Trouw*. [3] Hence many Turkish fathers in Holland give them to sons for their 17th birthday as a
kind of rite of passage.

To be sure, much about Murat's story calls for empathy. Friends later
spoke of his kindness, how he was always available to them. They said
he became more aggressive after his father went to prison, but never
appeared to be a killer. His intent, Murat himself insisted, had been
"only to frighten" Van Wieren—not to kill him. But speaking at his
trial, Murat Demir presented an image of himself that spoke as much
of him as of the values that his family and culture—isolated from
Dutch society—had taught him. "My intention was just to shoot him—
teach him a lesson," Murat explained. He'd assumed the teacher would
spend some time in the hospital, regret his behavior toward Murat,
and all would be set right. Speaking to the judge, he asked, "What else
should I have done?"

But while attentions focused on the killer and the cheering demonstrations of his fans, few paid much attention to the words of other
Muslim youth, those who condemned Murat's behavior—and saw an
opening in Dutch culture that offered a solution. Talking to a reporter
from the *NRC*, a 16-year-old boy with a Dutch mother and Moroccan father remarked, "In Turkey and Morocco, students have to stand beside
their chair if they talk back to the teacher. Here in Holland, kids just
laugh—not just at the teachers, but even at the cops. They need to be
handled much more strictly." Echoed another: "If someone hit me as the
teacher, I'd hit him right back. You need to compel respect," he told the
NRC. "Kids like Murat are looking for authority, testing the boundaries." [4]

This was hardly an earth-shattering new insight into adolescent youth—whatever the cultural or religious background: but it was one that no one seemed to want to hear—or do much about. Fortuynists simply argued, again, for a closing of borders and a ban on family unifications; their opponents responded with calls for sympathy, recommending an increase in government subsidies for Muslim community programs and a greater respect by the Dutch for Muslim mores. (No one noticed that Murat had never been forced to learn the values of Dutch culture: "What else could I have done?" he'd asked. Whose fault was it that he didn't know the answer to such a simple question?)

Murat Demir's crime reminded me—and still does—of the remarks my friend Roelof had made earlier about Moroccan culture and the differences in behavior regarding even the simplest things, like movie lines. True, Murat was Turkish, not Moroccan; but did that matter? Was the distinction based on geography, or the culture that surrounds a given religion and its mores?

Murat was tried as an adult—not because of his Turkish background, as many accused the courts, but because of the premeditated and violent nature of his crime. He received a sentence of five years. [5]

But if no one could agree on the role of Islam in the killing of Hans van Wieren in January, by March no one questioned any longer the fact that Muslim fury had arrived full force on Europe's shores. On the morning of March 11, ten explosions on four commuter trains took the lives of 191 people in Madrid. The attack, staged at rush hour, as millions of men and women casually started out for work, became the deadliest in Europe since the 1988 bombing of Pan Am Flight 103 over Lockerbie, Scotland, by Libyan rebels. Over 1,800 lay wounded in the streets, their blood falling on the scattered, severed limbs of others who had not been so lucky.

Though Spain initially suspected the Basque terrorist group ETA—and understandably so, having been hit by the ETA on numerous occasions—the rest of the world looked elsewhere. They were right; the Moroccan Islamic Combatant Group, a terrorist organization known to have ties to Al Qaeda, claimed responsibility.

Joeri Boom was wrong: it could happen here.

* * * *

Osama bin Laden took little time to issue a statement of explanation and demand: if Europe would retreat from Iraq, he promised, they'd face no further such attacks. "I also offer a reconciliation initiative," he stated, "whose essence is our commitment to stopping operations against every country that commits itself to not attacking Muslims or interfering in their affairs—including the U.S. conspiracy on the greater

Muslim world. The reconciliation will start with the departure of [Europe's] last soldier from our country."[6] (This, of course, opens new questions: *which* country? Afghanistan, where he presumably was hiding? Iraq, where the war was being waged? Saudi Arabia, bin Laden's homeland, where no European or American troops were fighting? How were these "our" country—Al Qaeda's, or the bin Ladens', perhaps—and, indeed, whom did he mean by "our"? Who was "we"?)

Spain, trembling from the attacks and preferring to find a scapegoat outside of its own culture than search for a failure from within, grabbed hold of bin Laden's seemingly outstretched hands. The bombings had strategically been set just prior to national elections, with the Popular Party of Prime Minister Jose Maria Aznar, who had shipped 1,300 Spanish troops to support coalition forces in Iraq—poised to win. Between the bombings and the statement of bin Laden, all that changed: within days, Spain voted in a new government, one which promised to withdraw its military as soon as possible from Iraq. In placing their votes, apparently, no one had paused to consider the fact that Al Qaeda operatives had been busy in Spain since long before Operation Freedom, as the 2003 invasion of Iraq was known; 40 suspected Al Qaeda members were arrested there shortly after 9/11.

Though the Moroccan Islamic Combatant Group (GICM) had ties to Al Qaeda—and several of its members train regularly at Al Qaeda camps in Afghanistan—they are a force unto themselves—with members, as the Madrid attacks revealed, who circulate freely within and among European cities. Neighbors of various Madrid bombers later described them to the media as "integrated" and "polite," with, according to the BBC, "a liking for football, fashion, drinking, and Spanish girlfriends."[7] The suspected leader of the group, the Tunisian-born Serhane ben Abdelmajid Fakhet, who was 35 at the time, had lived in Spain for eight years, coming initially to study economics at Madrid University; when he executed the attacks—all of which involved detonators attached to cell phones, rather than suicide belts— he worked in real estate and lived in a comfortable Madrid suburb. On occasion, he had traveled on a forged Belgian passport.[8] When police surrounded his home on April 3, however, he blew it up, setting off a bomb that also killed four fellow members of the GICM—and leaving much information about the background of the attacks forever beyond reach.

But what was clear to all was this: home-based Islamic radicals with ties to Al Qaeda had committed a terrorist attack on a European city; that many such extremists were fully integrated into European society, living ordinary, middle class, even Western-seeming lives; and finally, that a member state of the EU had bowed to terrorist demands.

Two weeks after the attack, Popular Party spokesman Gustavo de Aristegui issued a caution to incoming Socialist Prime Minister Jose

Louis Rodriguez Zapatero in the form of an op-ed published in the *Washington Post*. Above all, he said, the warnings about continuing to maintain troops in Iraq were "excuses." "And let us make no mistake," he wrote: "All the terrorists offer are excuses. For other governments to believe that only Spain's support in Iraq motivated the attacks against us, and that those who do not support what is going on in Iraq are therefore safe, would be a grave mistake. All democracies are targeted by these organizations because they consider freedom, and the sovereignty of the people, their worst enemies. The attacks here prove that terrorism has no boundaries, strikes where and when it can, and tries to influence, terrorize or force the surrender of democratic societies.

"The terrorists had more than one reason to strike against Spain. Islamists have been obsessed for years with the demise of Al-Andalus, the 800-year medieval Islamic caliphate of Spain, which they consider the zenith of their Golden Age. They believe that the historic humiliation that the West inflicted on Islam started with the end of that period in the 15th century and the Catholic conquest of Granada. In 1984, I had a long talk with a high-ranking Sunni cleric in the Omeyad Mosque in Damascus. He was very friendly when he learned that I was Spanish. After two hours of conversation about politics and theology, which are very much intertwined in that part of the world, he said to me: 'Don't worry. We will liberate Spain from Western corruption.' I understood then, that if even a moderate cleric was expressing this kind of thinking, then Spain's—and Europe's—main problem in the 21st century would be radical Islamism and the terrorism practiced in its name."[9]

Despite this, de Aristegui continued, "Already, unbelievably, some in Europe are talking about different approaches to dealing with terrorism, approaches that the terrorists could interpret as appeasement. There are those who say that poverty and the Arab-Israeli conflict are the root causes of Islamist terrorism, and if these two issues were resolved the terrorism would cease. This is risky thinking. Those are just two of the many factors behind the expansion of this phenomenon. If they were resolved, the terrorists would just make up new excuses to justify the unjustifiable. The Egyptian pediatrician Ayman al-Zawahiri, founder of Islamic Jihad and al Qaeda's number two, has already threatened France directly with attacks because of the banning of the Islamic head scarf in that nation's schools. That, of course, is a transparent excuse, since the terrorists cannot attack France on the basis of its having supported the war in Iraq. And France and others are aware of this. In the wake of the bombings here, both France and Germany, which also strongly opposed the war in Iraq, raised their antiterrorist alert level from orange to red."[10]

Within two years, despite heightened precautions throughout the EU, jihadists—many of them European citizens—would prove him right, with attacks that killed 52 in London (followed by a foiled attack in London again just two weeks later); a thwarted effort, one year after that, to blow up nine planes bound for the United States from London's Heathrow Airport; a series of planted bombs that miraculously failed to detonate in Koblenz and Dortmund, Germany; rioting in Paris, Denmark, and Amsterdam; and the killing of Theo van Gogh.

* * *

The woman known as Bat Ye'or has a theory about this way of thinking, described in countless articles and a half dozen books as the concept of "Eurabia," based on a cooperative pact settled between Europe and the Arab nations in the 1970s; and "dhimmitude," a neologism coined from the concept of the "dhimmi," an Islamic principle by which—in short—non-Muslims are "tolerated" by Muslim majorities in exchange for payment of an ample tax. (Because failure to pay that tax can and does result in death to the non-Muslim, I personally tend to think of it less as "tax" than as "ransom.")

"Eurabia" was the title of a policy report issued in Paris as the result of meetings between European and Arab leaders, according to Ye'or, aimed at guaranteeing oil supply to Europe in exchange for cultural support of Islamic initiatives in Europe (such as schools, mosques, and Euro-Arab cultural centers like the Institut du Monde Arab in Paris) and political and economic support of Palestine. The result, she argues, will be the inevitable overpowering of Western culture and ideas through the increasing introduction and infusion of Arab ones, and—more importantly—a Europe increasingly dependent on Arab oil, for which it will gradually be forced to make ever-greater concessions. Those concessions will become easier, too, as the Muslim population of Europe grows, and as Islamic culture spreads inside of Europe's borders. In short, Europe will be dhimmified.

There are many who think Bat Ye'or is absolutely brilliant. Many others think her absolutely nuts. Neither of these, however, occurs to me one way or the other when I meet her at a conference in The Hague in the winter of 2005. Diminutive and shy, she is, in person, nothing like the powerful warrior she becomes in the printed page. With the curiosity of a scholar and the politesse of an elite European, she engages strangers in conversation and is quick to make a friend.

Born in Cairo, Bat Ye'or (her pen name) left Egypt in 1955 with the expulsion of the Jews, escaping to London where she was granted asylum and, following her marriage in 1959, British citizenship. She and her husband, also a scholar in the area of human rights and radical

Islam, live in Geneva, where she has been known to face threats against her life for her writings.

While many mainstream thinkers, especially in the U.S., tend to dismiss the concept of "Eurabia" in its purest, undiluted version as "conspiracy theory," the attacks of March 11 in Madrid thrust the general notion into public view—in articles, on the Internet, and in debates across the Continent—prompting quite a few to reconsider the idea. Why *had* Spain so quickly surrendered? How much of France's refusal to back the coalition in Iraq could be explained by pacts made decades earlier, and a need for Iraqi oil? Had Europe forfeited too much to be sure of its own security anymore?

Whatever one made of "Eurabia" as an idea, the attacks in Spain should not have come as the surprise it did. Certainly other countries had become aware of growing Muslim radicalization within their borders; in Holland, only days before the Madrid bombing, the AIVD had published a study showing that second- and third-generation Muslims—Moroccans, especially—were being targeted and successfully recruited for jihad—in mosques, on the Internet, and in prisons, where juveniles serving time were assured that by taking to fundamentalism they could break from their wrongful pasts and find redemption.[11] Where previously, drug trafficking and street crime had been the lures—again especially in the Moroccan community—the call now was to religion and the conquest of the West: power, in other words, through intimidation, military preparedness, conquest, leadership, and in the end, immortality. For young, often (but by no means always) economically disadvantaged men and even women deep in the throes of adolescent insecurities, identity crises, and hormonal frustration, the call was—and remains—dangerously seductive. Add to this the promises of wealth, both for the recruits or, should they become martyrs, for their families, and it is unsurprising that the numbers of young jihadists throughout Europe has been growing.

"When kids come to me," Fatimazohra Hadjar tells me, "it's not because they are fundamentalists. They come to me with 'I have an education problem' or 'there's trouble at school.' Then I discover they won't shake my hand because I'm a woman, and that they spend the whole day in the mosques. So I find ways to occupy them. You have to keep a kid like this busy. I have to hold them tight, because if I let go, someone with money will come, and the next thing you know, he's strapped to a bomb."

None of this was lost on the rest of Europe in the aftermath of Madrid. France, which had already experienced threats from bin Laden in response to a national headscarf ban and tensions in its immigrant neighborhoods, especially Paris's Banlieu, immediately raised its terror alert to "red," its second-highest alert reading. *Time* magazine quoted a

French security official as saying, "We know if we're not next, we're after the ones who are next. And that is what everyone in Europe is thinking to themselves today."[12]

He was right. Within days, countries throughout Europe were re-examining their security and counter-terrorism policies, investing in intelligence, preparing new legislation, and upping their surveillance. In June, fifteen people were arrested in Belgium on suspicion of planning an attack, and an Egyptian by the name of Rabei Osman Sayed Ahmed, an explosives expert for the Egyptian military who was believed to be one of the main figures responsible for the Madrid attack, was arrested in Milan, Italy. In Holland, officials went on high alert; two men, one from Lebanon and one from Syria, were arrested on suspicions they planned to attack a sporting event in Nijmegen. Police also arrested the 18-year-old Dutch-Moroccan Samir Azzuz, who would later be convicted for his connections with the Hofstadgroep, based on evidence suggesting he, too, was planning an attack; authorities found blueprints of government buildings and Schiphol airport, along with bomb-making ingredients, including fertilizers, in his home. Writing for the *New York Times*, Marlise Simons reported that on July 30, four additional suspected Islamic militants—citizens of Saudi Arabia, Yemen, Suriname, and the Netherlands—were also arrested. According to Simons, police "raided three houses in Rotterdam" where they were said to have found various weapons and ammunition, along with a bulletproof vest. Islamic videotapes also found on the scene, according to Simons, included interviews with Muslim extremists planning suicide attacks. Additional arrests followed. "What we see in the Netherlands," a Ministry of Justice official told Simons, "is not one single organization but different, separate groups." [13]

And in England, several imams came under scrutiny as well, as did youth groups: in a town north of London, the *New York Times* reported in April 2004, a group of young, second-generation Pakistanis described the 9/11 hijackers as "the magnificent 19," as their leader spoke of the bombings in Madrid. At a tennis center community hall, reported the *Times'* Patrick E. Tyler and Don van Natta Jr., "their leader, Sheik Omar Bakri Mohammad, spoke of his adherence to Osama bin Laden. If Europe fails to heed Mr. bin Laden's offer of a truce—provided that all foreign troops are withdrawn from Iraq in three months—Muslims will no longer be restrained from attacking the Western countries that host them." And in Geneva, an imam at one mosque, according to the *Times*, "exhorted his followers to 'impose the will of Islam on the godless society of the West.'" [14]

Such statements, however gruesome, pose challenges. In a democratic state, free speech makes even incitement to violence potentially unassailable: and as they sought to recast their counterterrorism policies, Europe's leaders found themselves—and still do—struggling to find effective means to respond to those like Sheik Omar—or, for that matter, politicians like Dyab Abou Jahjah.

By now, Jahjah had become a familiar figure in Belgium and the Netherlands. The AEL had staged any number of demonstrations, and Jahjah, whose statements to the Western press consistently appeared mild-mannered, had also been quoted inciting violence against Israel in his closed-session speeches to Muslims. His motto, adopted from Malcolm X, was "by any means necessary," and he flaunted it on the AEL Web site and shouted it to his supporters. He and members of his League were repeatedly arrested, and repeatedly, too, released.

But in May 2004, Jahjah confronted a force he could neither intimidate nor inspire: Dutch filmmaker and commentator Theo van Gogh.

The debate took place in a sold-out city theater—the Stadschouwburg—on Amsterdam's Leidseplein, over questions of "idealism," pitting Abou Jahjah against D66 leader Boris Dittrich, a gay human rights activist who ran the liberal-social party and was known for having initiated several important laws defending victims' rights. Theo van Gogh was called to moderate.

But minutes before the third round of the debate was to begin, Jahjah expressed his disapproval of the selection of Van Gogh. In answer, Van Gogh stepped down, because, he said, "I find that the debate must stand above the moderator."

But he didn't leave it there; first, he explained to the audience what had happened, and announced that journalist Yoeri Albrecht, one of the organizers of the event, would take his place. "I find it odd, however," said Theo van Gogh, "that a pimp for the prophet, with Allah and a pair of enormous bodyguards on his side, is unwilling to enter a discussion if I am leading it."

That phrase—"pimp for the prophet"—would follow Van Gogh for the rest of his days.

Jahjah jumped from his seat and left the theater, followed by a crowd of his supporters. "Allah knows better!" Van Gogh called out after him. Outside the theater, fighting erupted between supporters of the two sides as debate organizers attempted to convince Jahjah to stay. Jahjah, however had "had enough of that pig," he said, and left. Van Gogh, despite urging to take a taxi for his safety, grabbed his bicycle and headed home. "Jahjah," he pronounced as he departed, "is the nail in the casket of free expression, and free expression must be defended. I will say whatever it is I think." And he mounted his bike and left.

Many—and I'm among them—found the events comical. But Holland in those days was not easily amused, and vulnerable to being set off balance by discussions of what may or may not be said. "Theo is asking for it," some argued. "Jahjah had it coming," others said. Had

Van Gogh tested the limits of free speech? It certainly would not have been the first time. Yet why point to him, when imams were known to call for the stoning of homosexuals from mosques throughout the country, and chants calling for the gassing of the Jews were commonplace?

In a small country, small dramas grow disproportionately immense. A similar example had occurred two years earlier, when Premier Jan-Peter Balkenende had expressed displeasure with *Egoland*, a series of six-minute, animated TV shows about the House of Oranje in which the royal family members were portrayed by clay figures. "Unacceptable," sniffed the premier, claiming the show could be "damaging" to the status of the royal house and proposing a parliamentary "discussion" about what could and could not be shown on TV. How had he arrived at this conclusion? Not, he admitted, by actually seeing the program; he was simply "adequately informed," he told the *Volkskrant*. "Words are being put in the mouths of people without allowing them to defend themselves," he argued. "Can we permit this?" The premier further pointed to a highly popular program, *Kopspijkers*, a talk show in which actors impersonated various prominent people—usually from the political sphere.

Unsurprisingly, Balkenende's ludicrous reaction caused the show's ratings to skyrocket. Said Boris Dittrich in a statement broadcast on *RTL News*, "This hardly strikes me as a job for the premier of Holland. There are, after all, more important issues that need solving." [15]

No one, as it turned out, could have agreed more than the royals themselves; one spokesperson for the family even noted, "The family can spend a whole weekend enjoying a good column by Youp van 't Hek in the *NRC* or [. . .] a broadcast of *Kopspijkers*."

Dittrich was, of course, right. By the time of the "pimp for the prophet" incident, concern about clay puppets had become practically obscene in its petty idiocy. Radicalism was growing. Honor killings had come into the open. Basic values of the state were being challenged. In France, they had banned headscarves by 2004, but the Dutch, by contrast, debated allowing Muslim policewomen to wear them, and KLM, the national airline, had designed scarves to match its uniforms. To do otherwise, it was argued, was religious discrimination. A parliamentary proposal to prohibit wearing burkas in public was quickly voted down.

One woman, however, took a different stance: Minister of Immigration and Integration Maria Cornelia Verdonk.

* * *

Known to most as "Iron Rita," Maria Cornelia Frederika "Rita" Verdonk was named Minister of Immigration and Integration as a leading member of the VVD under Balkenende's second administration in May

2003. A former Marxist (as a student in the 1980s, her activism had earned her the name "Red Rita"), she switched to the liberal VVD in 2002, prompting some former political allies to accuse her of having been a mole.

Throughout the 1990s, Verdonk worked in the prison system, first as the assistant director the Scheveningen Detention Center in The Hague, and then at the De Schie prison in Rotterdam. From there, she moved on to the Ministry of Justice until leaving the political and penitentiary worlds briefly as a manager at the global consultancy firm, KPMG. She returned to both with her appointment under Balkenende, falling into the role that, some would say, she had been born to fill.

From the beginning, Verdonk left no doubt that she had heard what Pim Fortuyn had said, and agreed. A woman little prone to social niceties and useless chitchat, she let her policies, for the most part, do the talking. Within six months of taking office, she ordered the deportation of 26,000 asylum seekers who, though their applications had ultimately been rejected, had spent five or more years in the Netherlands awaiting a decision. Some, argued Verdonk, had been turned down earlier and simply had appealed, allowing them to prolong their stay, in some cases more than once. She considered it abuse of the system.

But five years is enough time for lovers to meet and marry, for children to be born and grandparents to die. Boys and girls who had arrived clutching stuffed bears and favorite dolls had become young men and women old enough to serve a military and to vote. "What do you propose to do with these families?" Verdonk was asked in an interview, "as they are processed for return? Will you put families with children in detention centers, behind bars?"[16]

That, answered the woman soon to be known as "Iron Rita," "is not my choice or preference." But, she noted, "Children are the responsibility of their parents. That responsibility cannot be put into the lap of the Dutch state. They chose to stay here, not the state; the consequences are theirs to pay."

Verdonk's decision spurred an international outcry. In Holland, entire communities came together to protest the deportation of neighbors they had come to consider friends. Iron Rita stood unmoved. "Asylum seekers come of their own free will. If you demand a credible asylum policy, then rejection of applicants has to be a part of the equation," she said. "People forget that by sending away those people whose applications have been rejected, we make room for others who have a genuine right to stay in this country, who sit now in closed centers because we have no homes to put them in." The criteria for asylum, she added, involve "safety in the land of origin—not how well they've integrated here." It is time, said Rita Verdonk, to tell our neighbors, "Go back now. Nicely."

The 26,000 became a hallmark of Rita Verdonk's political career—and for many abroad, a shift in their thinking about Holland, that country they had previously considered a haven, tolerant and welcoming to all. Many Netherlanders bore the decision with shame. Verdonk tucked it, like a feather, in her cap, and went on working.

And work she did. By this time, she had already introduced measures to cut down on migration through marriage, a measure partially shaped by now fellow VVD-member Hirsi Ali's fight against forced marriages and the social and domestic problems they bring with them. She brought new force and urgency to an earlier, rarely enforced policy requiring foreigners to take a citizenship course to qualify for a green card, even suggesting that those who had lived in the Netherlands for decades, if they were still below the age of 65, be required to take the class as well. Most—other than immigrants from the United States, Australia, the EU, Canada, New Zealand, and Japan—would also be required to take an exam proving, essentially, that they understood and were prepared to live by the beliefs, values, and norms of Dutch society. In a truly extreme move, Verdonk further proposed that Dutch citizens who had been born and raised in other countries be required to take the exam as well.

And this was only the beginning.

* * *

By June 2004, I am following this story with growing astonishment and worry. The 600-hour course, some speculate, could cost about 6,000 euros, half of which would be refunded once the immigrant had passed the test. This, it is important to understand, is not for citizenship; it is for a residency permit, for the right simply to live in the Netherlands at all.

Fré and I carry two chairs from her apartment to the sidewalk of the Pieter Aertszstraat, where we chat and watch the neighbors we have not seen all winter passing by: a red-haired man with his curly, blonde-haired son; a woman, maybe 21, with straight blonde hair and a model's figure. Fré drinks sparkling water, and I a white wine spritzer made with South African (Dutch colony) wine and ice. We talk of work, of plans, and of Holland's closing doors. There will be a brain drain, I warn her, and she says, "you should write about that for the *NRC*." I tell her I will think about it. "Call them," she urges.

"Normally, you write the piece and just send it in," I answer.

"That's America," she laughs. "This is Holland. Here, you have to call and discuss it first. Everything must be discussed."

"People will leave," I say, "and people will stop coming." And it isn't just the Muslims, which are who this law is designed to keep away.

It will be the British and the Japanese, the Chinese and the Americans, the scientists, the teachers, the technical innovators, the corporations seeking to expand—and bringing with them, jobs. Who will want to start a business here, I ask her. What academic would bring his family so he could teach? American employees of companies like ABN and Sotheby's, or the coordinators of hotels, the curators of museums, the actors who have bought homes here, like Brad Pitt, will move on. Holland will become a wasteland, isolated and insular, without the technology or science or creativity to compete globally, alone with its beer and its war crimes tribunals, within its clenched and tightened borders.

Islam is a backward culture, they say.

What, I ask Fré, do they think theirs is going to become?

To escape the problem—or appear to—immigration officials arrive at what appears to be—but isn't—a way out: the "intellectual immigrant visa," which allows foreigners to live and work in the Netherlands without taking classes or passing tests. But the "intellectuals" they speak of are not, in fact, university professors, or writers, or artists, or curators, or composers. It is not Brad Pitt or Sotheby's employees. An "intellectual," according to the immigration service, is defined as someone whose salary will cap 50,000 euros a year.

In other words, if you earn enough money to pay a higher tax, you can live unhindered in the Netherlands.

It does not escape me that the architects of this system are the very people who write newspaper columns and shout warnings at various debates about "dhimmitude"—the Islamic state's tolerance of non-Muslims, as long as they pay the proper tax.

* * *

But for now, there is a Sotheby's, and it is hosting a group of journalists for lunch, starting with Moët & Chandon handed out at 11:30 A.M. as we arrive. By half past twelve, we all are a bit giddy, chatting freely with one another. We gather around the Old Master Drawings expert who is supervising this sale—the largest private collection of 18th-century Dutch works on paper ever to be offered at auction—and around Gary Schwartz, the Rembrandt expert who has come by as well. Schwartz thumbs through examples of the best of the collection—a few 17th-century treasures are among them—as the expert identifies the artists. We pause at a sheet containing four small pages from a sketchbook, each individually signed, which seems to all of us unusual; and at the freshness of cobalt blues and crimsons amongst the watercolors, clear enough to have been painted yesterday. The expert makes certain that we see a Lievens watercolor of London, where apparently he took up a whole new way of painting: a life, a history, told in the fading images of the Thames. The expert wears a blue suit and has brown eyes and graying hair and has a friendly smile and an accent much like Tony Blair's. He is cheerful and laughs when I ask obnoxious questions like how much did you reduce the estimates to attract the buyers and did you hold off on this sale until the market was particularly right.

Champagne is how we begin, in the low lights and modernist lines of the Sotheby's Amsterdam boardroom, but this indeed is Amsterdam and lunch is therefore *broodjes*—meat salads, mozzarella and pesto, roast beef, on various sorts of rolls. I take a mozzarella pesto on a whole grain bread and eat the mozzarella. We, all of us, civilized, European, and polite, address our sandwiches with knife and fork. No more wine is served (this isn't Paris) but instead, water, orange juice, and buttermilk—a standard for Dutch lunches. There is by now so little left of the Holland I came to live in over a decade earlier: the coffee or tea shopkeepers offered in China cups when customers came in are gone (smaller shops now offer nothing; larger ones have coffee machines with non-dairy creamer and plastic disposable cups instead); the warmth and curiosity toward strangers now a distant politeness, icy, and aloof.

Still, for all the changes the Netherlands has seen, for all its mosques and racial fights and questions around the future, one thing remains of who they are, and who they have always been: with lunch, they still drink buttermilk.

CHAPTER 14

I am early. She is late. We are meeting in a typical Amsterdam brown bar on the Keizersgracht, on the corner overlooking the canal and a flower stall on our side and the shops along the side street on the other. I wait, scribbling notes in a purple composition book about the man who shares my table as the whole café is full. They are regulars, yuppie Amsterdammers and a few more burly types, with big laughs and the Amsterdam dialect that is the Dutch equivalent of Cockney. They are all white: Four men at the bar, two on mobile phones, two in blue down jackets, all in jeans. A blonde woman and a youngish-looking man—young enough that, with his long hair, one has to look twice to see if he is not a woman—sit at the window, flirting with his mobile, the kind that apparently takes photos. She laughs and leans forward towards him. Above the bar, blue and white balloons in various stages of deflation form the sad reminder of what was once a festive moment, like a hangover across the ceiling.

You can see out these windows halfway down the block, which means, in essence, that anyone walking past here can see in, can see Ayaan when she arrives. It strikes me as excessively risky on her part, bodyguards or none.

But the guards do not appear. Over the pitched and gabled roofs of Amsterdam, the sky grows gray, and still the sun shines, the kind of light and paradox one sees in paintings by Vermeer and can't believe are real, the sun-filled, stormy light of *Nederland*. A taxi pulls up, but a bearded man emerges and enters the café, another "regular" here, it seems—or at any rate, not a bodyguard. Not a tiny black woman with almond eyes and cheekbones nearly at her temples. I wait. She remains, Ayaan, despite herself, disorganized and over-committed, and she will arrive (if she does arrive) babbling apologies, and all will indeed be forgiven. She has this effect on people.

I've been waiting forty-five minutes before at last I see them, two men in suit and tie across the Keizersgracht, standing, doing nothing. Only electronics salesmen and bodyguards wear ties in Amsterdam; the blue BMW on the corner, I decide, is obviously Hirsi Ali's. But the men don't move, and no one leaves the car. True, Brad Pitt has been in town, but I don't think he had bodyguards, and anyway, probably not the kind in suits. Ten more minutes pass. The men outside stay where they are. I've been waiting here for an hour now. She must not be coming.

As I pay at the bar for my coffee, I ask the bartender if he knows who Ayaan Hirsi Ali is. Of course he does. "If she comes," I say, "please tell her Abigail waited, and went home." The barman nods, and repeats my name: *Ahbigal*. "Yes," I say, and thank him, though I can tell he isn't certain what to do with this information. Hirsi Ali? Here? Is Abigail a friend or enemy? Is the message a kind of secret code?

The tram stop is at the corner of the Keizersgracht, and the car and the two men are still there. I pace the traffic island, annoyed that the trams so rarely come on time, and then a woman of about 28 approaches me and asks, in English, if I am Abigail. She is Ayaan's assistant, Iris, she tells me, and good that I'd not already gone, Ayaan is in the car—the blue BMW I'd spotted earlier—being interviewed by phone, shall we go back to the café?

Shortly after, two of Ayaan's guards arrive, scoping out the room, and then Ayaan follows, another guard on either side. We go upstairs to a separate dining area—one passersby cannot see into; the four guards stay down below. Because she is no longer allowed to spend the night in Amsterdam, even at her boyfriend, Herman Phillips' home, after she meets with me, after she dines with someone else, the guards will drive Ayaan back down to The Hague, arriving sometime around midnight. Tomorrow it will all begin again.

She has been at a lecture today, Ayaan tells me, and from her face I can tell she didn't like it. Besides, she's starving. (Frequently, her Muslim opposition will insist that she is crazy, using her thinness as evidence of sorts: at least she must be anorexic. But anyone who has ever shared a meal with Hirsi Ali knows otherwise: this is not a woman who leaves food lying on her plate. Despite her beauty—or perhaps because of it—she doesn't busy herself with makeup, with her weight, or with diets. Give her a three-course meal any time of day and she will eat it, full of energy, talking, arguing, bouncing new ideas around, giggling as she eats. If she is thin, it is because even when she is sitting, presumably relaxing, she is moving, she is fervently alive.) When a waiter finally comes, she orders *bitterballen,* the national snack of choice, and a glass of Beaujolais. Her assistant Iris orders Coke.

"You would not have believed it," Hirsi Ali says of the speakers she has listened to this afternoon. "These people are like fundamentalist Christians, speaking out in tongues. It's nonsense, what they say." She is talking about the multiculturalists, the ones who defend the ideas that she most passionately protests. "They say things like, 'we are for an individual multiculturalism.' Now, what on earth is that? It's meaningless. It's empty. It's an excuse, like 'liberal Islam.'"

Hirsi Ali does not believe in "liberal Islam," which she calls a contradiction in terms—the description of a thing that can't exist. "Islam" means "submission," she argues; if you submit your will to Islam, then according to the Koran, the rights of the individual are no longer protected. There is no more equality. "It's speaking," she says again, "in tongues." And she drums her tongue against her lips, "bthbthtbhthb. Like that." She cups one hand around her glass and leans towards me, across the table. "This cannot go on," she says. "This. Can. Not. Go. On."

Ayaan's hands move rapidly when she speaks, fragile, as if blown by the breathiness of her voice. It is hard to fathom that such a tiny woman has created so much uproar among so many. Magisterial as she appears in photographs or on TV, she is leaf-like, the kind of person you fear will be blown into the canals by a too-strong winter wind. Perhaps it is this near-vulnerability that makes her so self-protective, so defiant. Days earlier, while having lunch with fellow members of the Parliament one day, she had pulled a flask of pepper spray from her bag and sprayed it in the air. Though nobody was harmed, her performance was caught by the prying eyes of a gossip columnist for the national daily, *Telegraaf.* Pepper spray, it turns out, is illegal in the Netherlands. Holland's most famous politician had broken the law, as it were, while the film was rolling. "Hirsi Ali sprays fellow members of the Parliament with pepper spray!" the headlines screamed. Opinion columnists debated: should she be fined, as any private citizen would be, or, given the extraordinary conditions of the death threats out against her, be forgiven?

I found the conversations at once quaint and yet ridiculous. This was a woman whose life was so in danger that the government had assigned her, at one point, as many as eight secret service bodyguards divided among three cars—three riding with her, the others driving ahead or behind. No one else in government office in the Netherlands, in March 2004, had even a single guard for protection. This was a woman who may not even enter a public toilet unless it had first been properly cleared and checked for safety. But she may not carry pepper spray. You would think she'd fired gunshots in the air, then slipped her pistol back into her purse. But these things don't happen in the Netherlands. Pepper spray is radical enough.

Two cases of Muslim violence have appeared in the news the week Iris, Ayaan, and I all meet: the first was the murder of Gul, the 32-year-old Turkish woman whose husband shot her at the door of a battered women's shelter and whose brother threatened to blow the entire shelter up (and everyone who happened to be in it) if the children were not returned to the family immediately by the state, which had stepped in to protect them. In response, the Ministry of Justice had ordered the place evacuated; now the women on the run were on the run. And then there was the Moroccan man who brought his ailing wife to see a doctor. When the doctor extended his hand to her in farewell, the husband punched him in the face. At the police station later, he offered no excuses or denials. "Of course I did," he told the officer. "That's how things are in my culture, in my religion."

Pepper spray. Handshakes. In a country accustomed to acting by consensus, it is difficult to master notions about any bending of the rules.

I'm still stuck on the story about the pepper spray, but Ayaan's fury has long since moved on to all these other things. She is especially livid about the response to the bomb threats against the shelter.

"Evacuate," Ayaan says, "as if it were a war. This is what cultural relativism has brought with it: you don't get the aggressor. You just evacuate." Even worse was the suggestion of the local mayor: help these women leave the country, give them a new identity, and have them be protected there. Witness protection-type stuff. "More absurd, I can't imagine," Ayaan huffs. "First their husbands and their fathers want to kill them, now they have to become refugees?"

I suggest, and only half-joking, that potential honor killing victims— for that is what these women are—be issued cans of pepper spray.

The problem, says Ayaan Hirsi Ali, is that "the people who defend cultural relativism in Europe are people who were born and who grew up in freedom. They are told, 'minorities are weak, and you must pity them.' But the word 'pity' is, of course, not politically correct, so it becomes 'you have to sympathize with them; you must be tolerant.'"

And I say, "I am out of tolerance."

Ayaan Hirsi Ali's half-sister lives in England, where she continues the traditions of her culture to the letter, rising at dawn to pray, keeping her body completely veiled. Living with her, Ayaan declares, is torture. "'Ayaan, get up and pray,' she says, 'Ayaan, aren't you afraid of Allah, Ayaan, this world is temporary, Ayaan, get up and pray.'" It becomes a kind of chant itself: Ayaan, get up and pray, Ayaan, the hell,

Ayaan, get up and pray. Until the morning that Ayaan turned to her and said, "I don't care. I *want* to go to hell."

The words remind me that I have brought something to show her: a catalogue brought back from New York produced by a manufacturer of mannequins. The bodies come in all shapes and forms and colors.

"I thought this might be good for *Submission*."

She looks at it briefly, then puts it aside.

"I don't know. Maybe it's not a good idea. I'm not sure anymore."

"Why?" I ask her, surprised.

"Your friend, the artist," she says. "He frightened me."

"Arman?" I can't believe it. Arman is a gentle, kindly man. He was entirely supportive of her plans.

"He said that I'm courageous."

"Ayaan, everyone says you're courageous."

"Yes," Ayaan says, and turns her head from me. "But this was somehow different. And now I am afraid."

She looks at me, but I do not know how to answer. There is no time, anyway: Iris's watchful eye is on the clock.

"We have to go," she finally says, and nudges Hirsi Ali from her seat. "You have seven minutes left to get to dinner."

When we leave Café de Leeuw, Iris heads towards home. I stay with Ayaan. We hold hands along the Utrechtsestraat. Two Moroccan boys approach; one pumps his forefinger, staring at Ayaan. "Pepper spray!" he taunts.

"I'll use it on you!" Ayaan calls back, in English. Then she laughs.

I nudge her. "You mustn't say such things, Ayaan! The next thing you know, it's in all the papers."

"I can't help it," she says.

"Help it," I say. "I'm a journalist, too, you know."

The guards laugh. "Never happened," one says to me. "She never said it. Did she say it?" And they all look at one another.

I smile, satisfied. She is well-protected after all.

* * *

The multicultural debate in Holland had by now reached fever pitch, with a growing number concluding, as had Scheffer and Hirsi Ali, that the entire concept was only a disaster heading for even worse. Even as the United Nations Development Program's 2004 Human Development Report insisted that "immigrants should have the right to retain their own culture, without being forced to integrate," the British Neal Ascherson determined that the idea of a multicultural society was based on angst. Where once the idea had been to help "others"—minorities—assimilate: the "melting pot" idea—now, he argued, cultural relativism had taken over, with the result being that two conflicting sets of ethics and values should somehow find a way to live side by side in a larger society (the "salad bowl," as he put it)— a concept that is, for obvious reasons, utterly unachievable. "From traditional mixed communities," he wrote on OpenDemocracy.net in August 2004,[1] "We are back in the vast cities of modern Europe and America as they suck in migrants from every corner of the earth. Can those old forms of multiculturalism, in which ethnic groups stay distinct but live together peacefully, be reconstructed in London, Berlin, Toronto, Istanbul, Antwerp? Yes, they can—because after all, they already exist in those 'salad-bowl' cities. But they cannot exist forever, or even for long. The crucial point is this: western urban multiculturalism is not a destination. It is only a way-station on the road to something else."

Indeed. With reports in 2003 of rising criminality among Moroccan youth in Holland—this despite increased funding for neighborhood rehabilitation and youth counseling programs—the schism between *allochtoon* and *autochtoon* grew deeper. Nationalism raged, as if the city were being threatened with invasion (which, in many ways, it was), reaching into corners that had, until now, felt safe. In a meeting with the publisher of my earlier book that spring, I proposed a second, containing interviews with major artists from around the world.

"You'll need mostly Dutch artists," the editor responded.

The reaction stunned me. I could not imagine an American publisher requesting inclusion of an American artist simply on the basis of his nationality. And yet I realized, suddenly, that this had become the Dutch way: museum directors simply played musical chairs amongst the Dutch museums, rarely inviting anyone from abroad. Curators and gallerists exhibited the works of young Dutch art students even while non-Dutch students attended Holland's art academies in large numbers. Cultural relativism, the force behind the multicultural idea, had created a backlash, even in such traditionally Left-leaning social sectors as the arts, based—as Francis Fukuyama has noted—on a certain ethnic and cultural allegiance.[2]

Yet in so many ways, this was only another symptom of 21st-century Dutch culture—this closing of borders, this constant navel-gazing, this unwillingness to include itself in a larger, wider world, and embrace a wider world within itself. It was this, perhaps, that cut to the heart of the country's "multi-culti" quandary: in clutching to their Dutchness, the Dutch had failed to identify what "Dutchness" really is. Is it liberal, so much so that not only are homosexual marriage, euthanasia, and soft drug use accepted—but, therefore, so must religious groups that oppose them? Is it, as Dutch UNDP advisor Ad de Raad asked, "dependent on a border that was once drawn around a piece of land?"[3] Or is it a 400-plus-year-old culture, rooted deeply in its mercantile and marine histories, the water metaphors that guide its policies and structure, unbendable, lest the dam be broken and its people, as it were, destroyed? While France, in September 2004, put its foot down in the name of the separation of church and state, establishing a ban on religious symbols and accessories—headscarves as well as crosses and Stars of David—from the public sphere, Holland simply couldn't decide, wavered, debated, caved. Similar headscarf bans had been put in place in Turkey as early as 1997—yet Holland's parliament ruled against even banning burqas ten years later.

The problem, I realized, was not one of purpose; both sides of the debate defended the same fort: their culture. But no one asked—or attempted to—what that meant. And looming over all of it was the larger question not even Americans have asked since the World Trade Towers fell: as we fight on to spread democracy, preserve democracy, defend democracy, no one yet, it seems, has actually defined, for all of us, what democracy actually *is*.

That universal, Western—or certainly European—uncertainty, and Holland's wavering in particular, had turned the country into something of a playground for Islamic extremists by late 2003. The rules, after all, were weak. "When you were 15," Ayaan had told Iris, whom I judged to be in her early twenties, as we talked at Café de Leeuw, "there were discussions in Holland about what to do with the men who committed honor killings. It was decided that yes, they should be punished, but the punishment should be less than for other murderers."

"That can't be," Iris protested.

But it was.

So perhaps none of us should have been surprised, though we were, when reporters for *Trouw* uncovered the three-volume *Minhaj El Muslim* [*The Way of the Muslim*] available for sale in Arabic and in Dutch at mosques and ordinary bookstores throughout the country. Originally written in Arabic by Sheik Abou Bakr Djaber El Djezeiri in 1964, the *Minaj* was translated into Dutch by a woman named Jeanette Ploeger, who, in her introduction, called it "a standard work." The books, which call for female circumcision, advise that a man may strike a woman—as long as he leaves no detectable trace behind. Homosexuals, the guides counsel, are to be thrown from the tops of tall buildings head first, and thereafter "killed by the throwing of stones" (as if they could have survived in the first place). And should a Muslim find himself in a word of unbelievers, he must organize, rally his troops, and go to war—battling with words, with violence, with martyrdom, if necessary, to the end.[4]

What do you do, as a politician in a democracy, with such a book?

Holland's parliament demanded its removal from the bookstores, but the imam of Amsterdam's most radical mosque, El Tawheed—where the book had first come to public light—refused. The VVD threatened to close the mosque down entirely, and declared the sale of the book "illegal"—treading, in so doing, on a thin line between church and state, and free speech versus censorship. But by then, of course, it didn't really even matter. The guide was out there, and obviously, a good many Dutch Muslims had read it. Over the next years, it would reappear frequently, and the number of its followers would grow.

* * *

On a June afternoon in 2004, as Ayaan Hirsi Ali joined several colleagues for lunch at Dudok, a popular watering hole amongst members of the Parliament, a young, blond man approached her. He had acne, she later noted, and friendly eyes, and she assumed he was just an ordinary student, perhaps approaching with a political suggestion or a question about her work. "Madame," he said, speaking with the soft accent and dialect of South Holland. He tapped her on the shoulder. "I hope with all my heart that the Mujahadeen will find and kill you, *inshallah.*"

As the boy began to walk away—and to the surprise of those sharing her table—Hirsi Ali grabbed him by the wrist and pulled him back. With her other hand, she grabbed the knife from her plate and offered it to him.

"If you want me dead," she told him, "then do it yourself."

"Oh, no," protested the boy. "I don't dare. I'd be afraid of going to jail."

They exchanged further words. He called her (as many had) a "threat" to his religion.

"How is that possible," she asked him, "if your faith is so strong and will eventually conquer all? Why don't you just ask Allah to bring me back to faith?"

"Yes," admitted the young man. "That would be best."

Hirsi Ali wrote up the incident for her regular column in the *Algemeen Dagblad*. The text landed on the Web forums at www.marokko.nl, where members flocked to comment. Wrote "Jamal 64," "For some, death is the best solution." Added "Ouidath," "He should have stabbed her in the neck."[5]

* * *

A few days later, I receive a phone call from Ayaan, asking me about my summer plans—which, as it happens, will involve a great deal of travel. "What a shame!" she says. Her own plans for the next months include much time spent in Amsterdam.

I couldn't know it then, of course, and she could not have told me: but she would be spending her summer recess with Theo van Gogh, secretly making the film that would become *Submission*.[6]

I never saw Ayaan again.

* * *

Submission aired on the program *Zomergasten* [*Summer Guests*]—on Sunday, August 29. By then, the film—and some aspects of its contents—had been made public, though very few of us knew all of what it actually contained. I called Ayaan that afternoon from New York to wish her luck, then waited for the reports in the Dutch press.

It did not take long.

In the 11-minute film, a woman's voice narrates vignettes of the life of a Muslim woman (or perhaps it is three different women), while an actress stands half naked, covered only by a sheer veil that obscures her breasts, but only barely. Cut throughout the film are still shots of a woman, presumably the one who is speaking, with passages from the Koran calligraphed across her body—just as Ayaan had first envisioned it. The shock, she had told me earlier, would be felt in the response to writing Koranic verses on the bodies of women, and in this she proved right; but equally shocking, especially to Muslims, was the near-nakedness of the actress, an artistic maneuver that seemed entirely engineered only to provoke, without adding any substance to her message. As artwork, and as part of Van Gogh's film, that nakedness was entirely, of course, admissible; but *Submission*—Hirsi Ali's *Submission*—wasn't made as art so much as propaganda (even Van Gogh called it a "pamphlet," and the awkwardly-written, stilted script is aimed at making, first and foremost, a point). And after all, Ayaan was a politician, really, not an artist.

In this, the Van Gogh-Hirsi Ali collaboration could—should—have stirred a rich discussion on the relationship between art and politics, of the role of the artist in the making of the film and the role of the politician in its writing. In the Holland of the 1990s, I imagine, this would indeed have taken place.

But tempers and fears were far too hot for that in 2004, and a European Muslim community with virtually no exposure to concepts of art theory or artistic license, a community that had been so mollycoddled, protected and indulged that they had, in the process, missed out on learning so many critical, valuable aspects of Western culture (including, but by far not limited to, basic art appreciation—so commonplace among the Dutch) could not begin to understand. They viewed the film entirely as a political and religious act (within Islam, the two are anyway the same), a blasphemy, and they were outraged.

"Muwahhidin Brigade op weg naar HA en TVG," the announcement on an MSN-group site read: "Mujahadeen brigade heading for HA [Hirsi Ali] and TVG [Theo van Gogh]." And with this call to arms, posted on August 30, just a day after *Submission*, appeared, available to anyone with access to the Internet, Ayaan Hirsi Ali's—supposedly secret—address.

Within hours, she was on the run again.

She had, of course, anticipated such a response. What surprised her, she later admitted, was the uniformity of reactions, not among the Muslims but among Westerners around the world who viewed the film online and wrote about it on Web sites, on blogs, in newspapers, and reported on it on TV. To her disappointment (rightly), they, too, seemed distressed more by the fact that Koran verses had been inscribed on women's bodies than they were by what those verses actually *said*.

Had everyone gone mad?

That year, it almost seemed as if they had. In the annals of *anni horribili* of the 21st century, 2004 will surely be remembered among the worst, especially for Holland, where Queen Beatrix lost first her mother, the beloved Juliana, who died just shy of her ninety-fifth birthday in March, and then her father, Prins Bernhard, who followed at the age of 93 on the first day of December. It was year of numerous domestic honor killings, and the shooting of Hans van Weil. Outside the Netherlands, there had been the bombing in Madrid, a suicide bombing in Leganes, Spain, and, on September 6, just days after the airing of *Submission*, the hostage-taking of 1,300 students and teachers by Islamic Chechnyan rebels at a school in Beslan, Russia, which ended in the massacre of more than 350, many of them children.

And in November, with the brutal murder of Theo van Gogh, life—not just in the Netherlands, but all of Europe—would never be the same.

CHAPTER 15

Theo van Gogh was never an easy child. He cut school. He lost his class schedules. He talked back to his parents and expressed—loudly—his general opinions, even to those who didn't care to listen. He provoked often simply for the sake of provoking. Though his parents eventually learned not to react, that often only made him push that much harder. Like his famous great-great uncle, he was, from early on, fascinated with images, creating films almost every weekend with his friends even as an adolescent, working in eight millimeter until saved up enough to buy himself an old 16-millimeter set. Nonetheless, his application to the film academy, at the age of 18, was rejected. Undaunted, he set out on his own.

That stubborn willfulness may well have been as much a part of his genetic makeup as was his instinct for image. The day after a high-school principal sent the long-haired Theo home with money for a hair-cut, his mother marched into the principal's office, indignantly announced that neither she nor her husband had any problems with their son's shoulder-length blond curls, and promptly withdrew him from the school. [1]

So, too, with his interest in politics: both of Theo's parents came from leftist political backgrounds. His father worked for the secret service. During the German occupation, his father's brother, also named Theo, had taken part in the resistance, writing for the underground press; he was executed on March 8, 1945—thirty-three years to the day before the birth of Mohammed Bouyeri. As *Volkskrant* reporter Pieter Webeling noted in a beautifully-crafted, rare interview with the younger

Theo's parents, Johann and Anneke van Gogh, both Theo van Goghs, in the end, sacrificed their lives for the power of free speech.

Yet despite these strong connections to his forebears, at a certain point, reports Webeling, Theo considered changing his name. "You get fed up," he had said in an earlier interview in newsweekly *de Tijd*, "always having to show people that yes, you have both ears."

Theo van Gogh's first film, *Luger*, premiered on April 8, 1982. It was by no means a great film, or even, by many accounts, a good film. It was, however, certainly a controversial one, one which would have allowed its producer plenty of notoriety and recognition no matter what his last name might have been: it was for *Luger* that Van Gogh created his infamous scene, with the two cats in a washing machine. It was tasteless. It was an unnecessarily dramatic performance in the breaking of rules. It was shock for shock's sake. But it was quintessential Theo: he had something to say, and he was damn well going to say it.

Mohammed Bouyeri was barely four years old when *Luger* was released: Van Gogh was 23. By the time Mohammed had reached the same age, he was already known to the police, having (among other feats) attempted to stab an officer in the neck with a 22-centimeter knife.

Like Theo, he, too, soon began writing—penning articles he published on the Internet and in local newspapers under the pseudonym "Abu Zubair." His most renowned piece, "To Catch a Wolf," based on an ancient Eskimo story, appeared in March 2004—around the time of his twenty-sixth birthday. According to Eskimo legend, the way to catch a wolf is to cover the blade of a knife with snow that has been colored red. Attracted by the redness, the wolf will come and begin to lick the knife, cutting his own tongue in the process. He then continues to lick his own blood until, at last, he dies.

Such writings, along with Bouyeri's encounters with the police—especially his 2001 arrest for assaulting a police officer—did not escape the attentions of the Dutch authorities.[2] As early as 2002, the AIVD noted that gatherings were taking place at his home on the Marianne Philipsstraat in Amsterdam—gatherings, which occasionally included a Syrian asylum seeker (he was ultimately turned down) by the name of Mohammed Bassem Al-Issa, also known as Sheik Abu Khaled (both names would later prove to be stolen identities). It was he, most agreed, who was largely responsible for the radicalization of Mohammed Bouyeri and of a number of his friends. Soon they would form what the AIVD would eventually nickname the "Hofstadgroep"—two of whose members, it is worth noting, the brothers Jason and Jermaine Walters, were the sons of an American father.

In July, Mohammed Bouyeri, with assistance from fellow Hofstadgroep member Ismail Akhnikh, published a translation of a fourteenth-century

document, "The Obligation to Kill Those Who Insult the Prophet," originally written in Arabic by Ibn al-Taymiyyeh (1263–1328)—who, notes
Hofstadgroep and terrorism expert Emerson Vermaat, serves also as a
source of inspiration for Al Qaeda.[3]

For his part, Van Gogh was producing his own series of writings,
ranging from his book *Allah Weet Het Beter* [*Allah Knows Better*] to the
various columns in which he referred to Muslims as "goatfuckers."
That he, in spite of this, had by then already produced two films fea-
turing young Muslim actors, including *Najib and Julia*, a love story
(based on *Romeo and Juliet*) about a Dutch girl and a Moroccan pizza
courier, or that all the Moroccans with whom he worked frequently
expressed their gratitude to him for his support of their artistic careers
and the opportunities he had provided them—these things, to most
Dutch Moroccans—and especially Mohammed Bouyeri—made no difference. For Van Gogh, it was about freedom, language, and art; for
Bouyeri, it was about faith. The two forces could not possibly find
peace.

* * *

On the night of November 1, 2004, Mohammed Bouyeri invited several friends to dinner. It was Ramadan. They dined well, chatted,
exchanged memories and news. As it happened, the following day,
two members of their group were to marry, despite much disapproval
among the ranks. The bride-to-be, who called herself "Oum Osama"—
meaning "Mother of Osama," in anticipation of the son she hoped to
name after Osama bin Laden—was a student of one of the top members of the Hofstadgroep, Moroccan-born Nouredine el-Fatmi. Her
intended, however, Zine Labidine Aouragha, was viewed with some
suspicion by the other Hofstadgroep members, who questioned the
depth of his commitment to Islam, or specifically, to Takfiri, the
extreme form of Islam practiced and preached by the group. Moreover,
he was already married; his wedding to Oum Osama would have been
recognized in Islam, but not by the Dutch state. The single men in the
group, for whom the wishes of the woman mattered less than their
own desires for a wife, grew annoyed. Why should he have two wives
and they none? The members had argued throughout the day, phoning
and texting each other frantically. Ismail had even phoned the bride to
convince her not to go through with the wedding; furious, she
responded that if it was not to be, Allah, not Ismail, would prevent it.
And so the men conferred, now, further wondering what, if anything,
could be done.[4,5]

At the end of the evening, according to Vermaat, they took a stroll
around the neighborhood. It was well after midnight when and his

roommate, Ahmed Hamdi, returned home to the Marianne Philipsstraat and went to bed.

At half past five on the morning of November 2, the two young men, Bouyeri and Hamdi, rose to pray. In the United States, presidential candidates were making their last push before the elections, with John Kerry and George W. Bush running close in the polls. Went back to bed about an hour later. When he woke again at half past seven, Mohammed was gone.

* * *

Theo van Gogh's morning routine was relatively predictable. Bouyeri had, by the morning of November 2, already observed Van Gogh's movements a few times, watching him make his way along the Linneusstraat to his office in Amsterdam-Zuid. That morning, he, too, casually cycled along the same street, dressed, as he always was by that time, in his white djellaba. As he neared the regional city offices, the familiar, corpulent frame of Theo van Gogh came into view.

Bouyeri pulled a nine-millimeter HS pistol from his knapsack and fired. And again. Bystanders froze in horror. A woman who, with her small daughter, had been just leaving a shop, grabbed her child and pulled her back inside.

"Don't shoot!" Theo van Gogh cried out. "We can still talk! Don't shoot!"

Bouyeri fired again.

Van Gogh stumbled across the street and sank to the curb, protesting, still, as his body took eight bullets from his killer. He was still alive, officials say, when Bouyeri calmly approached him, ripped a 33-centimeter kukri knife—a kind of machete—across Van Gogh's throat, and began, according to witnesses, to cut off his head. (Police later found decapitation videos, along with some rather sordid pornography tapes and videos of men having sex with the bodies of dead women, in the Marianne Philipsstraat apartment.) When attempts at decapitation failed, he stabbed the same knife into the filmmaker's belly, plunging it so deep it touched his spine, virtually impaling him. Finally, Bouyeri plunged a filleting knife into his victim's chest, pinning with it the now-famous letter to Ayaan Hirsi Ali and the infidels of the West.

It was a quarter to nine in the morning—the same time American Airlines Flight 11 had struck the North Tower of the World Trade Center in New York City. [6]

Hoisting his knapsack back across his shoulder, Bouyeri walked away from Van Gogh's body and began, while walking, to reload his gun—a task that can challenge even the most experienced shooter.

Clearly, he had practiced. Police soon surrounded him, but he made no effort to escape; rather, he opened fire. His plan had been to die a martyr's death, killed by Amsterdam police in the shootout he imagined would follow the assassination. He was to be disappointed; of approximately a dozen agents who appeared on the scene, only one fired back, shooting him, per protocol, in the leg. It was enough to stop him in his tracks, but not to kill him. Police arrested him on the spot, charged him with the murder of Theodoor van Gogh, and brought him to a prison hospital in Scheveningen, just outside the Hague.

That night, George Bush defeated John Kerry, 286 to 251. It was 911 days after the killing of Pim Fortuyn.

* * *

What began as a peaceful protest of noise on the Dam the night of Theo's death quickly dissolved into violence throughout the Netherlands: within a week, 104 mosques, 25 schools, and 37 churches had been torched. Meantime, after some delay, the AIVD released the contents both of the letter Bouyeri had stabbed into Van Gogh's body, and of the testament—now known as *"in bloed gedoopte"* ("baptized in blood")—that he'd written in the expectation—and the hope—of his martyrdom. The testament, in verse, begins:

In bloed gedoopt
Dit is dan mijn laatste woord
Door kogels doorboord.
In bloed gedoopt.
Zoals ik had gehoopt
Ik laat een boodschap achter.
Voor jou . . . de vechter
De boom van Tawheed is afwachtend.
Naar jouw bloed smachtend.
Ga de koop aan . . .
En Allah geeft je ruimbaan
Hij geeft je de Tuin.
In plaats van het aardse puin.
Tegen de vijand heb ik ook wat te zeggen.
Je zal zeker het loodje leggen.
Al ga je over de hele wereld op Tour
De dood is je op de Loer.
Op de hielen gezeten door de Ridders van de DOOD.
Die de straten kleuren met Rood.
Tegen de hypocrieten zeg ik tenslotte dit:
Wenst de DOOD of hou anders je mond en . . . zit

Beste broeders en zusters ik nader mijn einde.
Maar hiermee is het verhaal zeker niet ten einde.

[This, then, is my last word
By bullets bored
Baptized in blood
As I hoped I would
I leave behind this message of insight
For you, who will go on to fight
The tree of Tawheed now awaits your wishes
For your blood, it languishes . . .
Grab it . . .
And Allah will open out to you
He gives you the garden
In place of earthly pain

To the enemy, I have something else to say:
You will surely find your lot
Death lies in wait
The knights of DEATH [*sic*] are at your heels
Coloring the streets in red
And in closing, I say to the hypocrites
Wish for death or shut your mouth and . . . sit

Dear brothers and sisters, I approach my end
But not the story, this does not end.]
[Translation by the author]

The "Open Letter to Ayaan Hirshi [*sic*] Ali," written in the same adolescent, melodramatic attempt at maudlin poetry, took a more threatening tone:

"OPEN BRIEF AAN HIRSHI ALI"[7]
   In Naam van Allah de BaRmhartige, de Genadevolle. [sic]
   Vrede en zegeningen op de Emir van de Mujahideen, de lachende doder Mohammed
Rasoeloe Allah (Sala Allaho alaihie wa Sallam), zijn familie en metgezellen en degenen
die hen oprecht volgen tot aan de Dag des Oordeels.
   Er is geen agressie behalve tegen de agressors.

Het volgende:
   Vrede en zegeningen op ieder die de Leiding volgt.
   Dit is een open brief aan een ongelovig fundamentalist, Ayaan Hirshi Ali, van de
Thaghoet partij VVD.
   Geachte mevrouw Hirshi Ali,

Sinds uw aantreden in de politiee arena van Nederland bent u constant bezig om de Moslims en de Islam te terroriseren met uw uitlatingen. U bent hiermee niet de eerste en zal ook niet de laatste zijn die zich hebben aangesloten bij de kruistocht tegen de Islam.

U heeft met uw afvalligheid niet alleen de Waarheid de rug toegekeerd, maar u marcheert ook nog eens langs de ranken van de soldaten van het kwaad. U steekt uw vijandigheid tegen de Islam niet onder stoelen of banken en hiervoor bent u door uw meesters beloond met een zetel in het parlement. Zij hebben in u een medestander gevonden in hun kruistocht tegen de Islam en de Moslims. Een medestander die hen alle "kruit" aanreikt zodat zij hun handen niet zelf vuil hoeven te maken. Aangezien u verblindt bent door de brandende ongelovigheid die in uw woedt, bent u niet in staat om in te zien dat uw slechts een instrument bent van de ware vijanden van de Islam.

U wordt gebruikt om allerlei vijandigheden over de Islam en de meest edele mens, Mohammed Rasoeloe Alla (Salla Allaho aleihie wa Sallam), uit te spuien.

Dit alles mevrouw Hirshi Ali neem ik u niet kwalijk, als soldaat van het kwaad doet u slechts uw werk.

Het feit dat u zo openlijk uw kwaad uit kunt spuien is niet aan uzelf te danken, maar aan de Islamitische Ummah. Zij heeft haar taak van verzetten tegen het onrecht en het kwaad laten liggen en ligt haar roes uit te slapen. Al uw vijandelijkheden tegen de Islam is dus alleen de Islamitische Ummah kwalijk te nemen.

Deze brief is Insha Allah een poging om uw kwaad voor eens en altijd het zwijgen op te doen leggen. Deze geschreven woorden zullen Insha Allah uw masker doen laten vallen.

Ik zou graag willen beginnen bij uw onlangs opgegooide voorstel om de Moslims te screenen op hun ideologie bij sollicitaties.

Uw voorstel is zeer interessant, temeer daar de invoering hiervan het rotte gezicht van uw politieke meesters tevoorschijn laat komen (wanneer het natuurlijk eerlijk op hen zou worden getoetst en zij openlijk hun ware ideologie kenbaar maken).

Het is een feit dat de Nederlandse politiek gedomineerd wordt door vele Joden die een produkt zijn van de Talmud leerinstellingen; zo ook uw politieke partijgenoten.

Aangezien u altijd "de hand in eigen boezem" propageert, zullen we dus uw voorstel in uw eigen politieke omgeving toetsen. Dezelfde politiek die met haar beleid zich heeft aangesloten bij het terrorisme tegen de Islam en Moslims.

Ik zou u graag de volgende vragen willen stellen:

Wat vindt u van het feit dat van Aartsen een ideologie aanhangt waarin niet-Joden als niet-mensen worden gezien?

Baba Mezie 114a–114b: Alleen Joden zijn mensen ("Alleen jullie zijn mensen genoemd"). Zie ook Kerlthoth 6b ondr sub-kop ("Oll of anointing") en Barakath 56a, waarin Gentile (niet-Joden) vrouwen dieren worden genoemd ("vrouwtjes-ezels").

Yebamoth 92a: Alle Gentile kinderen zijn dieren.

Wat vindt u van het feit dat er een burgemeester in Amsterdam aan het roer staat, die een ideologie aanhangt waarin Joden tegen niet-Joden mogen liegen? Baba Kamma 113a: Joden mogen leugens ("listen") gebruiken om een Gentile te misleiden.

Wat vindt u van het feit dat u deeluitmaakt van een regering die de Staat steunt met een ideologie dat genocide bepleit?

Sofarim 15, regel 10 (Minor Tarcctates): Dit is de uitspraak van rabbijn Simom ben Yohai: Tod shebe goyyim herog ("Zelfs de beste van de Gentiles zouden gedood moeten worden").

Aangezien u een voorvechtster bent voor gelijke rechten, zult u waarschijnlijk (nadat deze kennis tot u is gekomen) bij uw Joodse meesters in de kamer pleiten om de leerstellingen van de Talmud te verwerpen. U zult er waarschijnlijk ook meteen werk van maken om dit ook bij de Joodse gemeenschap van Nederland te bepleiten.

Uw optreden verraadt zo nu en dan uw laffe moed waarmee u aandacht vraagt vooor uw strijd. Zo heeft u de laffe moed gehad om Islamitische kinderen op school te vragen om een keuze te maken tussen hun Schepper en de grondwet.

Het antwoord van deze jonge reine zielen heeft u meteen gebruikt om argumenten te bedenken om uw kruistocht te rechtvaardigen. U heeft met al deze vijandelijkheden een boemerang losgelaten en u weet dat het slechts een kwestie van tijd is voordat deze boemerang uw lot zal bezegelen.

U krijgt de kans echter, mevrouw Hirshi Ali, om uw gelijk voor eens en altijd in de bladzijdes in te kerven.

Er is één zekerheid in het hele bestaan van de schepping; en dat is dat alles zijn einde kent.

Een kind dat ter wereld komt en met zijn eerste levenskreten zijn aanwezigheid in dit universum vult, zal uiteindelijk met een doodskreet deze wereld verlaten.

Een grasspriet die uit de donkere aarde zijn kop opsteekt en die vervolgens door het zonlicht wordt gestreeld en door het neervallende regen wordt gevoed, zal uiteindelijk verwelken en tot stof vergaan.

De dood, mevrouw Hirshi Ali, is het gemeenschappelijke thema van alles wat bestaat. U, ik en de rest van de schepping kunnen ons niet aan deze waarheid loskoppelen.

Er zal een Dag komen waarop de ene ziel de andere ziel niets kan baten. Een Dag dat gepaard gaat met verschrikkelijk martellingen en kwellingen. Een Dag dat de onrechtvaardigen afschuwelijke kreten uit hun longen persen. Kreten, mevrouw Hirshi Ali, die rillingen over iemands rug zullen veroorzaken; dat de haren op de hoofden rechtovereind doet staan. Mensen zullen dronken worden gezien (van angst) terwijl zij niet dronken zijn. ANGST zal op die Grote Dag de atmosfeer vullen:

Wanneer de zon opgerold wordt. En wanneer de sterren vallen. En wanneer de bergen bewogen worden. En wanneer de drachtige kamelen achtergelaten worden. En wanneer de zeeën tot koken gebracht worden. En wanneer de zielen verenigd worden. En wanneer het levend begraven meisje ondervraagd wordt. Voor welke zonde zij gedood werd. En wanneer de bladen opengeslagen worden. En wanneer de hemel afgestroopt wordt. En wanneer de Djahim (de Hel) ontstoken wordt. En wanneer het Paradijs nabij gebracht wordt. Dan weet een ziel wat zij verricht heeft. (81:1–14) Op die Dag vlucht de mens van zijn broeder. En van zijn moeder en zijn vader. En van zijn vrouw en zijn kinderen. Een ieder van hen zal op die Dag een bezigheid hebben die hem genoeg is. Gezichten (van de ongelovigen) zullen op die Dag met stof bedekt zijn. En een duisternis zal hen omhullen. Zij zijn degenen die de zondige ongelovigen zijn (80:34–42)

U als ongelovige extremist gelooft natuurlijk niet in de bovenstaande beschreven scène. Voor u is het bovenstaande slechts een verzonnen dramatisch stukje uit een Boek zoals velen. En toch, mevrouw Hirshi Ali, durf ik mijn leven ervoor te wagen om te beweren dat het ANGSTZWEET u uitbreekt wanneer u dit leest.

U, als ongelovige fundamentalist, gelooft natuurlijk dat er geen Oppermacht is die het hele universum bestuurt.

U gelooft niet dat uw hart, waarmee u de waarheid verwerpt, vóór elke tik toestemming moet vragen aan deze Oppermacht om te kloppen.

U gelooft niet dat uw tong waarmee u de Leiding van deze Oppermacht ontkent onderhevig is aan Zijn wetten.

U gelooft niet dat leven en dood door deze Oppermacht wordt geschonken.

Als u daadwerkelijk in dit alles gelooft, dan moet de volgende uitdaging voor u geen belemmering zijn.

Ik daag u met deze brief dan ook uit om uw gelijk te bewijzen. U hoeft er niet veel voor te doen:

Mevrouw Hirshi Ali: WENST de DOOD als u werkelijk van uw gelijk OVER-TUIGD bent.

Neemt u deze uitdaging niet aan; weet dan dat mijn Meester, de Meest verhevene, u heeft ontmasterd als een onrechtpleegster.

"Wenst dan de dood, als jullie waarachtig zijn" Maar zij zullen hem (de dood) nooit wensen, vanwege wat hun handen (aan zonden) hebben voortgebracht.

En Allah is Alwetend over de onrechtplegers. (2:94–95).

Om te voorkomen dat mij hetzelfde zou kunnen worden verweten als u, zal ik deze wens vóór u wensen:

Mijn Rabb, schenk ons de dood om ons te verblijden met het martelaarschap. Alla-hoemma Amien.

Mevrouw Ayaan Hirshi Ali en de rest van de extremistische ongelovigen: de Islam heeft de vele vijandigheden en onderdrukkingen in de Geschiedenis doorstaan. Telkens wanneer de druk op de Islam werd opgevoerd is hierdoor slechts het vuur van het geloof aangewakkerd. De Islam is als een afgestorven plant, die de jarenlange druk en extreem hoge temperaturen tot een diamant wordt gevormd. Een afgestorven plant dat door de grillen van de tijd gevormd wordt tot de sterkste edelsteen op deze aarde. Een edelsteen waarop de hardste moker zich kapot slaat.

AYAAN HIRSHI ALI JE ZAL JEZELF STUK SLAAN OP DE ISLAM!

U en uw kompanen weten heel goed dat de huidige Islamitische jeugd een ruwe dia-mant is dat slechts moet worden geslepen, zodat het haar aldoordringend licht van de Waarheid kan verspreiden. Uw intellectuele terrorisme zal dit niet tegenhouden, inte-gendeel het zal dit alleen maar bespoedigen.

De Islam zal zegevieren door het bloed van de martelaren. Het zal haar licht ver-spreiden in elk donkere hoek van deze aarde en het zal het kwaad desnoods met het zwaard terugdrijven naar zijn duistere hol.

Deze losgebarsten strijd is anders dan alle voorgaande strijden. De ongelovige fun-damentalisten zijn ermee begonnen en Insha Allah zullen de ware gelovigen deze eindigen.

Er zal geen genade voor de onrechtplegers zijn, slechts het zwaard wordt tegen hen opgeheven. Geen discussie, geen demonstraties, geen optochten, geen petities: slechts de DOOD zal de Waarheid van de Leugen doen scheiden.

Zeg: "Voorwaar, de dood die jullie trachten te voorkomen zal jullie zeker vinden, daarna zullen jullie worden teruggevoerd naar de Kenner van het onwaarneembare en Hij zal jullie dan mededelen wat jullie plachten te doen." (62:8).

En zoals een groot Profeet ooit heeft gezegd:

"En ik weet zeker dat jij, O Pharao, ten onder gaat." (17:102).

Zo willen wij ook gelijknamige woorden gebruiken en deze voor ons uitsturen, zodat de hemelen en de sterren dit nieuws op zullen pikken en dit als een vloedgolf over alle uithoeken van het van het universum zullen verspreiden.

"Ik weet zeker dat jij, O Amerika, ten onder gaat." "Ik weet zeker dat jij, O Europa, ten onder gaat." "Ik weet zeker dat jij, O Nederland, ten onder gaat." "Ik weet zeker dat jij, O Hirshi Ali, ten onder gaat." "Ik weet zeker dat jij, O ongelovige

fundamentalist, ten onder gaat." Hasboena Allah wa ni3ma alwakeel. Ni3ma alMawla
wa Ni3ma anNasseer. Saifu Deen alMuwahhied."

["In the name of Allah—the Beneficent, the Merciful [*sic*][8]

Peace and Blessings from the head of the Holy Warriors—the laughing killer
Mohammed Rasoeloe Allah—(Sala Allaho alahie wa Sallam), his family and
his companions who will steadfastly accompany him till on the Day of
Judgment.

There is no aggression except the against aggressors.

The following:
Peace and blessings on those who follow the Direction.

This is an open letter on a fundamentalist unbeliever, Ayaan Hirshi Ali, from
the Thaghoet Party VVD.

Dear Mrs. Hirshi Ali,

Since your appearance in the Dutch political arena you have constantly
busied yourself with criticizing Muslims and terrorizing Islam with your statements. You are hereby not the first and not the last, nor will you be the last, to
join the crusade against Islam.

With your attacks you have not only turned your back on the Truth, but are
marching in the ranks of the soldiers of evil. Because you do not hide your hostility towards Islam, your masters have rewarded you with a seat in parliament.
They have found in you an ally who provides them all the "ammunition" [they
need] so that they needn't dirty their own hands. So blinded are you by your
burning unbelief and in your rage you are not able to see that you are just an
instrument of the real enemies of Islam.

You are being used by all the enemies of Islam to siphon all kinds of hostilities towards the most noble person (Mohammed Rasoeloe Alla).

Mrs. Hirshi Ali, I don't blame you for all of this, as a soldier of evil, you are
just doing your work.

The fact that you so openly express your evil is not because of you, yourself,
but the Islamic Ummah. She has as her task to resist injustice and has let evil go
on and has been blissfully asleep. All of your hostility towards Islam is therefore the fault of the Islamic Ummah.

This letter is Insha Allah (God willing) an attempt to stop your evil and silence
you forever. These writings will Inshallah cause your mask to fall.

I would first like to begin with your recently launched proposal to screen
Muslims regarding their ideology on job applications.

Your proposal is very interesting, even more because its implementation has
exposed the rotten faces of your political masters (when of course it should, in
fairness, be tested on them and so make their own ideology known).

It is a fact that Dutch politics is dominated by many Jews and is a product of the
Talmudic Schools, including your colleagues in your political party.

Seeing as that you always propagate "the hand on one's own heart" [looking
inward], we would first like to test this proposal on you yourself. The same politics, which through its policies has joined in the terrorism against Islam and
Muslims. [*sic*]

I would very much like to put to you the following question:

What do you think about the fact that van Aartsen sees non-Jews as not being human?

Baba Mezie 114a–114b: Only Jews are people ("Only you are called (the) people"). Also see Kerithoth 6b under the sub heading ("Oil of anointing") and Berkath 56a, in which Gentile (non Jewish women) are called animals ("female donkeys").

Ybamoth 92a: All Gentile children are animals.

What do you think of the fact that the Mayor of Amsterdam is at the helm of an ideology whereby Jews are permitted to lie to non-Jews? Baba Kamma 113a: Jews may use lies ("listen") to mislead gentiles.

What do you think of the fact that you are part of a government that supports a State that pleads for genocide?

Sofarim 15, line 10 (Minor Tarcctates): This is the saying of Rabbi Simon ben Yohai: Tod shebe goyim herog ("Even the best gentiles must be killed").

Seeing as that you are a champion of equal rights, you will surely (now that this knowledge has been given you) plead with your Jewish masters to reject the teachings of the Talmud. You will most likely make it a point to deliver the same plea to the Jewish community in the Netherlands.

Your [media] appearances reveal your lack of courage now and then when you are asking for attention for your struggle. You even had the cowardice to ask Islamic children in school to choose between their creator and the constitution. You then immediately used the answers of these pure young souls to justify the arguments behind your crusade. With these hostilities you have unleashed a boomerang effect, and you know that it is only a question of time until this boomerang will seal your fate.

You have the chances now, Mrs. Hirshi Ali, once and for all to carve your own notch in the pages.

There is but one certainty in our entire existence, and that is that everything comes to an end.

A child who comes into this world and fills the universe with his first cries of life, will finally leave this world with the rattle of death.

A blade of grass, which emerges from the dark earth and is touched by the sunlight and fed by falling rain, will finally rot into dust and disappear.

Death, Mrs. Hirshi Ali, is a shared theme of everything in creation. You, I, and the rest of creation cannot escape this truth.

There will come a Day when one soul will not be able to help another soul. A Day of horrible tortures and painful tribulations which will go together with the terrible cries being pressed out of the lungs of the unjust Cries. Mrs. Hirshi Ali, which will cause chills to run up someone's spine, and cause the hair on their head to stand straight up. People will appear drunk with (with fear) even though they are not drunk. On that Great Day, the atmosphere will be filled with FEAR:

When the sun will be rolled up.

When the stars fall.

And when the mountains will be moved.

And when the beasts of burden will be left behind.

And when the sea will be brought to a boil.
And when all souls will be united.
And when the girl who was buried alive will be questioned.
About every sin for which she was killed.
When the pages will be flung open.
And the sky will be dripping.
And the heavens will be dripping.
And when the Djahim (the Hell) will be set aflame.
And when the Paradise will be brought closer by.
Then the soul will know what it has performed. (81:1–14)
On that day man will flee from his brother.
And the mother from the father.
And the woman from her children.
And every one of them on that Day shall have an occupation, which is enough for them.
Faces (of the unbelievers) will be covered with dust on that Day.
And they will be ringed in darkness.
These are the sinful unbelievers. (80:34–42)

Of course, you as an unbelieving extremist don't believe in the scene described above. For you, this is just a fictitious dramatic piece out of a Book like many. And yet, Mrs. Hirsi Ali, I would bet on my life that you will break into a SWEAT OF FEAR when you read this.

You, as unbelieving fundamentalist, of course don't believe that there is a Higher Power who runs the universe.

You don't believe that your heart, with which you repudiate the truth, must knock and ask this Higher Power for permission for every beat.

You don't believe that your tongue, with which you repudiate the Direction of this Higher Power, is subservient to His laws.

You don't believe that this Higher Power grants life and death.

If you really believe in all of this, then you will not find the following challenge a problem.

I challenge you with this letter to proof that you are right. You do not have to do much.

Mrs. Hirshi Ali: if you are really CONVINCED that you are right. [sic]

If you do not accept this challenge, you will know that my Master, the Most high, has exposed you as a carrier of lies.

"If you wish death, then you are being truthful." But they will never wish to die, because of what their hands (and sins) have brought forth".

And Allah is the all knowing over the purveyors of lies. (2:94–95).

To avoid the same fate coming to me as what waits ahead for you, I shall wish this wish for you:

Mijn Rabb (master) give us death to enrobe us in happiness with martyrdom. Allahoemma Amen.

Mrs. Hirsi Ali and all the rest of you extremist unbelievers, Islam has withstood many enemies and persecutions throughout History. Whenever pressure was put on Islam, it has been only a fire that has fanned the flames of belief. Islam is as a dying plant, which, through years of high temperatures and pressure, has formed into a diamond. A dead plant which was formed over the trials of time into the strongest precious stone on earth. A hard stone upon which will defeat any attempts to break it to pieces.

AYAAN HIRSI ALI YOU WILL BREAK YOURSELF TO PIECES ON ISLAM!

You and your friend know full well that the present day Islamic youth are raw diamonds that need to be polished so that they can diffuse the light of Truth. Your intellectual terrorism will not prevent this, on the contrary, it will hasten this.

Islam will be victorious through the blood of the martyrs. They will spread her light in every dark corner of this earth and will drive evil, with the sword if necessary, back into its dark hole.

This struggle that has burst forth is different than those of the past. The unbelieving fundamentalists have started it, and Inshallah it is the true believers who will end it.

There will be no mercy shown to the purveyors of injustice, only the sword will be lifted against them. No discussions, no demonstrations, no petitions: only DEATH will separate the Truth from the Lies.

Say: "Be warned that the death that you seek to prevent will surely find you, and you will be taken back to the All Knowing, and He will tell you what you attempted to do" (62:8).

And as a great Prophet once said:

"And I surely know that you, O Pharaoh, will be destroyed" (17:102).

So, too, will we use the same words and send this message out into the world ahead of us, so that the heavens and the stars will receive this news and it spread it as a tidal wave to all the corners of the universe.

"I surely know that you, O America, will be destroyed."

"I surely know that you O Europe, will be destroyed."

"I surely know that you O Holland will be destroyed."

"I surely know that you, O Hirshi Ali will be destroyed."

"I surely know that you, O unbelieving fundamentalists, will be destroyed."

Hasboena Allah wa nima alwakeel.

Nima al alMawla wa Nima anNaseer.

Saifu Deen alMuwahhied"][9]

[Translation by the author]

Such a text, the public sensed, could not simply be the ravings of an isolated madman. They were right. The afternoon of November 2, police arrested nearly a dozen other young Dutch-Muslim men for their connections to Mohammed Bouyeri and for suspicion of terrorism based on previous evidence, including phone conversations that had been recorded by the AIVD and items (including materials that could potentially be used in the manufacture of bombs) found in raids on several apartments. But how many others were there? How serious, how expansive, was the threat?

Well before dawn on the tenth of November, hundreds of police officers stormed into the Antheunisstraat in The Hague's Laakkwartier, accompanied by the counter-terrorism forces of the Royal Netherlands Marine

Corps. For fourteen hours, police stood off against the residents of a single home, while most of the rest of the neighborhood was evacuated. "Moroccans!" one officer was heard to call out, to which someone inside the building responded, "Go ahead—shoot me dead." Sharpshooters from the National Guard swarmed the rooftops. Someone inside threw a hand grenade, wounding an agent. Two others had been wounded when the raid began, having attempted to open a booby-trapped front door. Tanks were called in, and the airspace above The Hague closed off.

When it was over, near nightfall, police had arrested four Muslim youth, all allegedly members of the Hofstadgroep, including Zine Labadine Aouragha and Jason Walters, whose brother Jermaine had been arrested earlier that day in Amersfoort. Three others, living in Amsterdam, were also taken into custody that afternoon. Later, officials found several more hand grenades inside the Antheunisstraat building, all from the former Yugoslavia—a source, it turns out, for many of the weapons gathered and hoarded by European Islamic extremist groups.[10]

That evening, Holland's ministers of justice (Piet-Hein Donner) and internal affairs (Johan Remkes) penned a 60-page letter to the Parliament, revealing that Mohammed Bouyeri had been known to the AIVD for some time, and that the Hofstadgroep had already been classified as a terror network—but that as many as 20 similar groups might still be active in the Netherlands. Many of the Hofstadgroep members themselves had already been under surveillance for some time, and they had even been arrested on suspicion of terrorist activity in the past, only to be let go when gaps in the law made prosecution impossible. Given this fact, and given the AIVD's inability to prevent Van Gogh's murder despite all that they had known, the two ministers called for new laws and procedures to combat the spread of radical Islam, barring, for instance, those who incited violence and hate from certain public functions, and criminalizing the expression of endorsement or approval of violent crimes.

I couldn't help but wonder what Theo van Gogh would have had to say about that.

CHAPTER 16

"Something terrible has happened to Theo."

Hirsi Ali was in a private meeting at the Parliament when the phone call came. It was her former assistant, Hugo, who broke the news. Stunned and disbelieving, Hirsi Ali, by her own account, ran down the hall in search of more information. One of her own guards caught her on the way. Yes, it was true. Theo van Gogh was dead.[1]

Overcome with shock, Ayaan knew, too, that the risk had been there from the start. The AIVD had repeatedly urged Van Gogh to accept bodyguard protection. He had repeatedly refused, even going so far as to send them away.

"You are the apostate," he would tell Ayaan. "I'm just the village idiot."

But now the village idiot was dead, and what would soon become clear was the fact that he had died, at least in part, because his killer couldn't reach Ayaan. The letter, after all, had been addressed to her.

Immediately, Hirsi Ali was rushed to a safe house for protection, even as police stormed the country, arresting several members of the Hofstadgroep throughout the day. Soon after, former fellow VVD-member Geert Wilders was ushered away as well; the AIVD had earlier already uncovered a statement similar to one left on Theo's body, this time addressed to Wilders. It, too, had been signed by "Saifu Deen Al Muwahhied." (By the time of Van Gogh's death, Wilders, an outspoken right wing politician with signature bleached-blond hair, had, like Ayaan, already been under security protection; now, though, the urgency and danger were known and understood—and real.)

Speaking for the cabinet, Deputy Prime Minister Gerrit Zalm wasted no words: "We are declaring war on Islamic extremism," he announced at a press conference on November 4.

Many saw Wilders at the time as the "new Fortuyn." Others (wrongly) went further, pinning him as a white supremacist, a tag he earned partly thanks to the bleached hairdo he has insisted on sporting since the 1980s. An early opponent of Muslim immigration in Europe—his warnings about Islamic terrorism began as early as 1999— he'd made enemies of many of his non-Muslim political colleagues over the years as well, calling Holland "a country of mediocrity and compromise."[2] Previously, he had also worked as a speechwriter for Frits Bolkestein,[3] a position that surely reinforced and informed his views.

But beyond Hirsi Ali, Wilders had few supporters. Speaking to the NRC, Fatima Orgu, another VVD member, observed, "Geert is pretty much on his own in his inclination to see a terrorist in every headscarf. Naturally we need to be more alert when it comes to terrorism and security, but it is anti-liberal to ask the government to concern itself with something as individual as clothing choice."[4] By September, following a published statement from Wilders declaring that the VVD should lean further to the Right (raising speed limits and deporting radical imams were among his suggestions for an improved VVD), the party had had enough. In a motion reminiscent of Fortuyn, Wilders accepted his dismissal from the party and immediately established one of his own: the Party for Freedom (PVV).

But some of his opponents sought a different kind of punishment for Wilders' views; a 17-year-old Moroccan student from Sas van Gent, for instance, created an animation video, showing Wilders being beheaded. (It wasn't the first time, however. As early as 2002, a man known only as Bilal L., alias Abu Qataadah—there seems to be no public record of his real last name—had published threats against Van Gogh, Hirsi Ali, and Wilders; he served a three-year sentence, during which he actively recruited new jihadists from jail.)[5]

Shortly after leaving the VVD, Wilders and political essayist Bart Jan Spruyt published a manifesto of sorts in the Amsterdam broadsheet *Het Parool*, "Stop the Import of Islamic Culture."

"Freedom of religion is a great good," they wrote, "but it is not absolute. Not for nothing does this article of our constitution point to the individual's responsibility to the law. Yet that condition is scandalously ignored whenever the threat that Islam poses to our rule of law is ignored or excused. . . . It is our duty to stand up for our democratic state. Dutch culture must remain tolerant. Respect for minorities is important and the only litmus test of the power of a democracy. A culture that lacks this respect—as is the case in Islamic countries—is one no one wishes to live in. It is exactly with the purpose of continuing tolerance, democracy, and respect for minorities that we must finally and resolutely give up our nihilistic cultural relativism. The Netherlands must be protected against the import of an Islamist culture. . . ."[6]

As threats against Wilders in the aftermath of Van Gogh's death grew more dire, officials struggled to find a way to keep him safe without forcing him to leave the country. (Ayaan had earlier been spirited to the United States, where she took shelter on a military base.) Their solution: prison. In an irony worthy of a Greek tragedy, the leader of the fight for "Freedom" in the Netherlands was forced to spend his evenings and weekends literally behind bars—at the high-security prison in Zeist, in fact, that had held the Lockerbie bombers during their 2001 trial—while those who sought his death walked free.

He was not the only one.

In a desperate measure to aid the victims and potential victims of honor violence as domestic violence shelters reached capacity levels, the government by now had begun housing younger women in prison cells. Most of these women, too, were single, and the state had no proper safe houses for them; shelters were primarily geared to married women and not set up to handle the unique fears, dangers, and problems faced by younger, school-aged girls.

And yet here were girls who had done exactly what the Dutch had asked them to do: sought out a more emancipated life. They were guilty of no crime—not one that should send them to prison, and none that, in Western society, should have called for punishment by death. They simply wanted a non-Muslim friend at school, or to choose the man they wanted to marry, or to fall in love.

And now they were living their lives, these girls of 14, 15, 16, in jail. And not in special sections set apart specifically for them, either, but among the criminals, where ordinary prison rules applied. In trying to live the life of freedom Holland offered—even promised—them, they found themselves with none.

Meantime, the Dutch government scrambled to create new anti-terrorism laws, as did their counterparts across Europe. By the start of 2005, changes aimed at preventing attacks began to affect lifestyles everywhere. In Denmark, Prime Minister Anders Fogh Rasmussen won re-election in February, in large part thanks to his efforts to reduce the number of asylum seekers by nearly 75 percent, and according to *Time* magazine, "the right wing Danish People's Party [wanted] to go further by stripping citizenship from naturalized Danes found guilty of crime[7] and revoking foreigners' right to vote in local elections."[8] In France, where the country's High Council for Immigration reported that over 35,000 Muslim girls had been—or were under threat of being—genitally mutilated, then-Interior Minister Nicolas Sarkozy proposed quotas for immigrants. Only in Belgium did it seem that the right wing was losing strength: the country's highest court ruled that the 28-year-old anti-immigrant Vlaams Blok—one of the most powerful political parties in the country with 18 parliamentary seats—was racist, calling it "criminal." The Vlaams Blok was forced to close down, inciting party leader Frank Van Hecke to remark in a farewell statement posted on the party's Web site: "What happened in Brussels today is unique in the Western world: never before has a so-called democratic regime outlawed the country's largest political party."

In Holland, a number of new laws and practices went into effect, most notably the law requiring every person to present identification on demand. With great emphasis, the government insisted that this was absolutely not like the laws passed under German occupation requiring everyone to carry an ID. No, no, said the Parliament, we only ask that you show it. Those who could not or would not do so, however, would face a fifty-euro fine—and one might be asked at any time—say, if you were witness to a crime, or caught up in a crowd watching a house on fire, or stopped for riding a bicycle without a light after dark (in which case, failure to produce an official ID would bring two fines—a boon to an increasingly fine-happy Dutch economic system, but a ruling that many argued—and still do—violated European privacy laws). As one opponent to the law, Jaap van Beek, a member of an organization that bills itself as the "Anti-Fascism Action" group, the result is that anyone involved in a strike, demonstration, or similar activity—or even a bystander—could be registered with the authorities by name. "It is now no longer possible," he wrote on the group's Web site, "for a citizen to protest against the government anonymously"—a fact that forges a frightening affront to democracy.

But that was hardly all. That same year, cameras sprouted up on city streets, keeping careful, if discreet, watch on passersby. "Safety," said officials, but the "safety" they were talking about went beyond concerns for petty street crime and graffiti: cameras allowed police and other law enforcement officials to watch, systematically, the groupings of young men (and women) on the streets to ascertain patterns of behavior and personal connections—who was hanging out with whom. Added to this was, in some cities, a measure forbidding youths to gather in groups of more than two. On Rotterdam's Lijnbaan, a major shopping and commercial street, those who stopped even to chat with one another were asked to move along.[9] In most cases, they could also be asked to show their newly-required identification papers, as well, pairing names to faces.

And a name can tell a government official quite a bit in the Netherlands, especially if one knows the neighborhood—or even the city—where that person lives, as would likely be the case for kids hanging around a given street. From the time you are born, you are registered at the address of your parents in Holland, and from the moment you move out, you must register each and every new address with the city. This alone informs the government of your probable living costs (especially for those in subsidized housing), the size of your family, the gender makeup of your children, even the status of your relationships (if, say, been living with a partner, and one of you moves out). Add to this the information made available through the "koppelings-wet"—and, for those who joined it, AirMiles—and a detailed profile emerges.

Even so, after the discovery of the Hofstadgroep, they wanted more. A motion forced through Parliament—no vote was taken—gave police and other authorities access to health information, vacation plans, video rentals, book purchases, and more. Much of this had previously been at the option of those keeping this information; now it was mandatory. The expressed approval of terrorist or other violent acts became punishable by law. Overstepping the bounds of church and state once again, the government also ruled that it may close down mosques whose imams were found to incite violence or hate in their sermons or through other means.

And yet, arguably, none of this could do much about terrorism. While it might signal suspects, Van Gogh's murder had already made clear that this hardly was enough; police had, after all, been watching Mohammed Bouyeri and his cohorts for months before November 2, 2004, the day Theo van Gogh was killed. But should another Bouyeri emerge, would the police be likely to ask him, as he stood over the body, for his ID? Would it make a difference? Would closing down a mosque and silencing a preacher make a difference in the age of Internet—where most recruiting for jihad takes place, anyway? Besides, the beheading videos the Hofstadgroep members were known to have watched had hardly been acquired via Blockbuster or Netflix. Moreover, another Hofstadgroep member, Samir Azzouz, was found to have kept detailed drawings of government buildings and written notes of an attack. Such things would not have been discoverable through the new law.

Even so, as the year progressed, the government went deeper, demanding even membership lists of organizations and associations, including health clubs—not that this much mattered; most had cameras trained to their front doors, anyway.

But there were no cameras in Amsterdam's Diamantbuurt (Diamond District), with its streets named after precious stones. The neighborhood had originally paid tribute to the Asscher Diamond Factory nearby (where, among other things the Asscher-cut diamond was created). Rich as it sounds, the Diamantbuurt, just three streets away from the Pieter Aertszstraat where I lived at the time, housed largely immigrant families and refugees. And by late 2005, the word "Diamantbuurt" no longer suggested rare, cushion-shaped jewels; all over the country, the area instead became synonymous with street terror, and with the Dutch couple forced from their home by Moroccan *hangjongen*[10] who, for an entire year, stared into their ground-floor apartment, cursed them on the street, painted swastikas on the woman's car, and threw a stone through their living room window. Police did little. Certainly no one seems to have asked for the culprits' IDs. Eventually, their wills broken, the couple moved away—but not before their decision to leave had brought worldwide attention to their plight. Even an Israeli is said to have contacted the owners of the flat once the couple had left, offering to rent it.

"Do you know the story?" the owners asked him.

"Of course," he answered. "But in Israel, we are used to living with terrorists."

* * *

In February 2005, it is decided: a woman will be sent to murder Hirsi Ali. Women, the reasoning goes, raise less suspicion; and with their black abayas, it is so much easier for them to handle a concealed weapon. The talk on Internet forums grows excited. Still in hiding abroad, Ayaan has already announced that she is planning to return soon. When she does, the women will be waiting.

Muslim women, both in Europe and in the Middle East, were in fact starting to radicalize at a surprising—and alarming—rate. As early as 1993, Europe had begun to notice a rising interest in Islam among women, especially in the UK, where the *Times* reported on a growing number of middle-class Christians who were starting to convert, turning away from the "sins and chaos of Western culture." "Within the next 20 years," the author of a guide to the Koran predicted in the *Times* article, "the number of British converts will equal or overtake the immigrant Muslim community that brought the faith here."[11]

For many women, Islam, with its mandatory face- and body-coverings, provides an antidote to what they consider the view of women as "sexual objects"—a viewpoint other Muslim women would argue is entirely backwards: to some, the fact that women are forced to cover themselves stems from the idea that women are not people at all, but purely sexual objects that lustful, unbridled men will never be able to resist. (By contrast, by 2007, British police were being called in to protect Sikh and Hindu girls in the UK who were being threatened by Muslim boys—and occasionally beaten—to make them convert.[12])

By 2005, female suicide bombers, like the woman whose photo Ayaan had stared at in the *New York Times*, were sacrificing themselves for Allah, occasionally under duress, often of their own free will. Before year's end, three women would have blown themselves up in Iraq alone—including Muriel Degauque, a pale, 38-year-old Belgian woman. Degauque had earlier married a Belgian of Moroccan descent and had gone with him to live in Morocco for several years; when she returned, she was veiled and living the life of a fundamentalist Muslim "sister."

She was not alone.

In May, 2006, British police arrested a Dutch-Moroccan woman, Bouchra El-Hor, whom they claimed had offered to sacrifice herself and her six-month-old son as martyrs, according to the *Washington Post*'s Craig Whitlock.[13]

Much of what we know about radicalized Muslim women in Europe comes thanks almost entirely to the extraordinary work of two *Volkskrant* reporters, Janny Groen and Annieke Kranenberg, and to the courage and journalistic honesty of their editors.[14] During the Hofstadgroep trials, Groen and Kranenberg managed to gain the confidence of the wives and girlfriends of several of the group's members, three of whom were particularly forthcoming about their lives and their ideas. It was they who revealed the plans to have a woman kill Hirsi Ali. "If Hirsi Ali is murdered by a woman," one of them told Groen and Kranenberg, "it will have a much greater impact."

The three "women of the Hofstadgroep"—whom Groen and Kranenberg call "Fatima," "Naima," and "Khadisja—told the reporters that more and more women in their community were finding their way into a deeper Islam—often to the despair of their parents, first generation immigrants who do not share these views themselves.

"That doesn't surprise me," a woman I'll call Saskia tells me. Saskia, a Dutch woman who now sports a nose ring and tattoos, was wed to an Egyptian immigrant for ten years. He, too, demanded she live as a righteous Muslim.

"I didn't even realize what was happening," she says. Soon after the two met, she traveled with him to Egypt. "I didn't understand the language. I just did what he said, followed where he took me, and when someone finally explained it all to me, I was a Muslim and had been married in a mosque," she recounts. Saskia has another Dutch friend, she says, who also married a religious Muslim. "She no longer works," Saskia says, "because he wouldn't let her. Now she sits at home all day reading the Koran. She wears an abaya. And I can see, now, how it happens: you keep hearing that you're bad if you don't behave 'properly'—and you're crazy about the guy, so you end up going to extremes just because you want his approval. You want to be 'good.'

And the pressure comes not just from him, but from his entire family, from his friends—including the women."

Carla Rus, a psychiatrist who works with Muslim girls, agrees. "These girls want their boyfriends' approval. They conform to the group and pick up the norms and values of their subculture." Rus uses the example of a classic test, in which people are shown two lines and asked which one is longer. Researchers have found that 60 percent of subjects will go against their instincts and say the shorter line is the longer one if that's what the majority says.

Similar tests have also shown a proclivity toward bending to authority—a fact which can explain even the incidence of torture in the military. Rus cites a study in which Researcher A stands on one side of a two-way mirror while Researcher B and the subject stand on the other. Researcher B explains to the subject—often a medical student— that he is to issue an electric shock to Researcher A. It will cause pain, he is told, and each shock will be more painful than the one that preceded it. Dutifully, the subject will issue the first shock (which is not, in fact, real); Researcher A will respond by appearing to be in pain. Most of the time, the subject will refuse to continue; only when he is urged by the researcher at his side, who tells him things like "you have no choice" or "you will never be a good doctor if you cannot do this," will he issue another shock. And then another. "Eventually," says Rus, "the subject will go beyond his own boundaries in obeyance to authority or information suggesting it is 'for the good of' the other." Notes Rus, "The result shows, too, that in fact 60 percent of us are vulnerable to becoming torturers; we can be told that if we torture a subject, he will tell what he knows and this can save lives—and we can be made to conform."

It is a frightening truth.

Such factors would also explain the growing number of converts to Islam in the UK, for instance. Noted Lucy Berrington in the *Times* of London, "The surge in conversions to Islam has taken place despite the negative image of the faith in the Western press." Ironically, she pointed out, most British converts were (and remain) women—surprising, "given the widespread view in the West that Islam treats women poorly." Nonetheless, according to Berrington, in the United States, four times as many women as men converted to Islam in the 1990s, and in Britain, most of the estimated 10–20,000 converts to the British community of "1 to 1.5 million" were also women.

Moreover, Westerners, reported Berrington, had also become "despairing of their own society—rising crime, family breakdowns, drugs and alcoholism" and had "come to admire the discipline and security of Islam." But could that "security" and "discipline" explain four bombings and 52 deaths in London on the morning of July 7, 2005?

CHAPTER 17

"One minute the bus was there, the next minute it seemed to dissolve into millions of pieces."[1]

Jasmine Gardner was heading to work, about to board the number 30 bus, on the morning of July 7, 2005. Then the bomb went off. Debris flew. Shards and scraps jettisoned several feet away. "The scene was just carnage," one eyewitness later told the *New York Times*.[2] For Gardner, the shock was paralyzing. "I completely broke down," she said. "I was stuck to the spot. I turned away because I couldn't face to look at it. Someone had to tell me to run away as fast as I could. It was horrific."[3]

In four carefully orchestrated attacks on the London transit system, 52 people were killed and over 700 injured on the morning of July 7, 2005. The first explosion took place at the Liverpool Street Station at 8:51 A.M., ripping apart a subway car; the next, at King's Cross Station, occurred exactly five minutes later, and a third, at Edgware Road Station, at 9:17 A.M. The number 30 bus blew up last— at 9:47 A.M.

As in Madrid and Amsterdam, the timing appeared to be orchestrated to match the attacks of 9/11. As with the others, they were the work of Muslim radicals—suicide bombers, in this case. And three of them had been born and raised in England.

The British are a stoic lot; and like the Spanish, they had experienced terrorism in their cities in the past, actions perpetrated by the Irish Republican Army. The afternoon of July 7, my mother, who had been planning a trip to London (and was, by sheer coincidence, scheduled to fly out the next day), received a call from a nephew living there. "Everything is fine here," he told her. "Don't hesitate to come."

It was true. Post-attack London was nothing like New York City after 9/11, with its locked neighborhoods, its sidewalks filled with flowers, its posters asking for information about the missing, and the unceasing smell of smoke and death rising from downtown Manhattan. In England's capital, rather, while pronounced police presence secured the Tube and major thoroughfares in the days following the bombing, there was little that suggested an attack had just taken place, or fear another might follow—at least, not amongst the public.

In Parliament, however, lawmakers set immediately to work. If the bombings had been the work of British citizens, how could future such attacks be stopped? Where had they acquired the knowledge and expertise to manufacture these bombs, and how? What—or who—had instilled in them a hate so enormous, a commitment to Islam so perverted, that these British-born young men would kill crowds of innocent people—and themselves—for Allah? What had turned them against their own society? And were there more of them?

Within days, England had its answer: exactly two weeks after the bombings of July 7, four other young men attempted a similar attack, again on three metros and a city bus. As on July 7, the bombers used homemade weapons created with hydrogen peroxide and ordinary household flour. The bombs, however, failed: the proportions of ingredients had, according to experts, been miscalculated. In other words, the public had been saved entirely by the incompetence of the terrorists—not by dint of any action law enforcement might have undertaken.

For then Prime Minister Tony Blair, the shock of two successive terrorist attacks on England's capital quickly turned to indignation and to fury. "My point to you is this," he declared. "It's time we stopped saying, 'OK, we abhor their methods, but we kind of see something in their ideas, or maybe they've got a sliver of excuse or justification.' They've got no justification for it."[4] That anger grew only greater within the British public as it became known that the perpetrators of the July 7 attacks had, in fact, been known to Scotland Yard. The signals had all been there—but the laws and focus of attention—an awareness, perhaps, that an Islamic terrorist attack might actually take place on London streets—were not.

That would change. Though no one has ever established a connection between the July 7 bombers and the four who attempted a repeat performance on July twenty-first, the evidence of a growing domestic threat was clear. British officials, in fact, estimated that as many as 3,000 British Muslims had trained with Al Qaeda.[5] And as Blair had suggested, the war in Iraq, while it had by then become a center for training activity, was hardly the real cause: those 3,000 had been known to British forces as early as 1999. Rather, the primary force, it seemed, was coming from the mosques, from the Internet, and from Saudi-sponsored pamphlets available in bookstores and on the streets. Though England had not had a Hirsi Ali or a Janny Groen to bring these secrets into public view, it was now clear that the UK—indeed, all of Europe—confronted the same conflicts, the same challenges that had swept the tranquil tulip fields of Holland.

In fact, it turned out England had already thwarted a number of attacks before the bombings of July 7 and was becoming known, at least within European intelligence communities, as a power center for Islamic extremism in the West. "The Muslim Brotherhood and the group Hezb-ut-Tahrir, which Interior Minister Schily banned in Germany after the attacks of September 11, also maintain a strong presence in London," reported *der Spiegel* in July 2005.[6] "In addition, many radical Islamic publications—foreign issues of Saudi Arabian newspapers, for example—are printed in the city on the Thames. Hate sermons by radical sheiks are also posted onto the Internet in London. And despite crackdowns by the British police in recent months, radical Islamic propaganda continues unabated."

Moreover, radical imams—including a Jamaican convert, Trevor Forest aka Sheikh Abdullah al Faisal—had built a large following at mosques like Finsbury Park, which Zacharias Massaoui, one of the masterminds of 9/11—and said to have been a disciple of al-Faisal—frequently attended. (Al Faisal was arrested in 2003, and, according to a report from the Dutch National Coordinator for Counterterrorism [NCTb][7] was "found guilty on five counts of soliciting murder and four counts of using threatening and insulting words in a series of audio-cassette tapes bearing titles such as 'Rules of Jihad,' 'Declaration of War,' and 'Them versus Us.' Al-Faisal encouraged listeners to undertake violent jihad and to kill 'unbelievers' such as Americans, Hindus, and Jews. His trial provided the first opportunity for the rhetoric used by al-Faisal over a long period of time and intended only for sympathetic listeners to become more widely known. On conviction, he was sentenced to nine years imprisonment, later reduced on appeal to seven years. On reaching his parole date, he was deported back to Jamaica at the end of May 2007.")

Some of the strength of the UK as a center for radical extremism can be explained simply by logistics and convenience: most of the UK's Muslim immigrants hail from Pakistan, and are native English speakers. It is therefore easier for them to communicate with other European Muslims, many of whom speak English in addition to the languages of their country of residence (not many outside the Netherlands and Belgium, by contrast, speak Dutch). In most cases, they speak Arabic as well—something Mohammed Bouyeri, for instance, did not—acting as translators and go-betweens. And Pakistan, unlike, say, Morocco or Turkey, is already a primary center of terrorist activity and host to Al Qaeda (and other) training camps.

All of this has also made the UK appealing to radicalizing Muslim youth in other European countries, who thanks to a newly border-free EU, travel freely back and forth between their homelands and the radical mosques of England. Numerous Middle Eastern immigrants, too, who had joined the wars in the Balkans during the 1990s, had by then found their way to England, bringing their knowledge of the battlefield along with them. By 2005, the UK had essentially become the Western capital of Islamist recruitment and ideology.[8] According to an analysis by the late Michael Radu published in *American Diplomacy*,[9] "A May 2004 government report found that there were up to 10,000 active Al Qaeda supporters in the UK, while a joint report by the Home and Foreign Offices estimated that the number of British Muslims actively engaged in terrorist activity was 'less than one percent' of Britain's Muslim population, which would still be some 16,000." In addition, noted Radu, "A YouGov poll among British Muslims conducted after 7/7 found that six percent insist that the bombings were justified. Six percent amounts to about 100,000 individuals."

These are shocking numbers. Where, then, are the protests, the demands, of other Muslims in Europe? Why do we not hear more from those like the shop owner initially quoted in a story from the *Independent* and cited in Radu's report, who remarked, "Blowing up a bomb in London is not jihad. . . . We are British Muslims. We left our homes, our parents, everything, for the future of our children. Why don't these boys go to Karachi where there are bodies lying in the gutter and people are dying of poverty? Why don't they save those people?"

We don't hear from them because they, too, are often afraid. England, after all, was where so much of the cultural confrontations had centered for some time, most notably the Salman Rushdie affair. Even more, as many as half of Egypt's most-wanted terrorists live in England. The former imam of Finsbury Park Mosque, an international center for radical Islam in London, Abu Hamza, is, according to Radu, "wanted both in Yemen, for planning the murder of tourists, and in the United States for his role in a planned Oregon training site." And, lest it go unnoticed, Ahmed Omar Saeed Sheikh, also born and raised in England, provided substantial financial support to the 9/11 hijackers and was the force behind the 2002 kidnapping and murder of Daniel Pearl. (He, too, received much of his training in the Balkans.)

And then there is the problem of the converts.

One of the 7/7 bombers had been just such a recent arrival to Islam: Jermaine Lindsay, a Jamaican native who moved to England as a child and had changed his name to Jamal a year or so before his suicide bombing. And men with names like Don Stewart-Whyte, Oliver Savant, and Brian Young, were among those suspected of taking part in a 2006 plot to blow up United States-bound planes departing from Heathrow Airport. Richard Reid, the so-called "shoe-bomber" who was prevented from blowing up an American Airlines flight from Paris to Miami in December 2001, was another. Such names and backgrounds defy preventive measures such as profiling. And anyway, at the time of the failed July 21 bombings, few laws provided for prosecution of those who planned but did not actually succeed in (or actually engage in) terrorist attacks. Not only that, but one of the July 21 suspects, Muktar Said Ibraham (said to have masterminded the project) claimed to have learned to make the bombs through information he'd found online. If Europe was going to be better protected, it would need to enact stronger anti-terrorism laws. But how could a democratic EU counter the distribution of Saudi newspapers and access to the World Wide Web?

Within days, Tony Blair announced a "cross-party consensus" on new laws that previously might have been unthinkable. Though an overly-zealous police force had shot and killed a completely innocent Brazilian man in London's tube on July 22, believing him to be a potential terrorist, UK's parliament offered no apologies: a new world, they seemed to say, meant new rules, and possibly, new values.

And Blair's new laws did, indeed, suggest new values, including "the power to deport or refuse entry to people with a record of inciting terrorism." Like Holland, Britain now also introduced laws that would make praise or approval of terrorism a crime. But what the UK did not do—indeed, refused to do—was adopt Holland's supervision of telecommunications, or its long-term retention of private data such as phone conversations, health records, and book purchases.[10] And what the new British legislation also did not and could not do was address the challenge of the Internet, where sites like www.TurnToIslam.com encourage Christians to convert and where new converts were—and still are—often then targeted by recruiters for jihad.[11]

And new converts, especially non-Arabic speaking ones, are vulnerable: they want to do the right thing. They may not have read—and certainly not studied—the Koran and its various interpretations, making them dependent on others to tell them what it says and what they are to do. Like newly-reformed smokers, too, they can be the most adamant and inflexible in their thinking. For recruiters for jihad, the mosque, by 2005, was almost unnecessary anymore.

But the Internet is a formidable power. Radical imams broadcast speeches from abroad (even after being expelled from Western countries), while jihadist sites offer instructions on bomb-making and executions. Notes Clutterbuck,[12] "Jihadist groups and their supporters . . . may well be at the forefront of [the Internet's] exploitation as 'the size

and scope of the web resources being developed by jihadist sympa-
thizers today is enormous and maintained by thousands of highly IT-
literate individuals, broadly united by their adherence to a global Salafi
jihadist ideology.' "[13] Just as the Internet could bring tens of thousands
together across the Netherlands for a demonstration on the Dam within
hours of Van Gogh's murder, so could it bring thousands together
across the world to demonstrate, to riot, and to call for the destruction
of the West.

* * *

Among the most famous images for the year 2005 is a pen-and-ink
drawing of a Muslim man—presumably Mohammed—standing at the
gates of heaven. A caption beneath him reads: "Stop! Stop! We're running out of virgins!"

"Come on," a Palestinian-American friend writes me via e-mail
when she sees it the first time. "It's indisputably funny."

But not everyone was laughing.

The drawing was one of a series of cartoons that appeared in
Denmark's *Jyllands-Posten,* the country's largest-circulation daily.[14]
Angered by what he perceived—rightly—to be Europe's repeated capitulation to the demands of Muslim minorities and their threats against
art exhibitions, theater and opera performances, films (*Submission,* for
example), and books over the previous few years, cultural editor Flemming Rose lost patience when he heard that a Danish writer, Kåre Blut-
gen, had been unable to find a publisher willing to take his illustrated
children's book about Mohammed—or, for that matter, an artist willing
to provide the illustrations. The *Jyllands-Posten,* until then, had been
among the few European newspapers willing to take on the kinds of stories that the Dutch press—urged by Hirsi Ali—had been tackling since
9/11, investigating, for instance, honor killings and criminality among
Muslim Danes.

Rose commissioned twelve cartoonists to produce drawings of
Mohammed, which he then published in the *Posten* on September 30,
2005.

The initial response to the cartoons, which also included an image of
Mohammed with a turban shaped like bomb, seemed to be one of general indifference. It was only after a couple of weeks had passed that
some 4,000 people demonstrated quietly outside the newspaper's Co-
penhagen office. According to Pernille Ammitzbøll, a journalist for the
Jyllands Posten and Lorenzo Vidino, author of *Al Qaeda in Europe: The
New Battleground of International Jihad* (Prometheus, 2005), the demonstration had taken place largely at the urging of two radical Danish
imams, Raed Hillel and Ahmed Akkari, both of whom had been the

subjects of headlines in the *Jyllands-Posten* in the past.[15] Days later, the cartoons appeared in newspapers in Egypt and Indonesia, sparking no reaction whatsoever. Frustrated, the Danish imams reportedly contacted various Muslim diplomats based in Denmark, who then demanded an apology from Prime Minister Rasmussen. He refused. "I have no power to limit the press," he responded, "nor do I wish such power."

Battle lines were now drawn. While a number of European papers sided with the *Jyllands-Posten* and republished the cartoons in a show of solidarity, the Danish imams traveled to the Middle East to present a dossier on the cartoons—including additional, highly offensive images (one of which depicted Mohammed having sex with a dog) that had not, in fact, been among the *Jyllands-Posten* cartoons. By late December, it seemed that everything Flemming Rose had fought against had only resurfaced: more than 20 Danish ambassadors reprimanded Rasmussen for his refusal to meet with the Muslim ambassadors earlier, and the Council of Europe condemned Denmark's insistence of "freedom of the press." Even former president Bill Clinton spoke out against the cartoons, calling them "totally outrageous" and "against Islam." (One wonders if he ever actually saw them.)

But they were *not* against Islam, as even my Palestinian friend had noted. While strictly speaking, any graven image of the prophet is *haram*—forbidden—in Islam, the existence of one is not, in itself, an insult to the religion. In this case, the drawings not only served to emphasize the values of the West (which had arguably been insulted by the demands to close down and censor some of its greatest artistic achievements) but they poked fun, too, not at the religion but at the behaviors of those who used it to legitimize violence and hate. "You have to laugh at yourself sometimes," my Palestinian friend had written.

But instead of laughter came only more violence. As Western newspapers published (and republished) the images, the news passed immediately back to the Muslim region—and the reactions grew more and more severe.

Reading a timeline of the post-cartoon events is itself cartoonesque. Throughout the month of February 2006, every day witnessed a new battle, with more newspapers publishing the cartoons on one side, and increasingly violent protests against them on the other. Death threats and fatwas against the cartoonists became threats against Danish citizens in general, and then against Scandinavians, while the more geographically-challenged called for the destruction of the "Dutch" for their "newspaper that published those cartoons." On February 2 alone, a British Islamist group published a statement, "Kill Those Who Insult The Prophet"; Palestinian gunmen attacked the European Union headquarters in Gaza; and

France's *Le Monde* produced a cartoon of Mohammed formed from the words "I may not draw the Prophet." Days later, Chilean, Swedish, Danish, and Norwegian embassies were set aflame in Damascus, as violent protests broke out in Denmark. In New York City at the time, on the lapel where once I'd worn a ribbon for the victims of 9/11, I now pinned a Danish flag.

By March 2006, approximately 140 people had died during protests against the cartoons—nearly three times the number of victims of the London bombings the year before, and almost as many as had been killed two years earlier in Madrid.

* * * *

The Danish cartoons had been an effort to ward off the growth and influence of conservative Islam and Islamism in the West—and with them, the radicalization that often leads to terror.

It hadn't worked.

Radicalization within Europe's borders only intensified from 2005-2007—and it intensifies still. The problem of homegrown terror and radicalism extends from Northern Scandinavia down to the heel of Italy—even in the smallest villages and towns, along streets where not just Rembrandt and Spinoza, but Vermeer and Jan Van Eyck once walked.

In November 2005, the *Washington Post*'s Craig Whitlock reported from the "pastoral" town of Maaseik, Belgium[16]—once home to Van Eyck and now a European center for one of the largest international terrorism networks, the Moroccan Islamic Combatant Group (GICM)— the group responsible for the 2004 attacks on the Madrid underground. A month earlier, the GICM had been banned in the UK; the UN had already listed it as an Al Qaeda affiliate soon after the attacks of September 11.

At the same time, reports Whitlock, men in Maaisek's Moroccan community began wearing long beards. Many traveled to Afghanistan, where, in 1997, the organization had first originated with Moroccans at Afghan training camps, who sought to bring the cause to Morocco, and establish an Islamic republic there. Five years later, in May 2003, 12 GICM suicide bombers blew themselves up along with 33 civilians at various sites in Casablanca. Subsequently, according to the *Washington Post*, police in Italy, Belgium, Spain, France, and Holland broke up local GICM cells—but not, apparently, the Maaseik group. Not for another year did Belgian officials, with the aid of information acquired by Italian intelligence, pull off a large-scale arrest in the small village of Maaisek, rounding up close to twenty suspects in a town housing 800 Moroccans. Almost all were ultimately released.

To some extent, this outcome is surprising. The fall of the Vlaams Blok had been immediately resolved with the founding of the Vlaams Belang, an arguably even more right-wing party led by Filip Dewinter. And even Left-leaning Sweden, with one of the weakest military forces in Europe, had begun taking measures to address the prospect of a domestic terror attack, announcing an overhaul of operations and convicting two Stockholm-based men, members of Anbar al-Islam, a group that had killed hundreds in Iraq.

And yet, for whatever reasons, even with the presence of Jahjah's AEL on the one hand and the Vlaams Belang on the other, Belgium took little action.

The rest of Europe wasn't quite so calm.

* * *

One little USB flash drive can hold massive amounts of valuable information—and the very lives of thousands. On the night of August 9, 2006, British police, aided by intelligence gathered by Pakistani security services, busted more than 20 British Muslims suspected of planning mass murder on a devastating scale. In what they called "the great plan," the group aimed to detonate explosives on as many as 20 airplanes set to depart London's Heathrow Airport for destinations in the United States and Canada. One of the men, Abdulla Ahmed Ali (aka Ahmed Ali Khan), aged 27, carried a USB-stick in his pocket at the time of his arrest; it contained the flight information, schedules, security advice, and other details for seven flights departing between the hours of 2:15 and 4:50 P.M. from Heathrow's Terminal Three. Only one-way flights were studied—all of them Boeing 777, 767, or 763 aircraft—planes with a capacity to hold between 241 and 285 passengers and crew. In addition, the drive held a list of other potential UK targets, including an oil refinery in Essex, the Bacton gas terminal in Norfolk, and the gas pipeline between Britain and Belgium.

The bombers included mostly "middle-class, second-generation British nationals of Pakistani origin," according to the Hungarian National Security Office 2006 Yearbook report. Among those apprehended were a Muslim charity worker and a Heathrow airport employee with access to all areas of the airport—the world's busiest. An additional three of the suspects were British Muslim converts. One, remarkably, was a woman.

British intelligence had followed the suspects for some time before making their arrests, having identified them with help from the Bank of England, which, alerted by Pakistan, had marked substantial financial transfers from Pakistan to their accounts. It was a form of international coordination and banking surveillance that would have been virtually impossible before the institution of anti-terrorism banking laws that followed the September 11 attacks. Audio and video surveillance followed.

Anyone who has traveled on a commercial airline since the August 9, 2006, arrests has experienced the ramifications of the attempted attack. The plotters had aimed to inject hydrogen peroxide (again) into soda bottles, which they would detonate using another substance concealed in the batteries of cell phones or MP3 players. An entry in Ali's diaries, discovered after his arrest, noted: "Select date, five days before jet. All link up. Dirty mag to distract, condom. One drink use, other keep in pocket, maybe will not get through. Plus keys and chewing gum on the D in the electronic device."[17] (It can be pretty safely assumed that "D" stood for "detonator.")

The idea itself was complex, but its execution could not have been simpler. Moreover, had the plan not been exposed and the planes had actually exploded, the weapons would have been undiscoverable—clearing the way for additional such attacks in the future.[18] Indeed, while seven flights were marked on Ali's USB stick, apparently the plotters had considered executing their attacks on as many as 11 other flights departing from different terminals and over a period of 15 months.

Yet while the Heathrow plan, which resulted in the current ban on liquids and gels in carry-on luggage, failed, it refocused world attention on an area of terror attacks that had been thought to be secured: air travel. Despite increased precautions since 9/11, planes were evidently still vulnerable—and more and more people, it seemed, were prepared to use them as weapons.

* * *

Italy took the FIFA World Cup that year, beating out France in 64 total matches that brought over 3.3 million spectators to Germany. Players scored one hundred and forty-seven goals between the ninth of June and the ninth of July, with no one even once suspecting that the whole thing could have ended on day one, when officials foiled a terror attack at the Munich opening games. Reminiscent of the Palestinian kidnapping of nine Israelis during the 1972 summer games—also in Munich—the World Cup episode would prove to be the first in a series of failed attacks in Germany to take place over the course of the next 15 months.

On July 31, two abandoned suitcases were found on trains departing from Cologne—one heading north, the other south. Each contained a bomb set to go off at 2:30 P.M. Each would likely have caused the trains to derail, potentially killing and injuring hundreds. Each, thanks to defects in their construction, failed to detonate. The bombers were two Lebanese students in their twenties, whose images were captured by surveillance cameras at Cologne Station.

This fact alone indicates the extent to which opinions—and laws— have changed in Europe in response to Islamic terrorism and the fear of more attacks in the EU. No one believes for a moment, anymore, that "it's just about America." Germany, after all, did not even send troops into Iraq. Their involvement in Afghanistan had been one of peacemaking, with troops arriving only after the fall of the Taliban in 2001. But clearly, the *Bundesrepubliek*, too, was a target—and long-held beliefs, based on memories of an omnipresent Gestapo, were fading as realization of a different kind of threat emerged to replace them. Indeed, unlike the Netherlands, Germany has been reluctant to record or accumulate personal data about its citizens, and surveillance cameras have been among the means the public has most strenuously resisted. Yet in the aftermath of the failed bombings of July 31, as many as eighty percent of Germans now support the increased use of cameras.

That's not all. Motions were made by the country's Federal Criminal Policy Office (Bundeskriminalamt, or BKA) to increase monitoring of the Internet, and to require providers "to deny access to sites containing information on the assembly of explosive devices," according to a report from the Hungarian National Security office.[19] Officials also agreed to create an anti-terrorist data bank, which would include such personal information as religious affiliation and sexual preferences, though the more sensitive information would only be available to specific authorities.[20]

That October, 24-year-old Youssef Mahammed el-Hajdib, whom police had captured only hours after the bombs were found, received a life sentence in the German courts. (His accomplice had fled to Lebanon, where he was also intercepted and tried.) It was the harshest sentence the German courts had ever delivered for terrorism, but the public and the media embraced it. El Hajdib, a handsome young man who attended his sentencing dressed in a white djellaba, gave the judge the finger.

* * *

"It would have been an inferno," declared German weekly *Der Spiegel*.[21] Three men, said to be members of the Islamic Jihad Union, had been working on creating a bomb "with the power of 550 kilograms (1,200 pounds) of TNT," according to *Der Spiegel*, when German police moved in the fall of 2007. The components of the planned bomb, like those used in London and Madrid, included hydrogen peroxide. "The intention," *Der Spiegel* quotes one official as saying, "was to commit an attack and cause as many deaths as possible," targeting a U.S. air base, discos, and what one of the prospective bombers called bars "with American sluts." Two of the men, Fritz Gelowicz and Daniel Schneider, were German. Both had converted to Islam. The third, the Turkish Adem Yilmaz, had grown up in Germany, as had a fourth suspect, Attila Selek, arrested later.

A force of 600 police descended on the group during the afternoon of September 4, 2007. For over a year, Gelowicz and his cohorts had been under constant video surveillance, their cars bugged, their e-mails and phone calls tapped. So extensive had the infiltration been into the lives and activities of the home-grown terror suspects that at the time of their arrest, police had already replaced their barrels of 35-percent hydrogen peroxide with a 3-percent solution—not much more powerful than water. Nonetheless, when police moved in, they found all the makings of a so-called "Satan's Mother" bomb, including, in the living room of the vacation house where they worked, "two stainless steel pots and nine packages of flour," according to *Der Spiegel*, as well as military detonators, and "a canister of hydrogen peroxide was found under a white caftan in a closet."[22] By the time the case went to trial, *Der Spiegel* further reported, prosecutors had amassed enough material to fill 521 loose-leaf binders—"enough to fill up a shelf 42 meters (138 feet) long."[23] The presiding judge: Ottmar Breidling, the same man who had sentenced el Hajdib to life.

But despite all the evidence against them, the so-called "Sauerland cell" has one strong point in its favor: legally, the information obtained through the intercepted e-mails and taped conversations is, at this point, inadmissible in court. Neither can a newly proposed law criminalizing visits to terror camps or owning bomb-building instructions, though another law already in effect does allow for a ten-year sentence for membership in a foreign terrorist organization.[24] Either way, the changes in domestic policy show a distinct departure from the surveillance-averse culture that was Germany the day the World Cup opened. On that day, what Germany—indeed, all of Europe—feared most of all, was rain.

CHAPTER 18

Perhaps it was the copulating imams riding on an army tank named "Love," or the drawing of the imam being defecated on, or the one with feces spilling from his mouth—but when an exhibition of 26-year-old artist Rachid Ben Ali opened in January 2005 at Amsterdam's CoBrA Museum of Modern Art—part of a year-long, politically inspired celebration of the friendship between Morocco and the Netherlands—the death threats and the hate mail soon followed. Even a day after the exhibition opened, a car full of men followed him as he walked along the street. A few of them approached him on the sidewalk, pushing him, spoiling for a fight. "You'll be following right behind Van Gogh," they told him—and it was clear they didn't mean Vincent. The fact that Ben Ali is also openly gay did not help him. The artist, fearful for his safety, spent the next several nights away from home, staying with friends and in hotels.

At least, this is what he told the press.

But there are problems with this story. By some reports, for instance, Ben Ali was born in the Netherlands in 1978. Elsewhere, however, he has claimed to have been born in Morocco in 1975, arriving in Holland at the age of 15. In yet another version, he came to Holland in 1986—when he would have been either eight or 11. And after the reports of threats against him had filled the media for over a week, a reporter from the *Volkskrant* (which had earlier cited Ben Ali's year of birth as 1968) took the initiative of contacting the Amsterdam police for confirmation of Ali's claims. They had no record, the police told the reporter, of Ben Ali ever filing a complaint. The CoBrA Museum, too, the

Volkskrant said, denied receiving any threats. (Its director, however, stood fully behind Ben Ali's accounts.)

In a way, though, what matters far more than the question of whether Ben Ali was lying is the statement that is made by the fact that virtually everyone believed him—that the idea of an artist's life being threatened by Muslims in a European country because of paintings he'd produced had become not only credible, but likely. (It certainly was not, after all, as if Ben Ali needed the PR the media attention brought; he was already well-recognized in Holland. Shortly before his departure from the Stedelijk, Fuchs had invited Queen Beatrix to curate an exhibition, and Rachid Ben Ali was one of the artists she included. He had also received the country's "most promising young artist" prize in 2003.)

There is nothing one would be inclined to call "attractive" about Rachid Ben Ali's paintings. They are rough and fast and bloody scrawls, with an iconography of explosions and violence and homoerotic sex. Given what would take place less than two years later as a result of the cartoons in Denmark, it is almost surprising that the uproar—and there was some, at least, demonstrably proved by messages posted on the Internet—was not much greater.[1] But what it did signal, in any case, was that even in the aftermath of Van Gogh's murder, even after the arrests of the Hofstadgroep, even after the arson and the anger and the sorrow and the fear, even days after Hirsi Ali had bravely returned to the Netherlands and to work, nothing had really changed.

In fact, it had only gotten worse.

True, no further terror attacks had occurred in that time—though with ongoing arrests of Hofstadgroep members, a few may well have been prevented—but the tensions were becoming unbearable, and even hazardous; as one young woman remarked in a panel discussion hosted by *Sen* magazine, a women's magazine for Dutch Muslims, people began responding with the idea, "If you treat me like an extremist, I will act like an extremist."

And the numbers were there, too, to prove it. In April, the AIVD came out with yet another report showing yet another rise in radicalization among Muslim youth and growth of other local cells, warning that some young men may have gone to Iraq to train for domestic attacks. Even Turkish youth, the AIVD noted, were beginning to radicalize, in part in response to the events that followed Van Gogh's murder; until that time, the problem had largely centered around Moroccans. In Amsterdam, a study of 25 public schools showed a rise in "anti-Western" sentiment among Muslim students at all grade levels, and a growing intolerance of "homosexuals, women who—in their eyes—are too modern, and unbelievers."[2] Increasingly, according to the report, these kids did not "identify with Netherlanders, but [viewed] their Muslim identity as a binding factor."[3]

In July, a 17-year-old Dutch Muslim convert (his parents were Dutch and British) was caught with a homemade bomb in his home, which he evidently planned to use in an attack on Geert Wilders. Since Wilders at that point was still living under guard and in undisclosed, generally highly-fortified locations, the most likely place to have detonated it would have been in the area of the Parliament—which itself by now had been fortified with metal detectors and an increased police presence, none of which would necessarily have detected an explosive. And security was, anyway, never certain: A few months after Ayaan's visit to New York, she and I had met for drinks at a sidewalk café in the Jordaan. Her guards took their places at a nearby table. As we talked, a darker-skinned, Middle Eastern man made his way towards Ayaan and me and stretched out his hand. "Good for you," he had said in heavily accented Dutch: "stay who you are." Ayaan shook his hand, and he calmly had walked on.

In that case, she had been lucky. If the man had been carrying a knife, there would have been nothing the guards could have done to protect her. Now the boy with the bomb—like the boy at Restaurant Dudok—made it clear that even those you'd last suspect were suspect, and even places that should have been safe, were not.

Predictably, the Dutch were nearing the end of their patience. "Nederlanders Moslimmoe," announced a headline in *Het Parool*, the day after the 17-year-old bomber-wannabe was arrested, "Dutch tired of Muslims." The article presented the result of an American Pew Research Center study that showed Holland, with 51 percent of the Dutch viewing Muslims negatively, to have the highest anti-Islam sentiment of any of the seven European countries polled. (It did not help, however, that the same study found anti-Semitism to still be rampant in the Middle East, where 100 percent of Jordanians and 66 percent of Moroccans expressed hatred of Jews, thereby adding ammunition to arguments to close Europe's—or anyway, Holland's—borders.)

As a partial solution, the cabinet demanded revisions in the *inburger-ingswet*, the law that required naturalized Dutch citizens as well as foreign-born residents to enroll in citizenship classes. The proposals, which also addressed accusations of discrimination against non-native-born Dutch citizens, would now require all non-EU immigrants—including those already residing in the Netherlands; foreign parents or guardians of minors; and all naturalized Dutch receiving welfare, to take the courses and to demonstrate working knowledge of the Dutch language. In August, too, measures that had been established in January came into effect—including the right of law enforcement to engage in "preventive frisking" anywhere in the public arena, and at will.

It was hard to imagine that this same country had so resoundedly protested against national ID cards in the days following the Bijlmermeer disaster, just a decade and a half before.

By January 2006, all telecommunication traffic in Europe could be recorded and held on file—not for content, per se, but the names, phone numbers, and e-mail addresses contacted by every one of Europe's 450 million inhabitants, as well as the time contact was made. In Holland, arguments also were underway for a national DNA registry and a public transport system that would record the name and fingerprint of every traveler on every bus, tram, or train.

None, however, was so ludicrous as Section Two of the so-called "Rotterdam Code" of 2006, which stated that only Dutch should be spoken "at school, at work, in the streets, and in the community centers" of Rotterdam—or Rita Verdonk's suggestion that it be nationalized. That meant: No English. No Arabic. No Vietnamese. Anywhere. Should my family come to visit, we would not be permitted to converse outside the house. No foreign tourist could ask someone for directions. The Parliament actually discussed this. The media, predictably, roared.

What, for instance, would have happened to Theo van Gogh, who customarily had parted from friends and family with the words, "take care"? What of expressions like "Hasta la vista, Baby," and "Make my day" and "Bring it on"? Would the government, as one friend suggested only half-jokingly, issue badges to tourists on arrival, yellow stars emblazoned with a "V" for "visitor," say (or more likely, "B" for the Dutch word for "visitor," *bezoeker*)?

And the truth was, anyway, that there was little such a law could possibly have to offer—and in some ways, it stood to do harm. Abused Muslim women, for instance, take a tremendous risk when they summon the courage to seek help from the Dutch community. Because they are often not allowed to leave their homes, or are forbidden by their husbands to learn Dutch in the first place, how much more reluctant would they now be to reach out, thinking that in the very act of doing so, by speaking in their native language, they risked a confrontation with the law? More significantly, not only was it hard to comprehend how forcing people to speak Dutch in public actually helps them to better "integrate," but the majority of those being investigated or tried for terrorist activities in the Netherlands, the Hofstadgroep members— including Bouyeri—were Dutch-born, fluent in the language and the oft-praised, oft-repeated (as if it were a mantra) "norms and values" of the Netherlands.

The motion didn't pass. Months later, Rita Verdonk announced her candidacy for prime minister; she ended her announcement with the words, "Let's go"—spoken, that is, in English.

Unsurprisingly, reaction to Verdonk's proposal was mixed. Jeroen Adema, a junior member of the D66 party whose family comes from Germany, filed a lawsuit against her for discrimination. Members of the LPF, however, praised the suggestion as a "wise" move that would help discourage the "Arabization" of the country.

And non-Muslim immigrants? Their response was little less than fury. "I'll speak whatever f***ing language I want," one wrote on an online bulletin board. "Another reason to leave the Netherlands," a fellow American ex-pat chimed in.

The truth was, nothing the government was suggesting provided much of a solution. As an offensive strategy, it relied entirely on defense. It did little to address the spread of a problem that had already taken root. As one popular imam, the Dutch-born Abdul Jabbar (née Jilles) Van de Ven told *Trouw* shortly after the 17-year-old bomber had been arrested, "There are a lot of very angry young men walking around." [4]

Van de Ven first discovered Islam while a 14-year-old student at a Catholic elementary school, according to *Trouw*. He soon applied for a grant to study in Medina, Saudi Arabia, a request that was rewarded not just with schooling, but with accompanying airfare, visa, and housing. He received classes day and night. By the time he returned, he no longer felt a part of the culture into which he had been born.

"For us," he told *Trouw* of his social and religious circles after 9/11, "Afghanistan was the ideal. Anyone who refuses sharia, the formation of a state according to Islamic law, is an unbeliever. And the Taliban installed sharia. So I think there's probably not a single Muslim who believes America is not waging a war against Islam. Islam is not praying five times a day and for the rest, living just like everybody else. Islam is the sharia state." [5]

Faced with interviews with the likes of Van de Ven, many frequently responded (and continue to do so) that they represented a small minority of Muslims in the Netherlands—and in Europe. This is true. But others took note of Van de Ven's role as a popular imam, a leader and teacher of countless other young Muslim men, and one who, having been born and raised in the Netherlands, could not be accused of never having learned or absorbed Dutch values. To the contrary; he had simply rejected them, and was calling on others to do the same. And there were many others, all across Europe, like him.

In the UK, a post-attack government now proposed new measures against those like Van de Ven, making it possible to deport imams who stimulated or encouraged anti-Western sentiment, violence, or disorder—native British and immigrant alike. Even people found to frequent certain bookstores and Internet sites, according to news reports, could be subject to detainment and deportation.

But such laws were not under consideration in the Netherlands; and so, to a government they felt could not manage these challenges, many of the Dutch responded with dissatisfaction—and with a solution of their own: they left. Though the numbers proved to be lower than first suspected, the fact was that more people now planned to leave Holland than were arriving, turning it from a reluctant "immigration country" to an emigrating one. And those who were leaving were largely between the ages of 24 and 35, educated, high-income-earners—exactly the ones the country needed most.

When I first read reports of this, I thought of my earlier conversation with Fré. Now not only were the Dutch making it harder for intellectuals to come; they were chasing away the ones already there—including foreigners: as early as 2004, the International Organizations Staff Association found that 77 percent of expats in the Netherlands, including those working at the International Criminal Court, the European Space Agency, and Interpol, wanted out. For these expats, however, the reasons were largely different than they were for the Dutch. In their case, even for fellow Europeans, they simply did not feel welcome anymore. The Netherlands had become a country in which, it seemed, nobody really liked anybody very much.

* * *

On November 2, 2005, they hold a memorial for Theo van Gogh on the Linneasstraat. The mayor comes, and the prime minister, and people from the neighborhood, and they talk of harmony, and how we all are individuals, and of learning to live together.

Everyone is Dutch.

On television, the camera focuses on one lone, sullen-looking Moroccan, and that is all. True, we are watching only what the television cameramen choose to show us; but in photos of the crowd, there are no headscarves, no long beards, no dark-skinned faces.

Hours later, the United States of America memorializes Rosa Parks, a woman who would not give her seat up to a white man in an age when, as Bill Clinton says in his eulogy, gentlemen gave their seats over to a lady. It was, says Clinton, an act of peaceful resistance that changed absolutely everything.

Peaceful resistance.

Watching the services on CNN from my living room in Amsterdam, it occurs to me that this is precisely what is missing in the Netherlands. Europe has never really known such acts, such quiet revolutions. There were no blacks in 1953 to force into the backs of buses. And when the revolution came, it came to the United States, and Europe picked the ribbons up behind, like a bridesmaid carrying a bride's wedding train.

Maybe, I think, Rosa Parks belongs in Europe's classrooms, too.

Except the conflict in Europe by this time had gone beyond a fight for equal rights, or equal pay, or nondiscrimination. To the contrary, the battles were being led by extremists seeking to oppress gays and Jews and women. Can you win a religious battle at a soda counter, on a city bus, on the steps of universities that won't let you in? And here's the thing: Europe did let them in. It gave them jobs, and homes, and welfare when they didn't want to work—its own people's money with which to pay for the homes they came here voluntarily to live in, the homes they chose not to leave, even when they'd not been invited here to stay. Europe took them in, and made them comfortable, and when the time to leave had passed, extended their hospitality. Women did this. Jews did this. Gays. Christians. No one was brought against their will. There were no chains, no ships, no auctions.

The truth is, the Bouyeris, the Van de Vens, the Oliver Savants, and Richard Rieds don't want what the blacks wanted: equality. Dignity. Decency.

They want control.

They don't want us to let them in. They want us to let them take us over.

Which is why this has become about a world of "us and them."

It is not the Muslims against the whites, but the Islamists against everyone.

Perhaps that was the problem on the Linneasstraat. Muslim moderates are part of "us," not "them." Yet when they should have been there, just to make that simple statement, to present that one gesture of solidarity, they were not. And that they weren't makes me consider, on second thought, that maybe they aren't quite with us, after all. Perhaps, floating in some middle ground, they still are too close to "them": those who think Theo van Gogh "sort of deserved it," as they say. Their positions, their ideas, are still uncertain. They are vulnerable. And so they are therefore dangerous.

Perhaps, then, the answer is precisely the reverse: it is for us, the Westerners being beaten in the fields outside of Basra, knifed in the streets of Amsterdam, bombed on European subways and buildings in New York, who have the most to learn from Mrs. Parks. Sit where we believe we have a right to sit. Resist where they try repressing us. We will take our places, and we will not be moved.

* * *

By mid-2005, it had become clear that the so-called "terror war" had relocated almost entirely to Europe. While the United States busied itself with Terri Schiavo's medical conditions and family dramas,

Michael Jackson's acquittal on charges of child molestation, and, by summer's end, the devastation of Hurricane Katrina, Europe's newspapers, magazines, calendars, and parliamentary sessions, above all, focused almost without pause on the problem of Muslim extremism and the tensions in race relations. In New York, Christo and Jeanne-Claude installed "The Gates" in Central Park. In London, Prince Charles and Camilla Bowles were wed. YouTube was born. France and Holland rejected the European constitution. My friend Arman, the artist who had met with Ayaan earlier, died in November, and a colleague, journalist Steven Vincent, was kidnapped and murdered in Basra, Iraq, on August 2nd in retaliation for a story he had written for the *New York Times*. Saddam Hussein, bearded and defiant, stood trial in Baghdad.

In the Parliaments of Europe, you'd think they hadn't noticed any of it.

In December, Dutch culture minister Medy Van der Laan presented her own proposal for the creation of a re-united, happy society in the Netherlands. Museums, she declared, were boring. They were too predictable. They had vitrines with things in them, and pictures hanging dumbly on the walls. Like a woman startled by the disillusionment of discovering that books contain nothing more than words printed on the page, Medy Van der Laan called for a new "museal strategy," one that, with the help of gimmicks and tricks like videos and interactive installations, by lowering the threshold, so to speak, would attract more of what she called "urban youth." Those that failed to adopt this new strategy, the ones that insisted on hanging paintings on the walls, would receive reduced subsidies in future.

Rudi Fuchs picked up his pen.

In an op-ed for the *Volkskrant*,[6] he suggested dryly that perhaps he should best advise Ms. Van der Laan that "the Mauritshuis and Rijksmuseum are there to exhibit paintings because they have them." "We have a secretary of culture," he bemoaned, "who doesn't seem to understand that paintings are made to sit silently on a wall, even paintings by Rembrandt and Van Gogh." The magic of these works, said Fuchs, that "you can look at them, and let yourself be swept away by what you see; and while you look, your imagination blossoms, comes alive, filled with all one's individual knowledge and memories and longings. If ten different people stand before [Rembrandt's] *Jewish Bride*, each will see a different one—namely, his or her painting." Sure, said Fuchs, you can recreate a digitalized, modernized version of the *Nightwatch*, but would that really bring "urban youth" into the museum?

"Give me a group of 20 *allochtonen*," declared Fuchs, "and I can explain and convince them of the extraordinary beauty of the *Jewish Bride*. This, I know."

It was a challenge too good to refuse. Editors at the *NRC* took the dare, setting Fuchs up with a group of 15 students, ages 14 and 15, all of them *allochtone*. Then they sent along a reporter.

"This painting," began Fuchs, standing by the *Jewish Bride* and facing his group of students, "belongs to every *Nederlander*—and also to all of you."

How many others had ever said anything like this about a national treasure to these children? My guess is few, if any. Already at the door to the Rijksmuseum, according to the *NRC* account, one of the students had asked Fuchs if he was the owner of the museum. Not even their teacher had explained to these kids, who at 14 and 15 years old should have known already, that this was a national museum, a museum run by the people, with their tax dollars, that the state—and by extension, they themselves—were the collective owners, that Fuchs didn't even work there and never had. He was simply a man who loved art.

And so he posed his question: When you look at this painting, what do you see?

A handful of students offered up suggestions: a married couple. A brother and sister. A couple whose baby has just died.

For each student, another understanding, another vision, another way of seeing.

According to the *NRC*, these students had visited museums on school trips before. And yet, it seemed, no one had ever bothered to engage them. No one had told them stories, or asked them to invent their own, or suggested that one image could have so many interpretations, or that sometimes, you had to look beyond just what you could see.

After the visit, one student told the reporter of an event that he remembered having taken place at his aunt's house once, at a party celebrating the arrival of a new baby. Neighbors had written the word "Moroccan" and a swastika on the front stairs in benzine, he said, and tossed a lighted cigarette at the top. As with Rachid Ben Ali's tales, it almost didn't even matter if it actually was true. The story that it told was real enough.

* * *

Ayaan Hirsi Ali returned to the Netherlands on January 15, 2005, and to public life three days later, arriving at the Parliament surrounded by her customary phalanx of bodyguards and paparazzi. Facing her colleagues and the nation—those who admired her and those who willed her death—she spoke softly, but her voice rang out with the power of her mission. *"Ik ga door,"* she said: "I will go on."

Five days later, Mohammed Bouyeri faced the court to confess, unapologetically, to the murder of Theo van Gogh. The other members of the Hofstad network would be tried separately, each on specific counts, ranging from participation in a terrorist organization to planning to commit a terrorist act; from possession of weapons or their components to the promotion of ideologies of hate; from recruiting for jihad to training at a jihadist camp abroad. Among those tried was Martine van den Oever, a former Dutch policewoman who had also been affiliated with the group. Only one member of the Hofstad network would not be tried: Samir Azzouz, who had already twice been acquitted of charges (for which there had been abundant evidence) of planning terrorist attacks on Schiphol airport and various government properties. By law (and by logic), Azzouz could not be tried again for taking part, even as a group member, in crimes of which he had already been found not guilty—even if both acquittals had been based on technicalities. (Azzouz would eventually be convicted in December 2006, and sentenced to a prison term of eight years.)

In his own trial, the court gave Mohammed Bouyeri the chance to have the last word. He made full use of it, speaking largely to Theo's mother. "I have to confess," he stated, "that I do not feel what you feel. I do not share your pain. I can't. I do not know what it is to lose a child whom you brought into the world with so much pain and so many tears. In part, this is because I am not a woman. But it is also because you are an unbeliever." To the court, he added that he had not acted out of anger at Van Gogh. "The story about me being insulted as a Moroccan, because he called us 'goatfuckers'—this is simply not true. I acted out of my faith. If he had been my father or my brother, I'd have done the same. . . . I can assure you, were I to go free, I would do exactly the same. Exactly the same."

Bouyeri had requested the death penalty—the better to be martyred—but he was to be disappointed. On July 26, the court sentenced him to life in prison. As officers escorted him from the room, Lieuwe van Gogh, Theo's now-14-year-old son, called out after him, "I'll send you a card."[7]

* * *

But it was Ayaan who would soon receive a card, sent by Rita Verdonk, her colleague in the VVD. Since her return to Holland, Hirsi Ali had lived a dismal existence, moving from one safe house to the next, living in military barracks and hotel rooms, constantly on the move. At a given point, she—and Wilders, who was enduring a similar arrangement—had had enough. She demanded a home for each of them, and got it—in her case, in a towering, modern apartment building with glorious views in the chicest neighborhood of The Hague. But her happiness there was short-lived; neighbors soon voiced their annoyance at the heightened security measures they confronted, and argued that, as a terror risk herself, she was putting their lives at risk as well by living there. Not only that, they said, but she was affecting—negatively—the value of their homes. Together, they sued to have Hirsi Ali evicted, and won.

In May 2006, Hirsi Ali was profiled on a popular evening TV news program, *Zembla*. The report, which purported to be an investigative exposé of her life and activities in the Netherlands and prior to her arrival, included mention of the well-known fact that she had provided a false name—Ali, not Magan—on entering the country. There was nothing new in this. Hirsi Ali had spoken of it often, and had even pointed it out to the VVD before accepting their invitation to join them in the Parliament. According to *Zembla*, however, Ayaan had continued the charade when applying for citizenship in 1997, again using the name Hirsi Ali and a false date of birth. The problem was that doing so was against the law—a law that Hirsi Ali had herself defended.

The card arrived on May 15. "The decree that naturalized you," it read, "is void."[8] Verdonk had revoked her citizenship. Ayaan was not only without a home, but now, too, without a country.

The national uproar that ensued stretched into every corner of the Netherlands. "The law is the law," said Rita Verdonk. "Rules are rules." She had already deported others previously for lying on their applications. "My hands are tied," she had said then. It was what she said now. If they had had to go, so, too, did Ayaan.

Frustrated by her living situation, however, Hirsi Ali had already begun seeking a job in Washington, D.C. Now that she was no longer Dutch, she could no longer remain a member of Parliament, anyway. Quietly, she accelerated the negotiations that had already been underway with the American Enterprise Institute, a think tank based in Washington, D.C.

Complications followed. Stateless, she could not receive a visa to live and work in the United States. And yet she also could not remain in Holland. A crack legal team was assembled—ironically, from the same firm that had defended members of the Hofstadgroep. One able member of the team, researching frantically, found the solution: "Ali" had been the last name of one of her ancestors. By Somali law, this made it her last name, too—just as Magan was. Though she hadn't even known it at the time, technically, she hadn't really lied.

Within days, an agreement was reached. Verdonk would reinstate Hirsi Ali's citizenship if Ayaan would sign a statement accepting blame for the entire mess and agreeing to use the name "Ali" henceforth. Trapped in statelessness and with no other options, she signed.

News of the arrangement traveled quickly back to Parliament. On top of everything else, it seemed, Verdonk had now actually blackmailed Hirsi Ali. The D66 party entered a no-confidence motion, and matters only descended from there. On June 19, 2006, the government of the Netherlands collapsed again.

* * *

Hirsi Ali was not the only one driven away that year. In Holland, as elsewhere in Europe, Sinterklaas and his helpers arrive each year a few weeks before Christmas, parading through villages and cities, scattering gifts and leaving special surprises for young children. But lately, Sinterklaas's helpers, who appear in blackface, had been the subject of dispute: some said they looked this way because their faces had been blackened by soot as they ran down chimney after chimney distributing gifts to Europe's children; but others claimed the blackface harkened to colonialist days, and that the helpers were no more than slaves. As a result, resistance to the event had grown. In the Transvaalwijk, an immigrant neighborhood in The Hague, violence had even broken out the year before. And so it was announced in November 2006, that Sinterklaas would not be coming there this year.

Banished, too, that year, were the *negerzoenen*, literally translated as "nigger kisses," a chocolate-covered marshmallow treat that had been part of Dutch tradition since the 1940s. No more. Now they would simply be called "kisses."

I found this utterly inane. Also popular in the Netherlands is something called *jodenkoekjes*—Jew cookies. One imagines they were first invented by a Jewish baker, but no one seems to know for certain. And yet Jews had never protested—and neither had anybody else. No one shirked from the implication of Jews being put into the oven to bake. *Jodenkoekjes* they have always been, and *jodenkoekjes* they remain, tucked on grocers' shelves among the "kisses."

It wasn't just in Holland, either. A year earlier, Christopher Marlowe's 1580s *Tamburlaine the Great* was revised for London audiences—or, one might say, censored: a scene in which a Koran is burned was replaced by the burning of several generic books, and references to Mohammed were scrapped. In Germany, a Berlin opera house cancelled performances of Mozart's *Idomeneo*, in which the severed heads of Buddha, Jesus, and Mohammed are displayed across the stage. A furious Chancellor Angela Merkel responded, "It is not forbidden in Germany to feel hurt; you also don't have to go to the opera." But, she added, "about freedom of art, freedom of speech, the press, opinion, religion, there can be no argument about that. There can be no compromises here."[9] In the end, the play went on, without incident, after all.

And why not? It had been the *Jewish Bride* that Fuchs had presented to his Muslim students. They themselves had told the *NRC* that their favorite Amsterdam museum was the Anne Frank House. Rachid Ben Ali, despite the threats, never once considered pulling down his exhibition.

Theo van Gogh would have surely applauded Chancellor Merkel.

"Art," Rudi Fuchs had written in his response to Medy van der Laan, "encourages the agility of the spirit. That notion, that idea, I hold as one of the most important of all our 'norms and values.'"

CHAPTER 19

"Help wanted. Moroccans need not apply."

The memo circulated in July 2009, just as summer holidays were beginning and students were out seeking summer jobs. Sent to the managers of Albert Heijn express shops at train stations in Amsterdam and The Hague, it enumerated the qualities managers should seek in hiring summer help: no older than 18 years of age, willing to work from 7:00 A.M. to 10:00 A.M. or 4:00 P.M. to closing, and, the memo noted: "No Moroccans."

Sent—complete with a misspelling of the word "Moroccans"—by someone at Servex, the firm that ran these shops under license from Albert Heijn, the memo became public only after one employee happened to spot it in the trash bin of the store's computer, and sent it onward to anti-discrimination groups to investigate. When the story hit the press, the *NRC* opened up a discussion on its Web site: What did readers think?

"Shocking," came the first response, submitted by someone who also wondered whether Moroccans were subject to random ID checks on the street. The next poster, however, took a different point of view. "It's terrible," he said, "but the Moroccans have only themselves to blame."

Both were true.

The so-called "Moroccan problem" had continued to deteriorate in Holland even after Hirsi Ali's departure, as social and political tensions worsened. In October 2007, a young Moroccan man, known only as Bilal B., walked into a police station on the August Allebéplein in

Slotervaart—the same square where riots had broken out a decade earlier—jumped across the visitors' counter, and stabbed a policewoman in the chest. Then, as she struggled, he drove the knife into her back, perforating a lung. As another agent intervened, a wild Bilal plunged the knife again, now into the second officer's neck, and then yet again, jamming it into the man's shoulder. The woman he had first attacked grabbed her gun and fired.

As it turned out, Bilal, who died on the spot, had a history of psychotic behavior and had been in and out of institutions over the years. As it also turned out, he already had a file with the AIVD: he'd been associated with the Hofstadgroep and, what's more, had planned, with his brother, to blow up an El Al jet in the summer of 2005.

In the days after the attack, Bilal's family maintained his innocence, arguing that he was simply crazy, that he heard voices in his head. But Bilal had been released from hospital only a short time before the incident took place. Doctors there had found him reasonably sound of mind. Had they been wrong? And what of the friendship he'd had with Bouyeri, and the part about El Al?

Experts started coming forward. "*Allochtonen*," they said, "have a higher incidence of schizophrenia." The stress of living between two worlds, two sets of mores, was beyond what many of them could take. Others pointed to possible genetic factors, exacerbated by the inbreeding of marriages between cousins, common in Muslim culture. A third view, posed by Wim Veling and published in the *American Journal of Psychiatry,* argued that yes, *allochtonen* suffered a higher-than-normal incidence of schizophrenia—but only when they lived in mixed neighborhoods, surrounded mostly by Dutch. So long as they lived among their own, there was no problem.

Bilal lived in a largely Dutch-Moroccan neighborhood. Whatever the cause of his mental instabilities, it wasn't because of the people who lived next door.

And indeed, Bilal had plenty of local, also-Moroccan supporters, who made their views of the incident known in the days that followed. Cars burned. Riots exploded. Someone smashed the windows of the August Allebéplein police station, and others pelted policemen seeking to restore the peace with stones. This, after the area had just received a 400,000-euro subsidy for programs to reduce radicalization of young Muslims in the district. Inspired, at least in part, by similar riots that had recently broken out across Paris, the youth of Slotervaart tore through their neighborhood, terrorizing even their own parents, for weeks.

Or some of the parents. Others quickly defended them, scorning requests by local council leader Ahmed Marcouch (himself Dutch-Moroccan) to keep their children off the streets. Only boredom and fatigue, coupled with the arrival of colder, damper weather, eventually brought the riots to a stop.

Nonetheless, the rest of Holland cracked down. In Utrecht's Muslim neighborhoods, boys were forbidden to stand in groups of more than four. Cruising police vans circled the neighborhood, breaking up groups beyond the limit. Groups of four *hangjongens* stood several feet apart from one another—close enough to call out, but far enough apart to satisfy the law. Transgressions were punished with a 200-euro fine. "Stupid idea," one young man told a reporter from the *Volkskrant*[1]. It would only add to the criminality (which, according to police records, had increased 23 percent in the previous year). "You can't possibly think these guys are going to work to pay these fines, or that that their parents are going to pay them," he observed.

What is remarkable is the two-sided view many of these kids presented. While arguing that their neighborhood was "perfectly fine," that negative impressions were largely a result of media hype, the boys who spoke to the *Volkskrant* in Utrecht insisted, too, that no one in the area had much future. "See that sweet boy?" one of them asked the reporter, pointing to a dark-haired toddler passing by with his young mother. "When he's 16, he'll be bad, too."

Within a year, encouraged by a new trend among Moroccan boys of attacking ambulance drivers on duty and, in the town of Gouda, regularly throwing stones at the police, even the parents had had enough—as had lawmakers.[2] Discussions opened in defense of curfews: if children under the age of nine were found on the street after 7:00 P.M., their parents would be fined. Though efforts to create such a law failed at the time, the discussions still continue.

But again, would such measures make a difference? Many of these incidents took place during the day, orchestrated by kids who had dropped out of school or had finished their secondary education (which, in Holland, ends when a child is 16). Most of these kids lived with families who owned satellite dishes, from which they watched Arab-sponsored, highly propagandistic, TV. Moreover, the National Coordinator for Counter-Terrorism had, by January 2007, found some 100 to 200 Dutch Web sites promoting radical Islam—this over and above the hundreds, if not thousands, available in Arabic and English. Many provided detailed instructions on bomb-making. Keeping children at home and off the street, especially in homes wracked with violence and abuse, or with radicalized parents, was hardly going to save them. And no, younger than nine years old was not too young.

* * *

"America, I kill," said the five-year-old British boy, as his father, Parvis Kahn, cheered him. "Bush I kill."

Britain's MI5 caught it all on tape, and then some.

In June 2007, two more attempts on British targets failed: a burning Jeep Cherokee packed with canisters of propane gas slammed into the terminal building at Glasgow Airport on June 30, and, a day earlier, two highly-powerful unexploded car bombs were found in London's West End. The bombs, to be triggered by mobile phones, contained nails and 60 liters of petrol; flaws in their construction, again, had kept them from detonating. Investigators determined that the attacks were connected, and that both had been the work of Al Qaeda. Over the next week, police arrested five suspects—four men and one woman. Almost all were doctors and of Indian descent, living in the United Kingdom.

All were also linked to Duren Barot, a British citizen who had converted to Islam from Hinduism. Born in India, he immigrated to England with his family at the age of two. In the 1990s, he spent time in Pakistani training camps for Al Qaeda and allegedly then moved to the United States, where he surveyed American targets as an Al Qaeda agent. On his arrest in 2004, he confessed to plots to bomb the New York Stock Exchange and Citibank buildings, and the World Bank. He was sentenced to life imprisonment with a minimum of 30 years.

Police and MI5 immediately cracked down on South Asian immigrants, keeping an especially close watch on Indian and Pakistani Muslims in "hot" areas like Leeds and Birmingham. It was there they ran into Parvis Khan, a suspect in a plot to murder a Muslim British soldier. In the course of the investigation, officials began recording conversations in his home—conversations, according to the *Guardian*, in which he and his co-conspirator, Hamid Elasmar, appeared to be coaching a child in methods of beheading.[3] Soon, the boy would likely be sent to study at a local mosque, such as the one in Gladstone Park where British researcher Kerry O'Donoghue discovered that young boys were being encouraged to denounce their families and join the fight to retake the world from the Jews "who are assisted by Satan, as personified by all white Christians, especially the British and Americans."[4]

Eventually, too, according to the tapes, Khan's daughter would be married off to a terrorist—or even become one herself. At the time the tapes were made, the girl was three years old.[5]

* * *

Though it wasn't developed with such children in mind, Holland soon began work to create plans for a system that could, theoretically, protect children from such plans for their futures. But at what cost? The electronic children's health dossier, aimed at providing computerized national records of children's health and well-being, would be accessible not only to medical professionals, but also to organizations geared to watching "high risk" youth. Unclear, however, remains, even now, the question of whether doctors would require parental permission to access a file's content, or how the files could be protected from hackers. Even more unclear is the reasoning behind some of the information the government initially wanted these dossiers to contain—such as whether or not a child had developed pubic hair, and if so what color it is, whether it is straight or curly, or whether the child has ever engaged in sex with someone of his or her own gender. (As of this writing, the dossier project remains under parliamentary discussion and has not yet been put into effect.)

Yet despite such intrusive (and unnecessary) questions, the dossier plan does not seem to protect children like Kahn's from being turned into jihadists, or married off at the whim and fancy of their fathers—nor, by turn, does it protect the rest of society from them—even as it could. Questions to be posed do not, for instance, include things like "Do your parents want you to marry? Do you want this?", "Are you permitted to take swimming classes at school?", "Does your father punish you? How?"—all questions which both medical experts and social workers—those for whom the dossier is ostensibly intended—need answered.[6] To the contrary, in fact, lawmakers throughout Europe (and Canada as well) have, in some cases, acted to endanger such children, and with them, their mothers, defending and even encouraging the application of sharia law.

Dutch justice minister Piet-Hein Donner was among the first to broach the idea, stating in 2006, "If two thirds of all Dutch want to institute sharia tomorrow, then shouldn't that possibility exist? It would be scandalous to say that can't be. The majority counts. That is the essence of democracy."

Even earlier, however, had been the proposal from former Canadian attorney general Marion Boyd, who recommended the incorporation of sharia law in Canada in 2004, advising that it be incorporated into an already-existing system that permitted faith-based tribunals for Catholic and Jewish communities. The outcry reached across the Atlantic as Muslim feminists in Europe protested the motion. Ayaan Hirsi Ali even traveled to Canada to speak against the move. Supporters of the idea argued, in response, that Muslims could not abide by secular law and still be true to their faith; in their view, it was the only viable option. Though the tribunals would only be used to adjudicate family issues—marriages and divorces, primarily—and only with the consent of both parties, women argued that polygamy, valid under sharia but not Canadian law, would therefore be made possible—and yet, since those marriages would have no validity by Canadian law, second and third wives would be deprived of their legal marital rights. Divorcing women would lose custody of their children and rights by Canadian law to spousal support. Moreover, as many Muslim women in Canada further noted, women could be pressured into agreeing to a tribunal, or—especially in the cases of less-educated or illiterate immigrants—might not even know there was another option. Additionally, as a Dutch intelligence report noted (and as discussed earlier), such marriages often serve to help recruit women into jihad.[7]

In September 2005, a wise Premier Dalton McGuinty shot the proposal down.

But the seeds had already been let loose upon the wind. In early 2007, a German judge, Christina Datz-Winter, ruled against a German-Moroccan woman seeking an expedited divorce from her husband, who regularly beat her. (German law requires that couples be separated for a year before a divorce can be granted; that delay can only be waived under "extreme" circumstances.) According to Datz-Winter, the woman should have known, as a Moroccan herself, that her husband would execute his "right to corporal punishment" when she married him. Quoting the Koran's verse 34, sura 4, she noted that men are allowed to hit their wives: "As to those whose part you fear desertion, admonish them and leave them alone on the sleeping places and beat them."

Even the country's Central Council of Muslims decried the judge's ruling. She was soon removed, and a new judge granted the divorce.

Similar scenes, however, soon sprang up in England, Italy, and France, where a judge in Lille granted a Muslim couple an annulment on the grounds that the bride had lied to her husband about her virginity—as if to say, somehow, that the groom hadn't quite gotten what he'd paid for.[8] The ruling sent dozens of Muslim women scrambling for hymenoplasties—already a popular surgical procedure among these groups; the surgery restores a broken hymen, and is frequently performed in backstreet offices, as illegal abortions in the United States used to be.

Italy, too, bent its laws to "accommodate" Muslim culture, as Holland had done decades earlier. Apparently oblivious to the seriousness of honor violence, in March 2009, a Brescia court acquitted a Muslim family who beat their daughter for dating a non-Muslim. The court found that the child had been "beaten for her own good"—a verdict that was upheld by the Italian Supreme Court of Cassation.[9]

But even had the courts not ruled in the family's favor, local sharia tribunals would have—and their numbers were, and are, growing, despite the fact that reports of honor killings and forced marriages continue, not only among uneducated Muslims, but, according to a 2008 study by CIVITAS, a British think tank, among "immigrants who would usually be regarded as 'well-integrated.'"[10] In a horrifying incident in July 2009, two British Muslim men forced sulfuric acid down the throat of a 24-year-old man they accused of having an affair with a married Muslim woman. *Sky News* reported that the victim, according to a witness, "got up and ran straight into a tree, then staggered back to his house, tugging at his burning clothes and banging on doors shouting for water." Added the reporter, "Emergency services found the man wandering around in agony, unable to speak coherently. Firemen eventually hosed him down in the street. Later, it was discovered he had been stabbed twice in the back, hit with bricks and had sulphuric acid thrown over him and forced down his throat."[11]

Despite this, some 85 sharia tribunals stand active in the UK, according to a 2009 study also by CIVITAS. Of these, only five are legally recognized—but the actual influence and impact of the others on the Muslim community is powerful enough that, for the most part, recognition by the secular state doesn't matter. For fundamentalist Muslims, secular law has no meaning, anyway.

But it means a great deal to non-Muslims, or to most of them, and to moderate Muslims living in the West as well—which is why outcries continue as lawmakers, politicians, and communities in the West continue to compromise such laws, either in the name of "tolerance" or in efforts to restrain the influence of an intolerant, radical Islam.

Take, for instance, the case of Gregorius Nekschot, who was arrested in his bed on the morning of May 13, 2008. Officials searched his home and confiscated, among other things, his datebook, his computer, his cell phone, and his sketchbooks: Gregorius Nekschot is a Dutch cartoonist. (The name is a nom de plume, referring—it is said—to fascists, who shot their victims in the neck; his real identity is kept a close secret for security reasons.) Holland, however, is not Denmark, and 2008 was not 2006. Nekschot had published any number of cartoons insulting to Muslims—and they *were* insulting, albeit rather juvenile, with images of Muslims having sex with various wild animals, among other things—and the Dutch government was horrified. Apparently, they hadn't counted on the Dutch public being horrified, as well—by them.

In a way, though, it had been their own fault. After the fall of the cabinet following Hirsi Ali's departure from the Netherlands in 2006, new elections brought Balkenende back into power as prime minister, but with a dramatically changed parliamentary coalition. Voters this time had reached to extremes, electing a cabinet comprised almost equally of parties to the Far Left and to the Far Right. Consequently, though Balkenende's own party, the Christian Democrats, lost seats overall, the Christian Union (as well as Wilders' PVV) gained power, creating a strong Christian-Right base. From its inception, this government has squeezed out many of the "liberal" traditions for which Holland is so famous—proposing higher restrictions for abortions, increasing controls and limitations on "coffeeshops" (and entering into discussions of criminalizing marijuana again entirely), tightening the borders of Amsterdam's Red Light District, and, evidently, arresting cartoonists.

Nekschot's arrest made clear, however, that these restrictions had simply grown out of control. As writer Theodor Holman put it a few days later, "The arrests have begun."[12]

Indeed they had. In June 2009, AIVD agents invaded the home of Jolande van der Graaf, a reporter for national newspaper *De Telegraaf*. Van der Graaf, who was in the shower at the time of their arrival, was ordered into her living room where, guarded by an AIVD agent, she waited for six hours as inspectors ransacked her home, searching for documents they claimed had been given her by an AIVD agent accused of leaking state secrets. (It is a crime in the Netherlands to transmit documents from the AIVD to unauthorized parties, as well as to accept or to be in possession of such documents.) Van der Graaf had earlier written articles accusing the AIVD of irresponsibility in its handling of the situation in Iraq prior to the 2003 U.S. (and Dutch-backed) invasion, claiming they had simply copied reports from Britain's MI6. Other "state secrets" she had apparently published included the secret service's security provisions during a visit from the Dalai Lama.

The press reacted with understandable outrage. "It is absolutely unheard-of in a democracy that a journalist who simply does her work is invaded in her own home by the government," said Arendo Joustra, chairman of the Dutch Society of Editors-in-Chief. What made matters worse was the fact that, despite their insistence that they sought only "documents," the agents had departed Van der Graaf's home with dozens of other items, including things belonging to her young son. More than that, it later became clear that the AIVD had tapped Van der Graaf's phones, as well as those of three of her associates, including the paper's chief and deputy chief editors. Speaking to the press, the newspaper's attorney, B. Le Poole, accused, "All movements of Van der Graaf since 15 January have been minutely examined. Thus not only has a gigantic amount of information been gathered about the publications concerned, but also on other activities. They now also have information on sources that have nothing to do with the matter."[13]

An angry Afshin Ellian, as both a writer and professor of the philosophy of law, reacted strongly, writing in his blog for *Elsevier*, "State security is an extraordinarily large concept; pretty much anything could be considered a matter of 'state security.' Whoever endangers the security of the state potentially endangers our ability . . . to live in a free land. . . . But the concept of state security is also an extraordinarily dangerous one, for it can also be used to endanger democracy.

A country like Iran is a good example, where the powers running the state have, under the banner of 'state security,' confined and oppressed the legitimate freedoms of the country and its people."[14]

But it wasn't just the federal government imposing itself on freedom. In May 2008, local officials in Huizen removed stylized paintings of women with exposed breasts from the walls of their town hall in response to complaints from local Muslims. A week earlier, construction workers in Almere had been reprimanded when Muslims complained about their attire; the country was experiencing a heat wave, with temperatures near 90 degrees, and the men had donned T-shirts and shorts. "No more of that," they were told. Long pants it would be from now on, no matter how uncomfortable, no matter what the risk of heatstroke. That Christmas, the Amsterdam transit company, GVB, even went so far as to cancel its annual Christmas party, arguing that it was "too one-sided" (an observation that came as no news to the Buddhists, Jews, atheists, and others who had worked there for years). What they meant, of course, was that "Muslims would be offended."

Meantime, schools debated closing for Eid, the festival at the end of Ramadan, but not a single published calendar noted the dates of Jewish holidays like Chanukah or Passover (known to the Dutch as "Jewish Easter.")[15]

That wasn't all. In the fall of 2007, the director of the Gemeentemuseum in The Hague—one of the museums that had initially shown interest in exhibiting *Submission* while Ayaan still envisioned it as an art installation—removed photographs by Iranian artist Sooreh Hera from an exhibition of her work, declaring them "potentially insulting to some members of our community."

The images were part of a series of photographs of homosexuals in which the figures are disguised by masks. In one of the offending photos, titled "Adam and Ewald," the masks depict the prophet Mohammed and his son-in-law, Ali.

The response from the Dutch Muslim community was predictable: posts on Web sites like www.marokko.nl called her a "devil artist," "an agent of Zionists busy with plans against Islam." The new Islamic Democratic Party called for a mobilizing of forces. Muslim groups swore to attack the museum if the photographs were included in the exhibition. Dutch art lovers, in return, swore to boycott it if they were not. Hera herself received death threats and spent weeks before the scheduled exhibition on the run. Speaking on *Nova*, a TV news program, she observed, "It's as if an Islamist minority now decides what is and is not on view in a museum."

She was absolutely right.[16]

Unlike what had taken place years earlier in the cases of Chris Ofili, the British artist who incorporated elephant dung into a portrait of a

black Virgin Mary, or Andres Serrano, whose *Piss Christ*—a photograph
of a crucifix dipped into urine—caused an uproar in the United States
when it was shown in 1989, the Gemeentemuseum was not responding
to its own discomfort with the work, or to the discomfort of its sponsors. Ten years earlier, when New York City's Mayor Rudi Giuliani
had threatened to close down the Brooklyn Museum during the time
Ofili's paintings were on view, he was loudly shouted down. But no
one spoke of violence. There were no death threats issued to the artists
as there were to Sooreh Hera.

But that had all been in a different place, and in a very different
time.

* * *

And then there was *Fitna*.

It was going to be the force that did it: set off bombs from Groningen
to Maastricht, hostage-takings at Dutch embassies across the globe, flag
burnings, boycotts, riots in the streets. On March 27, 2008, the night
Fitna, a film by Geert Wilders, was scheduled to be released on a Dutch
Web site, my friend Andrew Bostom e-mailed me from Rhode Island
like an impatient child in the backseat of his father's car: Is it on yet?
he asked me. Is it on yet?

At 7:00 P.M., *Fitna* aired on LiveLeak.com before a Dutch audience of
three million. It lasted just 15 minutes. When it was over, I stood by
my window and waited for the explosions, for the sirens, for the
shouts.

Nothing.

Only silence.

The next day, the media reported that a handful of lone protesters
had stood near the Parliament building in The Hague, carrying a banner that stated simply, "Wilders is a Zionist."

That was all.

Fitna was Wilders' own *Submission* project, as it were—a film meant
to show the dangers of Islamic extremism and the threat it poses to
Western culture and society. Long before the film was even made, politicians, pundits, bloggers, and the media—not just in Holland, but
around the world—speculated about its contents. Wilders, eager to
feed the PR machine, encouraged all manner of rumors. He would
burn a Koran on camera, some said. He would rip a Koran to shreds,
one page at a time. He had, by this time, already compared the Koran
to *Mein Kampf*, a remark for which the courts threatened to prosecute
him on the grounds that it constituted hate speech. (A higher court
later dropped the charge, only to have it reinstated a year later.) Dutch
embassies abroad received evacuation plans. The Taliban, along with

Syria's Grand Mufti, threatened attacks on Holland should the film ever come to light. Prime Minister Balkenende made a show of distancing himself from Wilders, explaining that just because Wilders was a member of the Parliament of the Netherlands, it didn't mean he was a representative of the Netherlands. Dutch imams gave sermons calling for calm, in concert with instructions from the AIVD and local agencies. The *NRC* counted 50 articles and op-eds about the film in the *Volkskrant* alone, all in the first weeks after Wilders announced his plan to create it. All this for something that did not yet exist.

The unsurprising outcome of it all was the transformation of Geert Wilders from a local crank to an international star. By the time *Fitna* came out, the whole world was watching.

It wasn't that big a deal. The film consisted essentially of Koran texts that extol violence against infidels, intercut with film footage of terrorist attacks and Muslims calling for jihad. Voice-overs and graphics warned of more to come. While I stood watching for the bombs all expected, Muslims the world over shrugged their collective shoulders and continued with their days.

For non-Muslims, however, it was a wholly different story. Anti-Islam activists celebrated Wilders as their new hero, as the man who'd had the courage to confront the West with the truth of "Islamofascism" and the dangers it posed to our future. To other non-Muslims, he was a racist and a hatemonger, a bleached-haired neo-Nazi menace to the world.

Was it propaganda? The images he used are real. The suras from the Koran exist. There was nothing, in fact, untrue about anything that Wilders or his film had had to say. For Wilders, the West had spent too long denying and avoiding certain truths, hoping they would surely go away. They have not, of course, and we all know that it is folly to believe they will.

The problem was in what he didn't say: that not every Muslim is radical, that radical Islamists represent a powerful, but small minority of Muslims, that even Muslims themselves are in danger. These omissions, to more than a few, were unforgivable, and many responded to Wilders and his film with fury. The matter was only made worse with Wilders' repeated insistence that Holland ban the Koran outright—a statement that has been grossly misrepresented by most international media, who seemed to miss the point he's making: that if *Mein Kampf* is banned—and in the Netherlands, it is—so, too, should be the Koran. The truth is that Wilders is against all forms of book banning and the silencing of all free expression.

Nonetheless, between such assertions and the creation of his film, Wilders quickly became the great European pariah. In February 2009, a law introduced by Tony Blair in response to the July 2004 attacks that would deny entry to "those who would promote hate" was used to block Geert Wilders from entering the United Kingdom—even as days earlier, Dyab Abou Jahjah had been permitted in while in transit between Brussels and Lebanon. (A public outcry, however, resulted in his being refused entry on his return. In a statement posted to his Web site, Jahjah blamed "the Zionists and their stooges.") Noted *Financial Times* columnist Simon Kuper in an op-ed published in the *NRC Handelsblad* after Wilders was sent back to Holland, in a post-cold war era, "now that democracy seems safe in the West, it is easier to constrain it."[17]

At home, however, Wilders was only gaining popularity. Poll after poll showed that *Fitna* had hit a nerve; were Dutch Parliamentary elections to have been held in 2009, Wilders would likely have been made prime minister. (By contrast, the once-popular "Iron" Rita Verdonk received no show of support at all.)

Now politicians paid attention. In Rotterdam, measures to prohibit forced marriages were introduced in early 2009. Laws against the circumcision of girls were more strictly enforced, with penalties imposed on parents who had the surgeries performed abroad. Women were no longer permitted to refuse medical help from a male doctor—a problem in the Muslim communities in the past, especially in cases of childbirth.

In June 2009, Europe held its seventh parliamentary elections. If nationalism had been clear at the signing of the Maastricht treaty, now it had become deafening: 67 percent of voters stayed home, disillusioned with the entire notion of a unified Europe. Digging their heels in, they wanted, rather, their own cultures, their own societies, identities, "values and norms."[18] Those who did vote made clear just how much they meant it: Far Right, nationalist, and populist parties gained overwhelmingly. Europeans, it was clear, had had enough of Europe's immigrants, and enough of trying to appease them. They didn't want burqas, and they were tired of discussing it. They wanted something done about the honor killings, the gay hate, the demands for classes taught in Arabic by a population that could not even speak the languages of its homelands—German, Spanish, Italian, English, Dutch. They were tired of having intelligence agencies listening to their phone calls, watching their movements on the sidewalks, monitoring the books they read, and arresting cartoonists they didn't like. They were tired of seeing Mozart messed with, and photographers and comedians fearing for their lives.

The irony was: this time, it was the Muslims who decided to leave. Following Wilders' massive success in the elections (the PVV zoomed from zero seats of Holland's allotted 25 to four, putting them in second place, while the other Dutch parties all lost seats), the *NRC Handelsblad* announced, "More than half the people with Turkish and Moroccan backgrounds in the Netherlands say they would consider leaving the country due to the growing popularity of anti-Islam politician Geert Wilders. A third say they would definitely like to emigrate."[19] Moreover, another survey showed that not only were Muslims in Holland the most unhappy in all of Europe, but that while most second-generation Moroccan immigrants visit mosques less often than their parents, the trend is reversed in the Netherlands: half of the immigrants' children visit the places of worship, four percent more than the first generation.

Everything, then, had failed.

Once again, as they often had, pundits asked why it was that Europe could not get immigration and integration right, and the United States had done it all so well.

But had they?

CHAPTER 20

The ashes and the dust that whitened downtown Manhattan for months after September 11, 2001, are long gone now.[1] The fires that burned for nearly half a year where those two great towers once presided over the city skyline have grown cold. Once-welcomed security restrictions at airports have become the subjects of gripes, never mind late-night TV. American politicians who raise the specter of terrorism face accusations of fear-mongering and, for the most part, the media and the public have lost interest. All the major attacks since then—successful and no—have taken place on foreign soil, and unlike the 9/11 hijackings, have involved homegrown, not foreign jihadists. "America doesn't have that problem," various pundits pronounce on shows like *Larry King Live* and *Meet the Press*. "It won't happen here."

But it is happening "here."

In fact, in 2007, the Council on Foreign Relations stated in a backgrounder report, "Experts say it is quite likely that the next terrorist attack will not be the work of well-trained al Qaeda operatives sent from abroad, but rather that of an American citizen. As al Qaeda leaders focus more of their energy on trying to inspire others to commit acts of terror, most security and counterterrorism officials believe their message will resonate with at least some small number of Americans."[2]

In the United States, as in Europe, the Islamist threat is double-edged: violent and ideological. Ultimately, both point to the same goal: the establishment of an Islamic state, a planting of the flag of Islam where the flags of democracy now wave. Although the "terrorism" we hear about is the kind that invokes death and destruction, bombings and burnings and shootings, there is another kind of jihad, a more insidious, quiet version. It is this, what author Robert Spencer calls "stealth jihad," that has most American counterterrorism and intelligence experts concerned. And it is this form of jihad to which America remains the most vulnerable, as lawmakers sit by and do nothing.

But violence there is, too, and the link from one to the other, it appears, is one no one can predict—or, worse, control.

Daniel Patrick Boyd, a blond, all-American father of two, drove a brown pickup truck sporting a "Support Our Troops" bumper sticker on the back. Growing up in the suburbs of Washington, D.C., he played on his high school football team before moving to Raleigh, North Carolina, with his childhood sweetheart and their three sons (the youngest later died in a car accident). On July 27, 2009, state law enforcement, accompanied by four SWAT teams, arrested Boyd at his home on suspicion of "conspiring to support terrorists" and related charges. Earlier, having converted to Islam as a teen, Boyd had fought in Pakistan and Afghanistan, battling alongside the mujahideen against the Soviet Union. According to the *Washington Post*, court papers claimed that Boyd, on his return to the United States, "devoted himself to instructing young men that 'violent jihad was a personal obligation on the part of every good Muslim.'"[3]

Boyd was not alone. Arrested with him were his two sons, Zakariya (20) and Dylan (22), as well as Hysen Sherifi, a 24-year-old legal resident from Kosovo; Mohammed Oma Aly Hassan, 22; and Zijad Yaghi, 21, both U.S. citizens living in North Carolina. The group was charged with a variety of offenses ranging from "receiving a firearm through interstate commerce" and "making false statements in a terrorist investigation" to "conspiracy to murder, kidnap, maim, and injure persons abroad."[4] At their indictment, FBI Special Agent Owen Harris put the issue clearly: "The threat that extremists and radicals pose to America and our allies has not dulled or gone away. These arrests today show there are people living among us, in our communities in North Carolina and around the US that are honing their skills to carry out acts of murder and mayhem. Their ultimate goal is to wage war on freedom and democracy."

The North Carolina arrests came only months after the conviction of 44-year-old Ohio native Christopher Paul, who was sentenced to 20 years for conspiring to build weapons of mass destruction to be used against U.S. and European targets, and after American-born, Little Rock, Arkansas resident Abdulhakim Jujahid Muhammad opened fire on an army recruiting station, killing one soldier and wounding another. ("Tell me this isn't real," the surviving soldier, who was on break at the time, was heard to say as he crawled back into the recruiting station after being shot, "Tell me this isn't real.")[5] Even more ominously, the arrests followed by mere days the release of court papers in the case of Bryant Neal Vinas, another football fan who had also converted to Islam. A former soldier in the U.S. Army, Vinas had grown up in a Long Island suburb where he had been both an altar boy and Boy Scout; but in January 2009, he pleaded guilty to providing aid to Al Qaeda and conspiring to murder American nationals.

And as this was going on in the United States, rioters in the streets of Tehran protested against the ruling Ayatollah Khameini and President Mahmoud Ahmadinejad, calling for a free and democratic Iran. In response, the protesters—many of them women—were beaten, arrested, even killed.

There could be little argument with Owen Harris's statement.

After his arrest, Vinas turned informer, confessing that he'd provided Al Qaeda operatives with information about the Long Island Railroad. That information became part of a plot to bomb a Long Island Railroad train inside New York City's Pennsylvania Station, the city's main railway station located below Madison Square Garden and nearby Herald Square—home to the flagship Macy's department store. Five years earlier, just days before the Republican National Convention was to begin in New York City, police had arrested two other men, Shahawar Matin Siraj, a 23-year-old immigrant from Pakistan, and James Elshafay, the son of an Egyptian father and Irish mother who had grown up in Long Island City and graduated from Brooklyn College. The two were charged with plotting to blow up the New York City subway station at Herald Square/Penn Station, one of the city's busiest. (Officials noted, however, that at the time of their arrest, neither Siraj nor Elshafay had actually obtained any weapons for such an attack.)

The North Carolina case also closely followed the indictments of four men said to be planning to shoot down military planes at an Air National Guard air base in Newburgh, New York and to bomb two synagogues in Riverdale, the Bronx. I know those synagogues; dozens of my friends attended Hebrew school and were bar- or bat-mitzvahed there.

James Cromitie, the African-American leader of the would-be synagogue bombers, however, evidently did not. "I hate those motherfuckers, those fucking Jewish bastards," he allegedly told an FBI informant who had infiltrated the group early in the planning process. By the time of their arrest, the plotters had made significant progress, already having procured the bombs and missiles needed for their attacks. What they did not know was that the explosives and the missile had been supplied by the FBI, and were entirely inert.

Though at this writing, no evidence has indicated a connection between Cromitie and his American-born cronies (David Williams,

Onta Williams, and Laguerre Payen) and any organized terror network, authorities believe that they had all previously converted to Islam in prison, where several such groups actively recruit members—including most of those who have been involved in other foiled terror plots in the United States.[6]

Indeed, according to a 2006 report from George Washington University's Homeland Security Policy Institute (in conjunction with the University of Virginia's Critical Incident Analysis Group), "the potential for radicalization of prison inmates in the United States poses a threat of unknown magnitude to the national security of the U.S."[7]

Moreover, while a New York Police Department (NYPD)'s August 2007 report on radicalization in the homeland states that "unassimilated Muslims are vulnerable to extremism,"[8] the vast majority of the 24 foiled plots against the United States since 9/11 (and the one additional terrorist rampage of the Washington Sniper, who shot and killed eleven people over a course of three weeks in October 2002) have involved American-born, U.S. citizens—not unassimilated immigrants. Even before 9/11, U.S. natives like Clement Rodney Hampton-El were among those involved in the 1993 World Trade Center bombing. Hampton-El, a Brooklyn, New York, resident, was a member of Jama'at Al-Fuqra, a sizable, international organization founded by Sheikh Mubarik Ali Hasmi Shah Gilani, who is also alleged to have ordered the 2002 kidnapping and murder of journalist Daniel Pearl. (John Allen Mohammad, the Washington Sniper, is also said to have been a member.) Al Fuqra maintains locked communities throughout the United States with a headquarters in Hancock, New York, near the Catskills. Other Al Fuqra groups have formed in Virginia, South Carolina, Brooklyn, California, Tennessee, and Georgia, with an outpost in Combermere, Ontario.

Many of these settlements are unmistakable, particularly in Hancock, where signs identify Al Fuqra territory as "Islamburg." Generally speaking, however, Al Fuqra settlements are easy to spot, wherever they may be: they're the ones where members engage in paramilitary training, where gunshots ring out regularly and where children only attend schools inside the campground. Some members maintain jobs in the outside world. Others receive welfare. In either case, tithing is considerable—up to 100 percent, according to some reports. One former member told a terrorism expert I spoke to that people occasionally also carried as much as $10,000 in cash to Pakistan to fund Gilani's activities there.

Over the years, Al Fuqra members, including Hampton-El, have compiled a long list of convictions for violent crimes and terrorist incidents and plans, from the 1993 World Trade Center bombing to plots to bomb the United Nations, the Federal Building, and various tunnels and landmarks throughout the country. A March 2002 story in the *Weekly Standard* noted that "at least a dozen Fuqra members have been convicted of crimes including conspiracy to commit murder, firebombing, gun smuggling, and workers' compensation fraud in the United States and Canada. And Fuqra members are suspects in at least ten unsolved assassinations and 17 fire bombings between 1979 and 1990."[9] Evidence has also linked "shoe bomber" Richard Ried to the organization.

Al Fuqra is not new. Begun when Gilani visited the United States in 1980, the organization has relied on recruiting African-American Muslim converts, many from inner cities and from prisons, and another group, Dar ul Islam, for its growth. Some claim that Al Fuqra members frequently travel to Pakistan for training.

The organization first attracted public notice in 1989, when police raided a storage locker owned by Al Fuqra members in Colorado Springs. What they found there were the makings of a small war, described in an Anti-Defamation League document as: "a hoard of explosives, military manuals, bomb-making instructions and detailed plans of the sect's intended targets. The materiel found at the site included 30 pounds of explosives, three large pipe bombs, and ten handguns and silencers" along with other "bomb-making components such as electric wiring, fuses, mercury switches and timing devices."[10]

To deflect scrutiny, Al Fuqra now maintains various front groups, some of which act as charitable organizations. Hands to Hands, for instance, which poses, according to one investigator, as an "Islamic faith-based organization that brings disaster relief to Katrina victims," raises significant sums for Al Fuqra settlements and activities, and, possibly, for Gilani's operations in Pakistan.

Or there is the "Muslims of the Americas," a sort of nom de guerre for Al Fuqra, described by the Anti-Defamation League as "a virulently anti-Semitic, Islamic extremist group with ties to Al Fuqra."

But Al Fuqra is not the only organization busy in the prisons. Since September 11, 2001, according to the George Washington University study, "several individuals who were radicalized while incarcerated have been involved in terrorist organizations."[11] In a way, it makes sense: those who feel the United States has let them down, who may have felt the boot-heel of racism, who feel, in one way or another, betrayed, make ideal recruits. Some have even started their own groups or have organized attacks while serving time. Jose Padilla (aka Abdulla al-Majahir), the so-called "dirty bomber" convicted in 2008 of conspiracy to murder individuals in a foreign country, also encountered Islam—and radicalization—while serving time for manslaughter as a juvenile.[12] And Kevin James, an inmate at California State Prison in Sacramento since 1996, for instance, is believed to have been at the center of a 2005 terrorist plot described by the FBI as "the one that operationally was closest to actually occurring" since 9/11. Kevin James's organization, Jam'yyat Al-Islam Al-Saheeh, or JIS, which he founded in 1997, stands accused of orchestrating attacks against military recruitment centers, synagogues, and Israeli government agencies in the Los Angeles area, and attempting to finance these and other plots through gas station robberies. One-time Folsom State Prison inmate Levar Washington was arrested in conjunction with the robberies; he had converted to Islam and joined JIS at Folsom, where, a member of the California prison guards union claimed in a Voice of America interview, the organization had maintained a presence since even before the September 11 attacks. According to a statement from former attorney general Alberto Gonzalez, "Kevin James allegedly preached that it was a duty of JIS members to kill 'infidels'—perceived enemies of Islam. James's definition of the enemies of Islam included U.S. government personnel, supporters of Israel, and Jewish Americans. To achieve his extremist goals, James allegedly sought to establish 'cells' of JIS members outside of prison to carry out the violent attacks."

Not that finding religion in prison is anything new, of course—but so-called "jailhouse Islam" isn't the "religion of peace" many Muslims preach. Instead, it tends toward the kind of pro-jihadist, anti-Western, political Islam associated with terror groups and the most conservative forms of Islamism. A strong Saudi Wahhabist presence prevails in the U.S. jails, where Wahhabist propaganda and versions of the Koran circulate widely, and imams sanctioned by Saudi Wahhabists lead prayers and lessons on Islam.

Consequently, much of the radicalization that occurs in the U.S. prisons ultimately can be traced directly to Saudi influences: New York Senator Charles "Chuck" Schumer has stated, in fact, that "there is mounting evidence that Saudi-sponsored groups are trying to hijack mainstream Islam here in the United States—in mosques, in schools, and even in prisons and the military—and replace it with Wahhabism." Equally influential are members of the Muslim Brotherhood, the radical Islamist movement founded in Egypt in 1928 by Hassan Al-Banna, a schoolteacher, as part of an opposition motion against the British-backed Egyptian monarchy, and aimed at removing Western influences. Over the years, it has spread internationally, becoming one of the largest and most powerful Muslim groups in the world, with a solid, if secretive, presence in the United States. As a result, in many ways, despite the radicalization problem among Europe's immigrant Muslims, the influence of Muslim Brotherhood groups on Americans—and its success rate in converting new Muslims—may

make the United States an even more fertile source for jihadism than
is Europe.

* * *

In 2004, the *Chicago Tribune* published an extraordinary, in-depth ex-
amination of the Brotherhood, whose goal, journalists Noreen S.
Ahmed-Ullah, Sam Roe, and Laurie Cohen wrote, is "to create Muslim
states overseas and, they hope, someday in America as well."[13]

The Muslim Brotherhood slogan, "Allah is our goal; the Messenger
is our model; the Koran is our constitution; jihad is our means; and
martyrdom in the way of Allah, our inspiration," cogently sums up the
group's purpose—and its threat to Western culture. According to the
Chicago Tribune, the first U.S. chapter of the Brotherhood appeared in
the early 1960s, "after hundreds of young Muslims came to the US to
study, particularly at large Midwestern universities such as Illinois, In-
diana, and Michigan. Some belonged to the Brotherhood in their homelands, and wanted to spread its ideology here."[14]

And spread it, they have. One former Brotherhood member told the
Tribune that "the U.S. Brotherhood had a plan for achieving Islamic
rule in America: it would convert Americans to Islam and elect like-
minded Muslims to political office." "If the Brotherhood puts somebody up for an election," he told the *Tribune's* reporters, Muslims
"would vote for him not knowing he was with the Brotherhood."

Inamul Haq, a religion professor at Benedictine University in Lisle,
Illinois, also told the *Tribune,* "They're in a position to define American
Islam."

Over the years, the Muslim Brotherhood has further founded branch
groups such as the Islamic Society of North America (ISNA), many of
which have since distanced themselves from the Brotherhood—at least
publicly. In 1993, the group rebranded itself under the name "Muslim
American Society," (not to be confused with "Muslims of the Americas") which insists it is not really the Brotherhood anymore. "With 53
chapters around the country, however, the Society has raised $2.8 mil-
lion in 2003," the *Tribune* reports, "more than ten times the amount in
1997, according to Internal Revenue Service filings."

Like the Muslim Brotherhood, the Muslim American Society (MAS)
insists that jihad is a "divine right" of Muslims in order to defend
themselves and to spread Allah's word, and—also like the Brotherhood
and Saudi groups—the MAS subsidizes propaganda and the spread of
Salafist and anti-Western literature through youth centers, schools, and
mosques, as well as through its own schools, which train teachers and
imams—many of whom then take on jobs as prison clergy. The *Chicago*

Tribune reporters note that a Muslim American Society Web page geared to Chicago-area teens "states that 'until the nations of the world have functionally Islamic governments, every individual who is careless or lazy in working for Islam is sinful.'" It is a message that plays well with the recruiters and many imams at prisons, where, as in Europe, a literally captive audience of young criminals may be vulnerable to assurances of salvation and forgiveness for their crimes: Become active as a Muslim pursuing the goal of an Islamic state, and you will wash yourself of your sins. Such ideas marry well, too, with those of Saudi Wahhabists, whom law enforcement officials say have infiltrated not only prisons, but community centers, bookstores, university Muslim Student Associations, and schools.

Much of the literature distributed in the schools of Saudi Arabia promotes global jihad, asserts the justness of killing apostates and homosexuals, and declares the "Protocols of Zion" accurate. That material, which has reached the schools, mosques, bookstores, and community centers of Holland, the UK, Germany, and doubtless other European countries, is also very much a part of the Muslim experience in the United States. A New York Police Department report observed, "The jihadist ideology combines the extreme minority interpretation (jihadi Salafi) [*sic*] of Islam with an activist-like commitment or responsibility to solve global political grievances through violence. Ultimately, the jihadist envisions a world in which jihadi-Salafi Islam is dominant and is the basis of government. This ideology is proliferating in Western democracies at a logarithmic rate. The Internet, certain Salafi-based NGOs, extremist sermons/study groups, Salafi literature, jihadi videotapes, extremist-sponsored trips to radical madrassas and militant training camps abroad have served as 'extremist incubators' for young, susceptible Muslims—especially ones living in diaspora communities in the West."[15]

No one has had more power—or money—to do this than Saudi Arabia.

"In a costly and quietly insistent campaign to spread its state religion, Saudi Arabia has been trying for decades to induce American Muslims to become followers of the puritanical, Islamic sect that sustains the power of the Saudi royal family," declared the *New York Times* in October 2001.[16] In an article the likes of which we sadly—and strangely—rarely see anymore, the *Times* noted that the Saudis, "have spent hundreds of millions of dollars in an effort to stamp their austere version of Islam on the lives of Muslims in the United States."[17]

"Austere" is a measured word. Wahhabist Islam is the foundation on which Al Qaeda and the Muslim Brotherhood are based. Saudi monies subsidize ISNA, which in turn trains imams for the U.S. Bureau of Prisons—and the U.S. military. And the *New York Times* quotes a Saudi charity official who claimed that "half the mosques and Islamic schools in the United States have been built with money from Saudi Arabia."[18]

That money, of course, also subsidizes the materials used there—the same materials they use in the schools back home. Despite efforts by the U.S. government to restrict them, countless investigations have shown that these materials continue to be used, while many public schools are pressed to create presentations on Islam and the Koran. A New York City public school, the Khalil Gibran International Academy, came under fire in 2007 when its principal, Dhabah Almontaser, defended T-shirts emblazoned with the words "Intifada USA"; and in Virginia, the Saudi-funded Islamic Saudi Academy has been the subject of investigations by (among others) the U.S. Commission on International Religious Freedom, which found that its textbooks extolled violence.

What is especially remarkable about these efforts, as noted in the *Times*, is the deliberate focus on the African-American community; more than 200 black imams had received Saudi-sponsored training by October 2001, according to the *Times*. California imam Faheem Shuaibe told the *Times*, "There was a very deliberate recruitment process by the Saudis, trying to find black Muslims" vulnerable to their agenda. "They taught Islam with the intent to expand their influence," he said. The aim, he told the *Times*, "was to stop the indigenous Muslim leadership in America from tinkering with the religion." Over 30 percent of American Muslims are African-American.

What's more, blacks constitute a majority of the prison population, where until recently, Nation of Islam predominated. Approaching a Nation of Islam preacher and bringing him to the Wahhabi fold was not difficult—and certainly made access to incarcerated blacks much easier. "If you have a black American chaplain appealing to the prison population on the basis of Islam," says *Stealth Jihad* author Robert Spencer, "he will often be approached by brotherhood-linked groups and brought more in line with traditional Islam operating under the auspices of Nation of Islam while at the same time in conjunction with the Brotherhood." Beyond that, Spencer adds, "The Nation of Islam is then aided and abetted in its practice of grievance-mongering against whites in the US, which is then channeled towards [Wahhabi] Islam."[19]

In total, according to the October 2001 *Times* article, of two million American Muslims who regularly attend mosque, 25 percent subscribe to Wahhabist thought—which, if accurate, paints a horrifying picture of Saudi success. Do 500,000 Wahhabists really live among us, in U.S. cities and towns?

CHAPTER 21

The strength of Saudi influence, however, goes further—and it is here where the United States diverges most distinctly from its European counterparts. The relationships between Saudi investments and U.S. corporate, educational, and even military infrastructure form intricate, complex webs that represent a significant factor in the threat to U.S. security and democracy.

It is not, for instance, only Islamic schools that receive funds from Wahhabi interests: in 2005, Saudi Arabia's Prince Alwaleed Bin Talal, listed by *Forbes* magazine among the world's wealthiest men, donated $20 million each to Harvard and Georgetown Universities to fund Islamic study centers. He has also given $500,000 to the George H. W. Bush Scholarship fund at the prestigious Phillips Academy in Andover, Mass. In itself, this appears benign, even beneficent; United States-Muslim relations could certainly benefit from each culture learning more about the other. But given the educational materials circulating through other Saudi-sponsored schools, how can we be sure the same materials won't be part of the Phillips, Georgetown, and Harvard programs?

The answer is: we can't, and not just because the donor is a Saudi prince. The problem is that the donor is *this* Saudi prince, a man whose effort to donate $10 million to the city of New York following the September 11 attacks was accompanied by a statement essentially blaming the United States, urging the country to "adopt a more balanced stance toward the Palestinian state." Mayor Rudy Giuliani refused the offer. And well he might have; the prince's largess has also extended to Palestinian suicide bombers, to whose families he has given an estimated

$27 million in gifts—even more than he donated to Harvard and Georgetown, and nearly triple what he offered to the thousands of victims of the terrorist attacks perpetrated largely by his own subjects on the city of New York.

Unlike Giuliani, however, former treasury secretary Lawrence Summers, who was Harvard's president at the time, gratefully accepted the gift—even as enormous pressure from students had earlier forced him to return a $2.5 million gift to Harvard's Divinity School from United Arab Emirates president Sheikh Zayed bin Sultan al Nahyan, whose UAE-based Zayed Center promotes anti-American conspiracy theories and Holocaust denials. (Summers, notably, now serves as President Obama's director of the National Economic Council and Assistant to the President for Economic Policy.)

Prince Alwaleed's holdings—and his influence—do not end, however, at Harvard's gate. The billionaire prince also owns a five percent stake in Citigroup, as well as considerable shares in Apple Computers, Pepsi Cola, Kodak, Euro Disney, and the Walt Disney Company—great American institutions, all. In 2005, when French Muslim youth stormed the streets of Paris, setting fire to nearly 9,000 cars in 274 towns, and causing over 200 million euros (nearly $3 million based on 2009 rates) in damage over the course of less than three weeks,[1] American media uniformly referred to the events as "youth riots"—with one exception: Fox News used the term "Muslim" in its reporting. Rupert Murdoch, CEO and founder of the News Corporation, which owns Fox, received a call from Prince Alwaleed. Within half an hour, Fox had changed its terminology, describing the Paris unrest as "civil riots." Alwaleed owns more than five percent of the News Corp, along with wholesome shares of Time/Warner—owner of *Time* Magazine, Turner Broadcasting, HBO, CNN, and Warner Brothers.

At the 2006 conference in The Hague where I first met Bat Y'eor, former Muslim Ibn Warraq, author of *Why I Am Not a Muslim* (Prometheus, 1995), pointed to a Rand Corporation August 2002 study that described Saudi Arabia as "the kernel of evil, the prime mover, the most dangerous opponent." The report, said Warraq, went on to explain that "Saudi Arabia supports our enemies and attacks our allies. The Saudis are active at every level of the terror chain, from planners to financiers, from cadres to foot-soldiers, from ideologists to cheerleaders."

The UAE, to be sure, is not much better. Though the 2006 efforts of Dubai Ports World to purchase the Peninsular and Oriental Steam Navigation Company, which manages six U.S. seaports, ultimately failed, other efforts have not—including the purchase in 2005 by Dubai's crown prince Sheik Mohammed bin Rashid Al Maktoum of 230 Park Avenue, the building above New York's Grand Central Station; and the takeover by another Dubai firm, Dubai Holding, of the Doncasters

Group, a UK-based manufacturer of parts for military aircraft, tanks, and petrochemical markets, with plants throughout the United States and Europe. Doncasters'—now Dubai Holding's—biggest clients include Boeing, Honeywell, Siemens, and General Electric.

Meantime, Dubai Holdings also owns a $1 billion share of the former Daimler/Chrysler, makers of such commonly used U.S. and European military equipment as Jeeps, and of such vital military weapons as missiles. And Doncasters—now Dubai Holding—maintains close connections with General Electric—the company that not only produces turbine engines for Boeing (among others) but, as it announces proudly on its Web site, "Whether you're with a federal, state or local government agency, GE offers innovative technologies to help make your world safer. GE can integrate the latest advancements with your existing equipment and IT systems so you can increase security at embassies, borders, military installations, water treatment plants and other critical public infrastructure. Plus these integrated systems capture valuable data you can use to improve procedures, investigate events and prevent others from happening at all."

And yet, the UAE's views of the United States and the UK are hardly the kind you'd want from the owners of the company that builds military, water treatment, and border security equipment: to quote a piece in *Al Bayan*, a government-run UAE newspaper as cited by the Anti-Defamation league, ". . . but who planted the biggest and most dangerous virus in the region? Isn't it Britain and Europe who planted the Israeli virus? Isn't America protecting and injecting this virus in every aspect of life so it can penetrate and become monstrous?"

If this seems surprising, it shouldn't. Members of the UAE ruling family are known to have socialized frequently with bin Laden before the Al Qaeda leader went into hiding (and for all anyone knows, even since; the Taliban were warmly recognized by the UAE as the legitimate rulers of Afghanistan until U.S. pressure forced them to cut ties in September 2001). A military document submitted to the 9/11 Commission describes a February 1999 hunting trip members of the UAE royal family took with Osama bin Laden. According to the document, "the CIA received reports that bin Laden regularly went from his adjacent camp to the larger camp, where he visited with the emirates." In fact, having pinpointed the Al Qaeda leader at the camp, the United States chose nonetheless to refrain from attacking him for fear that, in the words of former CIA director George Tenet as cited in the 9/11 Commission report, "you might have wiped out half the royal family of the UAE in the process."

This is frightening stuff. A United States that cannot be conquered with rifles and with bombs, it seems, can, instead, quite easily be bought.

I realize that some people do not see this as a threat. They argue that the UAE has been an ally to the United States. When questioned on these events and connections, defenders are quick to pull the "racism card," and caution against angering our friends in the United Arab Emirates, who have, they maintain, supported and assisted some of the United States' anti-terror efforts. (That they have supported and assisted some of political Islam's most vicious terrorists is, apparently, not the point.) Besides, they say, in a globalized economy, international exchanges of businesses are not only likely but desirable; there should be no difference between selling a company to the UK and selling the same business to the Arab world—even to countries which have taken a pronounced, militant stance against Israel and whose anti-Semitic leanings and support of Hamas and of the Taliban are well-documented, or to countries that have served as financial centers for terrorists, countries that have, in fact, harbored the very terrorists who killed thousands on our own shores.

Even, it seems, in the face of history.

Others, however, like Mike Aldrich, vice-president of Force Protection, a manufacturer of military vehicles such as the Cougar, express other concerns. "Global war by Islamic extremists is becoming a business," he said when we spoke about this in 2006. "Tactics and procedures are being tested in Sri Lanka, bombs are tested in Indonesia, and suddenly they turn up in Afghanistan and Iraq." The UAE recognizes that military defense "is a growth business," he added, "and I think they know we are going to take a pounding."

* * *

How much of this, then, also explains the U.S. government's silence on the Saudi-sponsored literature and training materials in its schools and prison systems? For at least the past eight years, New York Democratic Senator Charles Schumer, Republican Congressman Frank Wolf of Virginia, and others have repeatedly pressed Congress and successive secretaries of state—Colin Powell, Condoleezza Rice, and Hillary Clinton—to take action on this issue. They have had no success whatever. Indeed, their actions—in the form of letters, memos, press bulletins, and Senate testimony—have largely been ignored. Further, Steven Emerson's organization, the Investigative Project on Terrorism, determined that, toward the end of its term, the Bush administration forged a policy prohibiting the use of the terms "Islamic terrorism", "Islamic militants," "Islamic radicals," or "jihad." Writing in *The Daily Beast*, Emerson, author of *American Jihad: The Terrorists Living Among Us* (Free Press, 2002) and *Jihad, Incorporated: A Guide to Militant Islam in the US* (Prometheus, 2006), stated, "These censorious vernacular prohibitions were the product of advice given by several Islamic advisors hired by Homeland Security. . . . The administration's reasoning here was the embodiment of appeasement; the goal: to protect Islam from any negative connotations." And yet, he observes, "the problem is not all Muslims. Far from it. It is radical Islam, just like German Nazism and Italian fascism were pinpointed as the devils in World War II. And in Christianity and Judaism, there are Christian and Jewish terrorists, terms no one is afraid of using." So why, he asks, can we not address "Islamic terrorism"?[2]

Similar silence has also met congressional expressions of concern over so-called "mainstream" Muslim groups in the United States such as the Council on American and Islamic Relations (CAIR), which many view as a legitimate civil rights organization. But in January 2009, the FBI, which had previously worked closely with CAIR, cut all ties as CAIR officials stubbornly refused to condemn Hamas and Hezbollah, both recognized by the United States as terror groups. CAIR was also implicated as a supporter of Hamas during the November 2008 trial of the Holy Land Foundation, in which five of the foundation's leaders were convicted of funneling millions of dollars to Hamas. Speaking on NPR's *Weekend Edition* on June 7, 2009, FBI assistant director John Miller explained, "During the Holy Land Foundation trial, evidence was brought to bear that two of the founding members of CAIR, who were still in those positions at the time, were related to Hamas organizers."

But beyond any alleged ties to Hamas, the problem with CAIR and ISNA and similar organizations has been their unwillingness to discourage the fomentation of radical Islam. Despite the lessons learned through Europe's investigations—and especially through the work of the Dutch AIVD—CAIR has systematically denied the spread of Wahhabist/Salafist literature or training. Court filings in the Holy Land case also connected CAIR (along with the Islamic Society of North America) with the Muslim Brotherhood. And former officials of the organization have been convicted or deported over the years on charges of fraud and aiding terrorist training, according to the *New York Sun.*[3]

For this reason, counter-terrorism experts have been expressing concerns about CAIR for years. So why was nothing done until the end of the Bush administration—nearly seven years after 9/11?

For its part, the Obama administration has also embraced CAIR despite concerns over its ties to terrorism. Steve Emerson believes that this is largely due to simple naïveté, to people "who believe that CAIR is a legitimate civil rights group. They want to believe it. It's an unjustified belief, but they want to believe these groups have gotten a bad hand." The danger, he cautions, is that if these people "become appointees to the Homeland Security Commission, they may find themselves [unwittingly] justifying groups like the Muslim Brotherhood."

Robert Spencer has another explanation. "American analysts in particular have decided that if a Muslim is not blowing something up, he must be moderate. But the distinction must really be placed between Muslims who want to impose Islamic law, and those who do not. There are many organizations working to bring Islamic law here, who believe that American law must give way when the two conflict. These people have the same goal as bin Laden, but they have a different means to that goal. To think they are benign because they are not working violently is extraordinarily shortsighted. Because if successful, they will undermine our values."

On Sunday, July 19, 2009, hundreds of American Muslims arrived at the Hilton Hotel in Chicago to join in the first meeting of Hizb ut-Tahrir to take place in the United States. Banned in many European countries—including Germany and the UK—the organization has claimed Abu Musab Al-Zarqawi, Al Qaeda's leader in Iraq, and Khalid Sheik Mohammad who orchestrated the 1993 World Trade Center bombings, as members. Imams from across America came to listen and to speak. The speech of one imam, made public by Steven Emerson, included the following words: "If [Americans] offer us the sun, or the moon, or a nice raise, or a passport, or a house in the suburbs, or even a place to pray at the job, on the condition that we stop calling for Islam as a complete way of life, we should never do that—ever do that—unless and until Islam becomes victorious, or we die in the attempt."

Robert Spencer, one might say, has a point.

Yet—as Senator Schumer and Congressman Wolf and others have learned—few are paying attention. Instead, the U.S. government has largely overlooked the problem of domestic radicalization and the imposition of Salafist and Wahhabist ideology and influences on our culture, focusing on violent jihad and protecting the homeland against attacks like 9/11—this, even as the NYPD (and experience) have shown that the September 11 attacks were rather an exception than the rule. [4] This, as we have fought a war since 2003 in Iraq, a country that had nothing to do with 9/11, and has never bought a single mosque—or jihadist—in our land.

* * *

"If you look at Middle Eastern society," Ayaan had said to me at our first meeting, "the way they relate in private life, and the public crisis these countries find themselves in is a reflection of the crisis in the home, and the helplessness, and the terror. Only if we see that is peace possible—and the end of terrorism. It's not just one or two

families, but millions of families, who teach their children by first hit-
ting them, and by first humiliating them; and why, with all the knowledge we have on humans and humanity and how they grow up, why
can't we ever make this link?"

It was Ayaan Hirsi Ali's focus on "terror in the home" that shattered
Holland's multiculturalist dream. "Look at the women," she said.
"Look at the children." And when Zarife was killed, and when her
teacher broke the secret, people began to see.

In America, no one will look behind those shuttered doors.

If the U.S. media rejected my efforts to reveal the honor killings
taking place in Europe, an even deeper silence has surrounded the killings that occur in the United States. Any suggestion that such killings
relate to Islam, too, bring accusations of Islamaphobia and racism.

And even if such crimes were not a part of Islam, they remain signals of something else: a clinging to fundamentalist and violent tribal
traditions and a mindset easily directed to jihad.

In February 2009, Muzzammil Hassan, 44, the owner of a television
station aimed at countering Muslim stereotypes in Buffalo, New York,
stabbed his wife, 37-year-old Aasiya. Then he cut off her head. Days
earlier, Aasiya had filed for divorce. (Perhaps not incidentally, it was a
Buffalo community that also bred the so-called "Lackawanna Six,"
who pleaded guilty in 2003 of conspiring with terrorist groups.)

Statistically, the most dangerous time for a woman in a violent relationship is the period after she leaves. Arguably, the Hassan case was
another tragic example of domestic violence. Except that Aasiya had
been *beheaded.* Dr. Mr. Zuhdi Jasser, an Arizona physician and the
founder and chairman of the American Islamic Forum for Democracy,
told Fox news, "It certainly has all the markings of [an honor killing].
She expressed through the legal system that she was being abused, and
at the moment that she asked for a divorce, she's not only murdered—
she's decapitated."

It was not the first time. In Atlanta, Georgia, a Pakistani man
strangled his daughter after he learned she wanted to end her arranged
marriage. She had fallen in love with someone else, he told police, so
he had killed her. Such affairs are forbidden in Islam. A *Boston Globe*
report says that a detective quoted the man in court: "God will protect
me. God is watching me. I strangled my daughter."

But the media is still. Government does not move. Jeanne Smoot,
Director of Public Policy at the Tahirih Justice Center in Falls Church,
Virginia, tells me, in fact, that efforts to locate information about the
frequency of honor killings in the United States, or about the severity
of the problem, are fruitless. She herself has hired interns, obtained the
assistance of interns at various law firms, checked LexisNexis listings—
all to no avail. Currently, she is assembling data on arranged, forced

marriages, though this, too, is elusive. Moreover, when she has been involved with such cases, she says, "child services often won't get involved, citing 'cultural considerations.'"

It is exactly what we saw in Holland in the days before Hirsi Ali arrived.

In one instance, Smoot recalls, a police officer told her of a girl from a local Afghan family, whose father regularly beat her for not being "modest" enough. Ultimately, she was sent back to Afghanistan, to—so the family said—live with her grandmother. Perhaps she did, and will spend her life veiled and sheltered in her grandmother's home. Perhaps her father took her there, as Zarife's took her to Ankara.

And the question no one asks is: Where do these families worship? And more: Who is their imam? What prayers does he recite? What sermons does he deliver? Where did he learn them? Who finances the mosque? Do these communities maintain Muslim and Arabic bookshops? What do they sell? Has Holland's *How to Be a Good Muslim* arrived on U.S. shores? How many neighbors agree that the father did the only thing he could? How many say "well, she should have known"?

We don't know.

* * *

After September 11, and while the country still stumbled, dazed and bruised, the Bush administration, with support of Congressional Democrats, passed the Uniting and Strengthening America by Providing Appropriate Tools Required to Intercept and Obstruct Terrorism Act, known as the USA PATRIOT Act—a comprehensive package of laws so enormous and comprehensive that (allegedly) some lawmakers never even read the whole thing before approving it. Condemned by civil rights advocates and lauded by conservative Republicans, the Act increased the reach and power of the FBI, the CIA, and the Department of Justice, opening the doors of private citizens to scrutiny through such measures as abandoning the need to obtain a warrant for wiretaps and requiring librarians to make information on book loans available to government investigators. Over the years, various measures in the original act have since been struck down as unconstitutional; others are simply bypassed, as with librarians who now reportedly often shred their records, and none of whom have ever been asked by the FBI to provide them, anyway. (Not that it would matter, really: libraries don't generally stock the kinds of material jihadists want. They stock material that students or that journalists—like me, for instance—might want. Jihadists find their resources at the Saudi-backed schools and mosques—the ones the Bush administration never did anything to deter. On the other hand, when Robert Spencer was asked to speak on

a panel discussion at the American Library Association's annual conference in 2009, CAIR officials protested. The ALA, under pressure,
cancelled the event.)

Also at issue in the original PATRIOT Act were the "sneak and
peek" laws, which effectively allowed law enforcement to enter and
search a person's home without that person's knowledge or permission. The law was struck down in 2007, after a man by the name of
Brandon Mayfield was imprisoned wrongfully on suspicion that he
was involved in the Madrid train bombings; in a court battle, a judge
ruled that the law violated the Fourth Amendment.

That, however, did not help Steve Kurtz.

In May 2004, Kurtz, then a 47-year-old art professor at the State University of New York at Buffalo, woke to the shocking discovery that
his wife, Hope, 45, had died during the night, having suffered total car-
diac failure in her sleep. Stunned, he called 911. Emergency workers
soon arrived, confirmed Hope's death, and briefly surveyed the Kurtz
home; as they left, the lead detective, according to Kurtz, casually
remarked, "I think the FBI is going to want to talk to you."

Sure enough, as Kurtz left the house to pay a visit to a nearby funeral home the following morning, several cars pulled up by his front
door. "They all lined up and each one said 'I'm sorry for your loss,'"
he recalls, "and then they all said, 'but we're going to have to hold
you and you can't go back into your house.'"

The Kurtzes were founding members of the Critical Art Ensemble,
an art and performance collective that focused on biotechnology and
its relations to daily life. Their work has been featured in exhibitions
from the Corcoran Art Museum in Washington, D.C., to the Whitney
Museum in New York City and the ICA in London; at the time of
Hope's death, they had been preparing to produce a project on geneti-
cally modified agriculture for the Massachusetts Museum of Contemporary Art (MASS MoCA), a major and highly-regarded museum. *New
York Times* art critic Randy Kennedy has described their projects:
"Occasionally the work is playful, verging on silly—serenading a strain
of *E. coli* bacteria with Engelbert Humperdinck's greatest hits to see if
that causes increased antibiotic production (it appeared to)."[5]

But police who had appeared at Kurtz's house in answer to his 911
call found the chemicals and Petri dishes they saw there suspicious.
Kurtz was arrested as the FBI seized his computer, various documents,
scientific equipment, and various other items. "They confiscated everything I had," he says, "including Hope's body and my pet cat. They
thought I was putting germs into it and letting it loose in the neighborhood to kill people."

A week later, the New York state public health commissioner tested
the samples that the FBI had taken from Kurtz's home, determined

they posed no threat, and ordered Kurtz's release. Only then did he recover his wife's body.

For the next four years, Kurtz found himself in a legal nightmare. His name appeared on terror watch lists and his home subjected to repeated searches as the FBI pursued a 20-year sentence against him on charges of bio-terrorism. Meantime, in the very same city, no one even thought to investigate the home of Muzzammil Hassan.

In 2008, U.S. District Judge Richard Arcara dismissed all charges against the artist. He is now working to rebuild his life.

Yet even in the face of cases like Steve Kurtz's, despite public protests and legal actions against the loss of civil rights in the "war on terror," all told, Americans have sacrificed far less than many Europeans, protected largely by the U.S. Constitution and various civil rights groups. But the United States has committed horrors of its own, through measures embedded into the PATRIOT Act and other laws—some secretive—passed under the Bush regime that violate the very principles of democracy. While memos that circulated within the Bush White House remain classified and Senate investigations—and calls for further investigations—continue, the fact that America has engaged in torture in violation of human rights laws and principles under the Geneva Convention can no longer be contested. The despicable acts of humiliation and cruelty that took place in Abu Ghraib remain a blemish on U.S. history that we will never, ultimately, live down. They are the shame of our legacy, as much a mark of the end of American innocence as were the towers that fell that bright day in September.

And yet—to what end? For even as we press prisoners for information about potential attacks from abroad, American lawmakers still fail to address domestic risks. Intelligence officials have, thus far, managed to use PATRIOT Act measures to prevent over a dozen possible terrorist strikes by plotters within our borders; but even as they do, "stealth jihad" is spreading, undeterred.

"We're doomed," Steven Emerson stated flatly the last time we spoke. "America is asleep at the wheel." Quoting Winston Churchill, he added, "Democracies only act when there's blood in the streets."

Robert Spencer is less fatalistic. "I understand how he feels," he tells me when I mention Emerson's despair. "Saudi Arabia owns a whole lot of American politicians. They have a roster of former ambassadors and lobbying groups and they've been able to provide for a very significant presence of the Saudis in government. It's not paranoia. It's an urgent threat, though one needs to be informed about sharia and the goals of the Muslim Brotherhood in particular to be aware of the urgency. Those who are not aware of that will not be able to understand it as anything but hysteria and fear mongering. The difficulty comes from the fact that Islam is a religion—and people from Jewish and

Christian backgrounds have a whole lot of trouble understanding that Islam is not a religion in the Western sense—or rather, it is *more* than a religion in the Western sense. It is also a comprehensive framework for society and the rule of the state. So people think of it as simply a religion, and that people who oppose these things are bigoted or hysterical or both, when in fact they are opposing the socioeconomic aspects of Islam that are a threat to the equality of rights and more."

Still, he adds, "while I breathe, I hope."

But are we defending ourselves against their "threat to the equality of rights" by establishing our own? Can we do it any other way?

In the United States, as in Europe, the threat continues. The US hasn't really succeeded, after all; and if we continue blindly along this same thicket-covered path, we never will.

CHAPTER 22

So what are we to do? Are we to be forced to choose between an Islamist or a secular, but totalitarian, state? Can multiculturalism work, given more time? How much time? What do we risk in the meanwhile? Is it worth it?

Here, I think, is what we can say safely, and needing no paranormal powers of clairvoyance: little that the West has done so far has helped much, nor is it likely that it ever will: not the crackdowns that inspire rebellion, not the compassionate efforts of tolerance and moral relativism, not hard love and not soft. Born of all the best and kindest of intentions, the concept of the multicultural society, at least where Islam is concerned, has, in the end, done more harm than it has good. Islamic extremism is growing, and tensions between the Islamic and Western worlds tightening with it. Justices and governments around the globe now debate questions to which we'd long thought we'd had the answers: how "free" can free speech be? Can an emotion—like hate—be punishable by law? Can thoughts? Is a thought, even a fantasy, an act of terror?

Do we know, even, what "democracy" means, anymore?

For decades, the multiculturalist—and by extension, often liberal democratic—view has been that democracy demands respect for and tolerance of minorities and, accordingly, the lifestyles and beliefs of the "other," whoever the "other" may be.

On the face of it, this argument makes sense. In practical terms, however, the gaps it leaves are wider than we can possibly traverse. When religious laws conflict with the law of the land, for instance, which prevails? Does freedom of religion include the right to practices that violate our laws and moral values? If we make allowances for some and not for others, is that not discriminatory—and so, counter to the multiculturalist ideal? How tolerant must we be of intolerance? Is there a line beyond which such intolerance cannot cross? Who determines it? Conversely, if we do away with multiculturalism as a whole, we confront other dilemmas equally confusing: is one view "right" and the other "wrong?" Is there any kind of universal moral absolute? If yes, what is it—and if not, who arbitrates?

Arguably, this is the problem of theism at its base: my god and only my god, and the (narcissistic) notion that any god (especially one's own god) can and does dictate the rules for all humanity. But the truth is, for better or worse, we live in a theistic world. Under those circumstances, how do these questions find answers?

Paul Cliteur, a colleague of Ellian's at the University of Leiden, published an essay in 2006 addressing the problems of multiculturalism in part as a response to Ian Buruma's *Murder in Amsterdam*, a portrait of the Dutch situation and the murder of Theo van Gogh.[1] In his words, "Multiculturalists . . . reject the universality of Enlightenment ideas of democracy, human rights, and the rule of law, viewing them instead as isolated preoccupations of no universal appeal. It is preposterous and a manifestation of cultural arrogance, on this view, to invade foreign countries to export democracy and other Western ideals; it is likewise ridiculous to expect that religious and ethnic minorities in Western societies should be expected to adopt these ideas and integrate into liberal democracy. Minorities should live according to their own customs; and, insofar as national culture is at variance with non-Western ideas, the national culture should adapt itself to new conditions." Cliteur clearly fears the ramifications of such views, which, he claims, "lead to a bowdlerizing 'purification' of the whole Western tradition of literature, art, cinematography, and even science." (Ironically, but importantly, the same could be said of many of the actions and expressions of the Christian Right in the United States and those put forth during the George W. Bush administration—think of former Attorney General John Ashcroft's insistence on veiling the breasts of Lady Justice, and the Bush era efforts to promote creationism over evolution and ban stem cell research.)

Multiculturalists, in return, frequently argue that those who, like Ellian, Hirsi Ali, and American scholar Bernard Lewis, insist on the superiority of post-Enlightenment over pre-Enlightenment perspectives are fundamentalists themselves—"fundamentalists of the Enlightenment." Buruma, says Cliteur (and I would say, many others), views the Enlightenment as "not significantly better [than] or preferable to an orientation toward radical Islamic ideology. Radical Islam is a fundamentalist position, but the same could be said about 'radical Enlightenment.'" Both parties, says Cliteur, "believe in universal values. Both parties believe they are struggling for a righteous cause." And he quotes Buruma, "the same could be said, in a way, of . . . the modern holy warrior, like the killer of Theo van Gogh."

Cliteur, rightly, finds the analogy ludicrous. "Are these two positions really 'the same'?" he asks. "Is someone who is a warrior of the pen really the same as someone who conducts his war by killing people and decapitating them? Both Chamberlain and Hitler had moustaches, but it would be absurd to attribute any significance to this similarity."

(I confess that this is one of the sharpest, most astute critiques of the multicultural viewpoint I have ever encountered.)

It also hits directly at why, in fact, multiculturalism has failed. Sociologists, psychologists, counterterrorism experts and social workers all agree that a significant factor contributing to radicalization is the search for identity and belonging. For Muslim immigrants in the West, particularly, the sense of tribal unity that engenders not only identity but self-confidence is evasive: unlike the challenges that face American blacks, for example, they have no history, no commonality, either with their homelands (or, even more so, with the homelands of their parents) nor with the country in which they (now) live. Islam, and the embrace of a group, provide this community in the form of the "ummah"—the global community of Muslims; and if there is no other perspective available that demonstrates such clear conviction, such certainty, it is not surprising that this is the direction in which they turn. A parent who enforces no rules raises an unruly child. What do we offer these youth if we cannot even show conviction in what we believe, in the rules of our society—those things that make us who we are and, by extension, what we expect them to become?

Others have argued for a so-called "European Islam." But what exactly does that mean? Is it an Islam that sacrifices some of its own central tenets in exchange for the offerings and advantages of modern democracy? One difficulty here, as a few people have observed, is that Islam has no pope. It has no one who can dictate for all 1.5 billion Muslims in the world that it is no longer acceptable to beat your wives and kill your daughters, that Muslims who choose to live in the West must accommodate themselves to Western law. It has no one who can condemn the imprisonment and calls for execution of a British teacher in the Sudan who names a teddy bear "Mohammed," as happened in the fall of 2007. Nor, as Mat Herben, the former advisor to Pim Fortuyn, said when we spoke in The Hague, is there even a measure by which multiple forms of Islam can co-exist—a problem which confronts Muslim communities from Somalia and Iraq to Amsterdam and Madrid—and, evidently, even Buffalo, New York.

Testifying before the Judiciary Subcommittee on Terrorism, Technology, and Homeland Security in 2003, Michael Waller, Annenberg Professor of International Communication at the Institute of World Politics in Washington, D.C., explained, "[A] great battle is taking place today within the Muslim faith around the world. Many Muslims have come to me and to my colleagues with information about how their mosques, centers, and communities have been penetrated and hijacked by extreme Islamists who have politicized the faith and sought to use it as a tool of political warfare in the United States."[2] At the same time, Wahhabist and Salafist Muslims would argue that those who approach Waller and others are traitors. If the Islamic world cannot agree on what Islam is, how can we expect to define a "European Islam" to replace it? And how would such a "reform Islam," as it were, survive in the face of violent Islamists who would consider it simply another form of apostasy? Would it even serve any real, nonredundant purpose?

Zuhdi Jasser, an American-born Muslim and former lieutenant commander in the U.S. Navy who now practices nuclear cardiology in Phoenix, Arizona, has touched on what might be the beginnings of a possible solution—though the tenuousness of this wording indicates the cautiousness with which I think his project needs to be regarded. The American Islamic Forum for Democracy, which Dr. Jasser created in response to the silence of the Western, supposedly-moderate Muslim community in the face of Islamic terrorist acts against the West, emphasizes the value of Western liberties for Muslims, encouraging them to practice their religion as religion—not politics—and to view democracy as a force to make them even better Muslims. The organization publishes literature for distribution, such as a booklet Jasser describes as "a positive message on America—not necessarily patriotism, but on liberty and the concepts of separation between mosque and state." The aim, he says, is to "show that political Islam is the risk to freedom." Which does God value more?" he asks. "If you fast in a society that is mixed, that doesn't all come to a stop as Saudi society does for Ramadan, it is more of a real choice."[3]

In Jasser's view, Americans and other Westerners have not yet fully understood the nature of the threat, or its severity. To a significant extent, this is the fault of a cowardly, popularity-based media—one which calls honor killings in the West "too inflammatory" to report, or which—as in the case of Yale University Press, who in August 2009, censored images of Mohammed from a book about the Danish cartoon controversy—either does not see or does not care what it gives up in giving in.

Adding to the challenge is the fact that, as the NYPD report observed, "Entering the [radicalization] process does not mean one will progress through all four stages and become a terrorist. However, it also does not mean that if one doesn't become a terrorist, he or she is no longer a threat. Individuals who have been radicalized but are not jihadists may serve as mentors and agents of influence to those who might become the jihadists of tomorrow."[4] We don't, in other words, always know what is going on next door. Again, a frightened media and intelligentsia is partially to blame—even as, as Jasser observes, what the public needs most is to understand "that terrorism isn't just about radical militants, but about a core idea that is in conflict with what makes us free in America."

But fighting the Saudi/Wahhabist machine isn't easy, and Zuhdi Jasser admits his progress to date has been minimal. "It's a generational change," he concedes.

The country's recent refusal to acknowledge the concept of Islamic terrorism, a trend begun under George W. Bush but which continues in the Obama administration, doesn't help. Muslims and non-Muslims, liberals and conservatives alike I spoke to on this issue agreed on this one point. In keeping with later Bush administration decisions to drop the term "Islamic terrorism" from its lexicon, in March 2009, the Obama White House did away with the phrase "global war on terror," choosing "overseas contingency operation" in its place—leaving open the question of what we should then call the homegrown terrorists responsible for the majority of attacks over the past eight years. Not that it's clear what "overseas contingency operation" actually means, anyway: contingency regarding what? Where "overseas"? Anywhere? Are all foreign combatants terrorists? Or is terrorism to be handled the way we would handle all the actions of all enemies abroad? If this is not a war, is not defined as "armed conflict," then what is it? Equally important, if it's not a war, does that mean that the rules regarding the humanitarian treatment of prisoners apprehended during times of armed conflict as proscribed by the Geneva Conventions (and Obama's own directives regarding the use of torture) no longer apply? Is this yet another circumvention of the Geneva Conventions of the kind for which Obama himself so vehemently criticized the administration that preceded him? What treaties and laws regulate the options and restrictions that apply to a "contingency operation"?

Moreover, with no word left for "Islamic terrorists," what do we call home-based Muslim terrorists now? Why are we able to speak of "Basque terrorists" and "environmentalist terrorists" but not "Muslim" or "Islamic" ones? For that matter, if it's not a war, why isn't it? Aren't the lives and rights of women and girls, of cartoonists and filmmakers and photographers, of Jews and Hindus and Christians, of homosexuals and atheists and musicians and the guy blogging down the street worthy of a war? Mat Herben even argues that in many ways, an interchange with Islam can be nothing else: Mohammed, he says, "does not belong with Jesus so much as with Alexander the Great: he was first and foremost a statesman and a soldier. Islam would never have existed without a conquering army."

This is not to say that a war against terrorism—Islamic or otherwise—must or should be fought entirely on a battlefield with arms—a fact the Saudis have known and exploited to their advantage for some time. As the NYPD report points out, "Implementation of Sharia law and replacement of the system of nation-states with a worldwide Caliphate are the ultimate political aims. . . . Contemporary Saudi (Wahhabi) scholars have provided the religious legitimacy for many of the arguments promoted by the jihadists."[5] In New York, the report adds, "Salafism comes in many forms to include sermons given by visiting radical imams, the sale of jihadi tapes, extremist Web sites, lectures and other activities sponsored by extremist student associations, as well as traveling jamaatis or pilgrimages to and from extremist madrassas and mosques, and radical literature from Saudi Arabia."[6]

Consequently, if we are going to protect our way of life and the values of democracy that define Western civilization, then paths such as the one set out by Zuhdi Jasser (who is also working to produce films and videos) are vital: essentially, Jasser is fighting the (Saudi) Wahhabists on their own terms, using their weapons, in what may in some ways be the most effective strategy of all.

But it is not without problems of its own; like Hirsi Ali, writer Daniel Pipes, and many others, Jasser is often charged with being a "racist" (despite the fact that he is an observant, practicing Muslim who prays five times a day himself). Noted Dr. Waller, "Significantly, our research shows the most virulent of [such] denunciations have come from the self-proclaimed Muslim 'leaders' who are tied to foreign or domestic terrorist organizations; foreign—mainly Wahhabi—funding; and in critical cases, the Muslim brotherhood. [One] reported Muslim Brotherhood member, who had built a political pressure group in Washington that the FBI certified as 'mainstream,' frequently assailed the arrests of bona fide terrorists as bigoted actions that would harm the American Muslim Community."[7]

Moreover, on a practical level, for all its potential, it is difficult to determine how Jasser's strategy could effectively be put in place—even if he were to secure private funding to compete with the Saudis. (Government funds would likely be deemed unconstitutional, as the case could be made that his materials constitute religious discrimination and pro-American propaganda.) How and where would such materials be distributed? Certainly not in the mosques and schools governed by Wahhabi institutions. With an illiteracy rate nearing 70 percent, prisons, too, would hardly be ideal. Could messages instead be broadcast on TV, like the old anti-drug "this is your mind on dope" commercials? Can we urge the media to address the issue as they have, say, cigarette smoking and drunk driving? The audience, of course, is so much smaller—who would see such a topic as worthy of the expense? Concerns arise, too, over the safety of those designing, publishing, or broadcasting such campaigns; not for nothing did Ayaan Hirsi Ali leave even the name of her ghostwriter a secret. On the other hand—can Muslims remain silent without being, essentially, complicit? Writing of Paul Hall, a.k.a. Hassan Abujihaad, a former naval officer accused of "taking part in a conspiracy to kill military personnel by supplying terror suspects with information," Jasser has said, "Islamism will continue to be a threat to national sovereignty as long as Muslims remain silent against its anti-American and un-American goals." Muslims, he declares, must clearly articulate a separation of our national political identity from the global political Islamist identity.[8]

The quandary here is: if radicalization in the Muslim community is growing in "logarithmic proportions," then, too, the number of those prepared to fight against it is declining equally. If Jasser is right—and I think he is—that this is a situation that will only be resolved over generations, then we must find a way to equip the next generation to resist the forces we want them to reject. If we no longer are engaging in a "global war on terror," then, too, we must give up the idea of a "battle" over hearts and minds. It has become, rather, now, a race.

* * *

As I prepared to write this chapter, the United Nations Development Programme published an update to its "Arab Human Development Report," which first came out in 2002—just after the September 11 attacks. As Thomas Friedman so succinctly phrased it in his *New York Times* column, "the bad news: things are getting worse, and many Arab governments don't want to hear about it."[9]

What does "worse" mean, exactly?

To start with, some 40 percent of Arab women are functionally illiterate. UNESCO estimates within the region predict that illiteracy by 2010 will be at 57.2 percent in Iraq, 19 percent in the UAE, and 42 percent in Morocco. The total illiteracy rate in the region comes to about 60 million people.

Sixty million people is nine times the population of New York City, or virtually the entire population of the United Kingdom. Imagine if none of them could read or write.

Moreover, investments in science, innovation, education, and the arts are minimal; as Friedman notes, the 2002 report showed that "Greece alone translated five times more books every year from English to

Greek than the entire Arab world translated from English to Arabic."
Belief in traditions and folk medicine often supersedes scientific
understanding.

Meantime, in the United States, an American National Adult Literacy
study revealed that more than 60 percent of the country's prison
inmates are illiterate as well, with reading ability below the fourth-
grade level;[10] and according to Family Literary Centers, the Department of Justice has found that "the link between academic failure and
delinquency, violence, and crime, is welded to reading failure."

In other words, Islamic fundamentalism and jihadi violence seem to
flourish in two specific environments where reading levels are low to
non-existent.

This matters.

* * *

"The poets," wrote British romantic poet Percy Bysshe Shelley in his
"Defence of Poetry," "are the unacknowledged legislators of the
world." These, I believe, are words to live by. For Shelley, "poets"
meant artists, writers, dancers, architects—"the inventors of the arts of
life." It is the storytellers, after all, who introduce us to people we otherwise would never know, places we may never travel to, lives that we
otherwise might never encounter. It is the storytellers who help us to
see what these people see, to feel what they feel, to live inside their
lives. It is the poets who teach us that, in the words of Archibald
MacLeish, "a poem should be equal to/not true," that "an empty doorway and a maple leaf" can stand for "all the history of grief." It is the
artists who invite us to recognize universal balance in a crossing of
three lines, or to see gold where there is none—only paint. It is this
understanding of symbol, of metaphor, that allows us to see the nuances in things, to rise beyond the literal and what we think we see, and
to look deeper. It is this that distinguishes those who read religious
texts—the Bible, the Koran—as directives, as history and law, from
those who recognize the same words as allegory and idea. It is the
entering of lives that literature gives, the intimacy of reading, the cap-
turing and feeding of imagination, that breathe life into compassion
and innovation and possibility.

This is why the Taliban forbid them.

This is why we will not survive without them.

I am certainly aware of how utopian this sounds. And yet: several
studies have shown clearly that learning about art improves children's
abilities for self-reflection, their willingness to experiment and to per-
sist in the face of setbacks and obstacles to their goals. Students of visual art, according to Ellen Winner and Lois Hetland, co-authors of

Studio Thinking: The Real Benefits of Visual Arts Education, (Teacher's College Press, 2007), learn to look—and to look deeply. "Seeing is formed
by expectation," they wrote in an editorial in the *Boston Globe,*[11] "and
expectation often gets in the way of seeing the world accurately."

But it doesn't stop there: art classes encourage envisioning—the ability, essentially, to ask and answer the question: "What if?" What if you
moved this square to here? What if you added a tree in that corner?
What if you were looking at this fruit bowl from below and not beside
it? What happens to a child's mind when you move him into a world
where there are no "right" and "wrong" answers, but only different
ways of seeing and expressing an object, a vision, an idea? John Dewey
called imagination "the great instrument of the good."[12] The ability to
make aesthetic valuations, he believed, sharpens our ability to make
moral ones—a view I also heartily embrace.

And there is so much more than simply this. The students who
viewed *The Jewish Bride* with Rudi Fuchs had also visited the Anne
Frank House. But a child growing up in Somalia or Iran or Riyadh
who is told by his parents and his teachers and his imams that the
Holocaust never happened, and who cannot read himself, will never
engage with the *Diary of Anne Frank.* Other world views, other truths,
are lost to him. And yet Fuchs, in that one afternoon, endowed his students with the gift of something found: "this painting," he said,
"belongs also to all of you." This history, the culture, the greatness of
Holland's achievement, became their greatness, their culture, too. It
became their pride—something far more graspable than concepts of
"freedom" and "tolerance," less controversial than legal prostitution
and gay marriage. That identity with the land in which they, the immigrants and children of immigrants now live, could not be more critical
to nurturing a sense of pride and self—not national, but socio-cultural.
Deep in this painting, in their engagement, whether they knew it then
or not, these children found not just a community—an *ummah*—but
their honor.

* * *

Still, I know it would be utter silliness to suggest that any of this is
enough. Mohammed Bouyeri and certainly Osama bin Laden are fully
capable of reading and of writing, and familiar with many of literature's greats (despite the shocking fact that they are not taught in most
Dutch—or Arab, for that matter—public schools). The direct relationship between literacy and violence cannot be said to apply to them—
much as it can—and does—to Muslim converts in the prisons, and the
jihadi foot soldiers among school dropouts in the cities and the villages, not just of the Muslim world, but all across the West; and an

army without foot soldiers is no army at all. The more, then, that we can do to strengthen youth resistance to the propaganda and indoctrination of Wahhabi and other extreme and political forms of Islam, the weaker the enemy—and the stronger we—will be.

That said, more immediate and critical measures remain urgently necessary. American journalists have got to take on the task accorded them, as Dutch journalists have done, observing the inner workings of American mosques, the content of Islamic literature distributed in the United States, and the nature of the country's Muslim communities—and their editors must allow them the space and freedom to report on all they find there. At the same time, tired arguments about "poverty" and "disenfranchisement" as the sources of radicalization (oft aired in the media and by multiculturalist believers) have long since been disproved (the 9/11 hijackers were neither of these things, and neither, among others, was Daniel Boyd); and the press must take responsibility here, as well, for stating so.

And then there is the specter of the Holocaust, often raised by Europe's multiculturalist camp and others who contend that Europe's Muslims are "the Jews of the 21st century." Anti-Muslim sentiment, the argument goes, has forced Muslims into unemployment, robbed them of decent housing, and threatens to transform itself into another bout of genocide.

In fact, nothing could be further than the truth; and one critically urgent measure now is to put this myth, once and for all, to rest. In fact, if anything, the situation is the diametric opposite: It is Muslim extremists who, like the Nazis, call for the destruction of those they consider inferior, the "apes and pigs" who live Judeo-Christian lives (never mind the atheists) and who are systematically rounded up for slaughter. It is not the non-Muslims, but the Muslims themselves, who seek martyrdom by blowing up other, less-orthodox Muslims, in the marketplaces and on the streets of Iraq, Egypt, Jordan, and the rest of North Africa and the Middle East. It is we, not they, who are threatened with a violent destruction, and the end of all that we believe in.

Nonetheless, Europe particularly has a long way to travel in its handling of its minority populations: the overt "No Moroccans" memo in the Netherlands is but one example of a system in which, Europe-wide, résumés bearing Muslim-sounding names are routinely trashed without even a first glance. While this hardly constitutes ethnic cleansing, it remains utterly inadmissible in our society and in the democracy we claim to be protecting. What we refuse to accept among our Muslim populations, we can neither accept within our own.

Europe, however, also carries burdens in this respect that the United States no longer does. During the 1980s, for instance, successful American blacks—actors like Eddie Murphy, basketball players like Michael Jordan, for instance—actively took on the task of becoming role models to black inner-city youth, replacing the pimps and drug dealers who had held this place before them. Now the president of the United States of America is a black man—way cooler than some stoner doing time.

Tragically, this is hardly possible in Europe now. While Dyab Abu Jahjah soars to fame on a chariot driven both by his own ego and the cheers of his disciples, the models of Ayaan Hirsi Ali, Wafa Sultan, Irshad Manji, and the occasional Muslim comedian find most of their applause among non-Muslims, seasoned liberally with death threats from the very communities they are hoping to inspire. It simply doesn't work in the same way.

In response, for their part, many European politicians would silence those threats, and any similar incitement to violence, by law. But can we, in a culture that calls out so passionately for the free word? Should we? How far does such silencing go?

This, too, is part of the dilemma we face now, in the West. "Threats of violence must be completely banned," suggests Afshin Ellian, "and anti-Semitism must be punished. Life has to be made unbearable for these immigrants and their families who do not assimilate—or they must leave." In his view, the Salafist mosques of the Netherlands should be closed down if they continue to spread literature and lessons of violence and hate.

But has the state, in a secular democracy, the right to silence angry words? Has it the right to step into a house of worship and declare what may or may not be said there?

Robert Spencer and Zuhdi Jasser would say yes, arguing that calls for violence against the United States and the replacement of American government with a caliphate run according to Islamic law, whether written or spoken, constitute sedition. As such, even if spoken in or distributed through a house of worship, the government, they maintain, can and should step in. They have a strong point: Title 18, Part 1 Chapter 115 of the Sedition Code states:

"Whoever knowingly or willfully advocates, abets, advises, or teaches the duty, necessity, desirability, or propriety of overthrowing or destroying the government of the United States or the government of any State, Territory, District or Possession thereof, or the government of any political subdivision therein, by force or violence, or by the assassination of any officer of any such government; or Whoever, with intent to cause the overthrow or destruction of any such government, prints, publishes, edits, issues, circulates, sells, distributes, or publicly displays any written or printed matter advocating, advising, or teaching the duty, necessity, desirability, or propriety of overthrowing or destroying any government in the United States by force or violence, or attempts to do so; or Whoever organizes or helps or attempts to organize any society, group, or assembly of persons who teach, advocate, or encourage the overthrow or destruction of any such government by force or violence; or becomes or is a member of, or affiliates with, any such society, group, or assembly of persons, knowing the purposes thereof—Shall be fined under this title or imprisoned not more than twenty years, or both, and shall be ineligible for employment by the United States or any department or agency thereof, for the five years next following his conviction."

And yet, as Saudi-sponsored anti-American literature fills the mosques and Islamic schools of the United States, and American imams promote the institution of a sharia state to replace the U.S. Constitution, sedition laws have barely been enforced in over 50 years. Is it even possible to enforce them without returning to McCarthyism? How? And do such acts constitute civil crime, or terrorism? If those responsible are convicted, how wise would it be to house them in our prisons, where radicalization is already taking place? If not, though, in conventional prisons, then where?

To his credit, President Obama has done away with the forms of humanitarian abuse sanctioned and committed under the previous administration, redacting laws and regulations that permit torture of prisoners of war. But he has also accepted the hospitality of the Saudi royal family, and has shown no indication that he intends to freeze U.S. business dealings with them. What message does that send? What risks do we expose ourselves to so long as we accept as friends and partners those who help to finance suicide bombers, who subject women not just to utter subjugation, but to torture and to stoning? What does that say of our own values?

So far, solid intelligence has helped us to avoid dozens of attacks; and such intelligence should continue. But the term "probable cause" is one that seems to have been lost in the years since 2001. Who is the government investigating? If FBI agents have reason to suspect jihadist leanings within a certain mosque or group, then by all means, investigate, and hire an informant, if needed. My computer is filled with Web pages from Salafist Web sites and information downloaded about Islamic groups. I see no reason why FBI officials wouldn't be watching, and I can't blame them for it. But do they need, too, to observe the habits of, say, my friend who works at an auction house in Manhattan? Of the shoemaker and his wife on the Pieter Aertszstraat in Amsterdam?

When fighting terrorism brings us to the point of treating artists as conspirators against the democratic state, when books are banned and cartoons forbidden and even libraries provide no sanctuary—and still terrorist plots continue, and mass murders are narrowly escaped—we have failed.

This is why I turn back to education as our greatest weapon against the forces of jihad. In the words of Hannah Arendt, "Education is the point at which we decide whether we love the world enough to assume responsibility for it." We need to take back that responsibility. We need to start again.

It won't be easy.

Edward Albee, the great American playwright, wrote in his classic, *Zoo Story*, "Sometimes, it is necessary to go a long distance out of the way to come back a short distance correctly." I believe that this is one of those times. As we continue to struggle towards a solution, Afshin Ellian, for instance, suggests temporarily closing the borders to the Netherlands—an idea that I once would have rejected, but no longer can. "Solve what we have," he says, "and then think about how to handle the situation before reopening the doors." Similarly, in the United States, I think it is time to reconsider our openness to Saudi sponsorships—of our schools, of mosques, of community centers, and associations—and to allowing countries that fail to uphold our own democratic values to invest in our businesses: not banks, not manufacturers, not even real estate. If literature or other material is found to be seditious, remove it from circulation. These are not moves that should necessarily be made permanent, but perhaps scheduled to sunset within, say, 15 years—enough, in other words, to reach the generational change both the fighters for democracy and the jihadists believe that it will take to win. They are the long distance out of the way we must go to come back a short distance correctly. In the meantime, make art education mandatory in the schools. ("A nation devoid of art and artists," proclaimed Kemal Atatürk, founder of the only democratic nation in the Muslim world, "cannot have a full existence.") Teach our children not only how to fish, but how to read, how to think, how to move beyond frustration until a problem can be solved, to explore and innovate. Teach them to follow the seduction of metaphor, and to know the power of compassion. Armed with these abilities, they will—one hopes—stand against the efforts of extremists to turn them away from a world they have already made their own.

We must stop behaving as if democracy is negotiable. It is not. We cannot bend to a limitation of freedoms, simply in the name of freedom in itself. We must demand a hierarchy in which democratic values of dignity and respect and liberty remain paramount. This is the paradox of democracy—a paradox made greater by the fact that, while in itself a demand for hierarchy in a system based entirely on equality appears hypocritical, the failure to meet that demand is even more so. Radical Islam will not compromise, will not bend. Radical conservatives and, in equal measure, radical liberals, do; both forsake the very principles of justice and liberty they seek most to defend. This is why they will lose. Between the two shines the flame of the Enlightenment—the flame that guides our path to knowledge, to learning, to growth, to self-overcoming and, on, from there, to freedom. We must keep the candle burning.

Vrijheid, blijheid.
Abigail R. Esman
Stockbridge, Massachusetts
August, 2009

Notes

PREFACE

1. Francis Fukuyama, "A Year of Living Dangerously," *The Wall Street Journal*, November 2, 2005.

2. David Reiff, "An Islamic Alienation," *The New York Times Magazine*, August 14, 2005.

INTRODUCTION

1. Hafid Bouazza, "Nederland is Blind Voor Moslimextremism," *NRC Handelsblad*, February 20, 2002.

CHAPTER 1

1. Pieter Webeling, "Jezus, Theo, moest dat nou?" *Volkskrant*, February 25, 2005.

CHAPTER 2

1. *Funding Universe Web Site*, http://www.fundinguniverse.com.

2. *Amsterdam Info Web Site*, http://Amsterdaminfo.com/Netherlands/population.

3. CBS (Centraal Buro Voor Statistiek), September 20, 2004.

4. Bianca Stigter, "Islamitische Architectuur in Nederland; Waar de Kameel knielde," *NRC Handelsblad*, August 9, 1991.

5. CBS Nederland report, March 14, 2005.

6. Eddie Nieuwenhuizen, "Het Schijntaboe over minderheden en criminaliteit: Dat mag ook wel eens worden gezegd," *Zebra Magazine*, June 2, 2002.

CHAPTER 3

1. The more likely alternative, of course, is that the RRP had simply refused to authenticate paintings which were, indeed, by Rembrandt—which is Schwartz's entire point.

2. "The Netherlands, 1990–1991," Elise Consortium, Center for European Policy Studies, Brussels, Belgium.

3. Ibid.

4. Ibid.

5. "De Komst van de Moskee," VPRO Broadcasting, February 1, 2005.

6. "On the Collapse Of The Soviet Union," Address to the Liberal International Conference in Luzern, September 6, 1991.

7. Kees Versteegh, "Aparte schools voor moslims," *NRC Handelsblad*, February 1, 1992.

CHAPTER 5

1. Van der Burg, Jos. "De Dood In Het Leven," *Filmkrant*, February 1993, 131.

2. Loet and Edith Velmans, conversations and e-mails.

CHAPTER 6

1. Siem Eikelenboom, *Jihad In de Polder: Radical Islam in Nederland* (Amsterdam: Uitgeverij L.J. Veen, 2004), 202.

2. Youssef M. Ibrahim, "Europe's Muslim Population: Frustrated, Poor, and Divided," *New York Times*, May 5, 1995.

3. "Study shows syringe exchange programs effective in reducing the spread of AIDS," University of California at Davis Health System report, July 2001, http://www.universityofcalifornia.edu/news/article/3451.

CHAPTER 7

1. Report of Centraal Buro voor Statistiek, September 20, 2004.

2. Wim Kohler, "Een Kwestie van Ethniciteit," *NRC Handelsblad*, September 7, 1996.

3. "Europees Racism," *NRC Handelsblad*. December 23, 1997.

4. Derk-Jan Eppink, "VVD-leider Vindt Dan Moslims Zich Moeten Aanpassen; Bolkestein: Compromis Met Rechstaat Is Niet Mogelijk," *NRC Handelsblad*, September 12, 1991.

5. Herman Pleij, Hollands Welbehagen: Amsterdam: Ooivaar Uitgeverij, 1998.

6. Monique Snoeijen and Herman Staal. "ME Ingezet Bij Rellen in Buurt Amsterdam," *NRC Handelsblad*, April 24, 1998.

7. "SCP: jeugdcriminalitiet harder, verdachten jonger," *NRC Handelsblad*, April 17, 1998.

8. "Geen Mohammed, maar ook geen Willem," *Op de Grens!*, May 4, 1999.

CHAPTER 8

1. Though the term literally means "foreigner," it has come to be used as an adjective to describe specifically non-Western, non-white immigrants—chiefly Muslims.

2. Dyab Abou Jahjah, *Tussen Twee Werelden: De Roots Van Een Vrijheidstrijd* (Amsterdam: Meulenhoff/Manteau, 2003), 265.

3. A version of this passage about the shoemaker, entitled "A Foreign Bond That Unites Us," by Abigail Esman, appeared in *The Christian Science Monitor*, May 2, 2002.

4. Douglas Frantz, "A Top Boss in Europe, An Unseen Cell in Gaza, and Decoys Everywhere," *The New York Times*, September 23, 2001.

CHAPTER 9

1. Kustaw Bessems, "Invloed Moslim-radicalen in Nederland neemt toe," *Trouw*, September 27, 2002.

2. S. Eikelenboom, *Jihad In De Polder* (Amsterdam: L.J. Veen, 2004).

3. Ayaan Hirsi Ali, "Integratie is een cultureel probleem," *NRC Handelsblad*, August 31, 2002.

4. On April 16, 2002, Prime Minister Wim Kok rode his bicycle to the home of Queen Beatrix in The Hague to render his resignation. A report days earlier, issued by the Dutch Institute for War Documentation (NIOD), had shown that the 1995 mass murder of 7,000 Bosnians by Serbian rebels had occurred on Holland's (peacekeeping) watch. Kok assumed full responsibility as the country's leader, and the government collapsed.

5. Cited in "Leefbaar Rotterdam opent aanval op Fortuyn," *De Volkskrant*, August 31, 2001.

6. Frank Poorthuis and Hans Wansink, "De Islam is een achterlijk cultuur," *De Volkskrant*, February 9, 2002.

7. Stephen Castle, "Anger, remorse, and confusion in a country famed for its tolerance," *The Independent*, May 8, 2002.

CHAPTER 11

1. Ambrose Evans-Pritchard, "EU 'covered up' attacks on Jews by young Muslims," *Telegraph*, April 1, 2004.

2. These passages describing Jahjah's early years appeared in a slightly different form in Abigail Esman, "The Arabian Panther," published on Salon.com, June 14, 2004.

CHAPTER 12

1. Kustaw Bessems, "Eerwraak/de onzichtbaar grens," *Trouw*, June 29, 2006.

2. Ibid.

3. Massoeme Abbrin, "De Namus Gebroken," *Trouw*, August 28, 2003.

4. Marie Brenner, "Daughters of France, Daughters of Allah," *Vanity Fair*, April 2004.

5. Carolijne Vos, "Na het ja-woord begint de ellende," *De Volkskrant*, March 19, 2004.

CHAPTER 13

1. Hans Werdmolder, "Een Turk of niet," *Trouw*, January 17, 2004.

2. E. Mulder, "Murat is een doodgewone jongen," *Trouw*, August 15, 2005.

3. "Vanaf 700 eur heb je een pistol," *Trouw*, August 15, 2005.

4. "Ik wreek me niet, los het op met woorden," *NRC Handelsblad*, January 17, 2004.

5. In addition to the five years in prison, Murat Demir was sentenced to additional time in TBS—a part of the Dutch penal system in which criminals are comfortably housed in psychiatric clinics and take part in group therapy sessions. TBS is generally imposed for no more than 50 months.

6. "Full Text: 'Bin Laden Tape,'" *BBC News International*, http://news.bbc.co.uk/2/hi/middle_east/3628069.stm.

7. "Piecing together Madrid bombers' past," *BBC News*, April 5, 2004.

8. Ibid.

9. Gustavo de Aristegui, "Euroworried: It's Folly to Think They Struck Us Simply for Iraq," *The Washington Post*, March 21, 2004. Reprinted with permission from Gustavo de Aristegui.

10. Ibid.

11. "AIVD: Jongeren gevoelig voor djihad," *Trouw*, March 10, 2004.

12. Aparisim Ghosh and James Graff, "A Strike at Europe's Heart," *Time*, March 22, 2004.

13. Marlise Simons, "Dutch Tell of a Spate of Threats from Islamists," *New York Times*, September 15, 2004.

14. Patrick E. Tyler, "Militants in Europe Openly Call for Jihad and the Rule of Islam," *New York Times*, April 26, 2004.

15. "Balkenende wil meer respect voor koningshuis," *RTL Nieuws*, November 2003.

16. "U moet waardig en netjes vertrekken," Interview Verdonk with Marcel ten Hooven and Cees van der Laan, www.askv.dds.nl/archief/interviewverdonk.htm.

CHAPTER 14

1. Neal Ascherson, "From Multiculturalism to Where?" www.opendemocracy.net/node/2052, August 19, 2004.

2. Francis Fukuyama, "Identity And Migration," *Prospect*, February 2007, 131.

3. "Gedwongen integratie fout," *Trouw*, July 16, 2004.

4. "Moskee promoot homohaat," *Trouw*, April 21, 2004.

5. See http://forums.marokko.nl/showthread.php?+=287629.

6. It is unclear whether Van Gogh first approached Hirsi Ali about the project, as she reported in her memoir, *Infidel*, or whether she first came to him, as some newspapers stated at the time. Either way, the project was funded in full (to the tune of some $20,000) by Van Gogh. Regardless, the decision to produce a film to air on television rather than an art exhibition staged at a museum certainly would—and did—prove safer to the general public. It was a wise choice.

CHAPTER 15

1. Pieter Webeling, "Jezus, Theo, moest dat nou?" *Volkskrant*, February 5, 2005.

2. According to a report from the AIVD, Bouyeri had also clashed with a security guard at the Amsterdam Social Services offices in May 2004. "I'll kill you!" he had cried, "I'll rip your heart out!" (Van Straelen, F. W. M. "Stand van zaken onderzoek moord Theo van Gogh," Openbaar Ministerie, Amsterdam, January 26, 2005.)

3. Emerson Vermaat, *De Hofstadgroep: Portret van een radical-islamitisch netwerk* Amsterdam: Uitgeverij Aspekt, 2005.

4. The following day, Oum Osama reportedly greeted the news of Van Gogh's death with the exclamation, "It is a beautiful day. Van Gogh is dead, and I am getting married." But Allah did, indeed, have other plans: Labadine was arrested that afternoon in association with the murder, and the wedding never took place.

5. Janny Groen and Annieke Kranenberg, "Hofstadgroep op dag voor de moord vooral bezig met trouwerij," *Volkskrant*, July 25, 2005.

6. For reasons I have never understood, the significance of the time of this attack has never been noted by Dutch authorities or other writers about the event.

7. Published by the Algemeen Nederlands Pers (ANP), November 5, 2004.

8. All grammatical errors appear also in the Dutch version and are authentic to the text.

9. Translation my own, based on a previous translation provided by MilitantIslamMonitor.com.

10. Vermaat, 96.

CHAPTER 16

1. Ayaan Hirsi Ali, *Infidel* (New York: Free Press, 2007).

2. raymond van den boogaard, "Kruisridder tegen Moslimfundamentalisme," *NRC Handelsblad*, May 3, 2004.

3. Ibid.

4. Ibid.

5. Soon after his release, in July 2004, Bilal was arrested again for plans to launch a suicide attack.

6. Geert Wilders and Bart-Jan Spruyt, "Stop import islamitische cultuur," *Het Parool*, October 22, 2004. Reprinted with permission from the authors.

7. This measure may well have been stimulated by the fact that Bouyeri held both Moroccan and Dutch passports.

8. Aatish Taseer, "Getting Tougher," *Time Europe*, February 20, 2005.

9. Derk Walters, "Een avond stappen in de stad kan niet meer anoniem," *Volkskrant*, July 18, 2005.

10. A Dutch expression for boys who hang out on the street.

11. Lucy Berrington, "The Spread of a World Creed," *London Times*, November 9, 1993.

12. "Police protect girls forced to convert to Islam," *Daily Mail*, February 22, 2007.

13. Craig Whitlock, "Terrorists proving harder to profile," *Washington Post*, March 12, 2007.

14. It is worth noting that the bravery and openness of the Dutch press and intelligence agencies received deserved recognition from abroad, including from *New York Times*, which as early as October 2001, ran an article titled "Dutch

Frankness On Immigrants Treads Where Many Nations Fear To Go: Europe's Muslims: A Difficult Debate."

CHAPTER 17

1. Alan Cowell, "After Coordinated Bombs, London is Stunned, Bloodied, and Stoic," *New York Times,* July 7, 2005.

2. Ibid.

3. Ibid.

4. Sarah Lyall, "Strict Terror Laws Advance in Britain," *International Herald Tribune,* July 27, 2005.

5. Mark Follman, "The enemy is closer than we think," Salon.com, July 19, 2005.

6. Andreas Ulrich and others, "Radical Islam's Rising War In Europe," republished on Salon.com, July 12, 2005.

7. Lindsay Clutterbuck, "Radicalization and Extremism in the UK" in *Radicalisation in broader perspective.* National Coordinator for Counterterrorism, Ministry of Justice, the Netherlands (no date).

8. Michael Radu, "London 7/7 and Its Impact," *American Diplomacy,* July 30, 2005.

9. Ibid.

10. *"Strict Terror Laws Advance in Britain."*

11. That particular site no longer exists, but new ones appear—and disappear—almost daily.

12. Clutterbuck.

13. Gabriel Wieman, "How modern terrorism uses the internet," U.S. Institute of Peace 116, March 2004, as quoted in Clutterbuck.

14. Although it has been reported that the *Jyllands Post* received a prize in 2005 for "anti-discrimination" reporting, this is not entirely true; the paper had in fact been reprimanded several times for its anti-immigration stance over the years. That specific award was given not to the newspaper itself, but to one of its reporters, who had developed a series of stories about successful immigrants in Denmark. However, it is worth noting that the accusations of "anti-immigrant" leanings may not have been either accurate or fair.

15. Pernille Ammitzbøll and Lorenzo Vidino, "After the Danish cartoon controversy," *Middle East Quarterly,* Winter 2007, 3–11.

16. Craig Whitlock, "How a town became a terror hub," *Washington Post,* November 24, 2005.

17. Haroon Siddique and agencies, "Bomb plot targeted seven Heathrow flights, court told," *The Guardian,* April 3, 2008.

18. This fact actually calls into question the origins of unexplained explosions on flights such as Air France 447, which vanished en route from Rio de Janiero to Paris in June 2009.

19. NBH Yearbook 2006.

20. Ibid.

21. Matthias Gebauer and yassin Musharbash, "Islamic terrorists planned massive attacks in Germany," *Der Spiegel,* September 5, 2007.

22. Marcel Rosenbach, "Terror from the German heartland," *Der Spiegel Online,* September 4, 2008.

23. Yassin Musharbash and Marcel Rosenbach, "Germany prepares for home-grown terror trial," *Der Spiegel Online,* April 16, 2009.

24. Ibid.

CHAPTER 18

1. Not surprisingly, a gallery in Denmark was among the first to show Ben Ali's work outside the Netherlands.

2. "Morokkaanse leerlingen Amsterdam anti-Westers," *Volkskrant,* June 17, 2005.

3. Ibid.

4. Romana Abels and Kustaw Bessems, "Jonge Fondamenten," *Trouw,* August 15, 2005.

5. Ibid.

6. Rudi Fuchs, "Wat Mevrouw Van der Laan zegt is heel erg," *Volkskrant,* December 6, 2005. Reprinted with permission from Rudi Fuchs.

7. "Zwaarste straf voor moord op Van Gogh en terreur," *Volkskrant,* July 27, 2005.

8. Ayaan Hirsi Ali, *Infidel* (New York: Free Press, 2007).

9. Associated Press, "Germany might restage opera despite fear of Muslim outrage," Associated Press, October 4, 2006.

CHAPTER 19

1. Charlotte Huisman, "Utrechtse toestanden," *Volkskrant,* October 20, 2007.

2. In addition, in November 2008, a group of Muslim boys in Gouda also firebombed a local church; similar firebombings took place around the same time at Jewish centers in Amsterdam.

3. Vikram Dodd, "'America kill. Bush I kill. Blair kill,' said the five-year-old boy," *The Guardian,* February 19, 2008.

4. Report by Kerry O'Donoghue, 2005, obtained from the author.

5. Ibid.

6. In a report on Muslims in Germany published in *Der Spiegel* in March 2007, one middle-school principal in Ruhr noted that "About one-third of Muslims wear headscarves, 'and one in two are unhappy about it.'" Another educator in Berlin remarked, "girls from conservative families say that their fathers and brothers have the right to hit them."Yet, said *Der Spiegel,* which also pointed to "poor students with gold chains who routinely use anti-American, anti-Semitic, and sexist language, often addressing German women as 'whores, "German authorities "are generally aware of little of what happens in families." Source: "Paving the way for a Muslim parallel society" *Der Speigel/Spiegel Online,* March 29, 2007.

7. *Informele islamitische huwelijken—het verschijnsel en de (veiligheids)risico's,* Dutch Ministry of Internal Affairs, 2006.

8. Many European countries, as well as Canada, have also now introduced sharia-compliant banking. My first inclination is to view this as akin to having, say, kosher and vegetarian restaurants available for those who want them; I do not see how such options can violate humanitarian principles. But as I've no

expertise in the world of economics and banking, I leave this discussion to those who do.

9. Olivier Guitta, "Sharia's inroads in Europe—Italian Court: Beaten up for her own good," *HudsonNY.org*, March 5, 2009.

10. CIVITAS, "Crimes of the Community," CIVITAS Centre for Social Cohesion, London, 2008.

11. Martin Brunt, " 'Honour' Attack: Two Charged With Murder Bid," *Sky News*, July 23, 2009. Reprinted with permission from *Sky News*.

12. Joep Dohmen, " 'Humor of haat': feiten en dilemmas van de affaire-Nekschot," *NRC Handelsblad*, July 5, 2008.

13. "Press sector sues state for eavesdropping *Telegraaf* journalists," *NIS News Bulletin*, July 9, 2009.

14. "AIVD, houd je bezig met echte staatsveiligheid!" *Elsevier Weblog Afshin Ellian*, July 24, 2009.

15. Few non-Jewish Dutch have any idea of the actual meaning of the event, which marks the Jews' flight from Egyptian slavery under Pharaoh. For most Dutch, matzo, the unleavened bread the Jews prepared for their escape, is considered a traditional Easter breakfast food.

16. In the end, Sooreh Hera declined to be included in the exhibition at all, stating, according to a post on the official Web site of the City of The Hague, "I am not budging. My project will be shown in its entirety or not at all. So it won't be shown in The Hague. Maybe it will be shown in Gouda. Maybe I'll be shot dead. Just as long as nobody thinks of sending my corpse back to Iran."

17. Simon kuper, "Veiligheid gaat dus voor vrijheid," *NRC Handelsblad*, February 12, 2009.

18. Speaking at a conference in New York in June 2009, Bas Heijn, a writer for the *NRC*, explained, "The aversion to Europe is now as strong as the aversion to Muslims. There's a feeling that 'Holland isn't Holland anymore.' Because of its reputation for tolerance, the Netherlands was not traditional—and now our identity, not only our freedoms, is threatened. We want our identity to be firm—but Muslims want to be firm as well. No one wants a dynamic identity."

19. "Wilders makes half of Dutch Muslims want to emigrate," *Expatica/NRC Handelsblad/Radio Netherlands* report, July 8, 2009.

CHAPTER 20

1. Portions of this chapter appeared in different form on the Web site of WORLDDEFENSEREVIEW.COM.

2. Eben Kaplan, "American Muslims and the threat of homegrown terrorism," Council on Foreign Relations backgrounder, May 8, 2007.

3. Carrie Johnson and Spencer S. Hsu, "From suburban DC childhood to indictment on terror charges," *Washington Post*, July 29, 2009.

4. Department of Justice press release, July 27, 2009.

5. Steve Barnes and James Dao, "Gunman kills soldier outside recruiting station," *New York Times*, June 1, 2009.

6. It should be noted that some have argued that the FBI's involvement in this case constitutes entrapment, and that the informant led the four suspects into action. The nature of the defendants' statements and their openness to the idea of killing scores of innocent people, however, clearly suggests otherwise.

7. "Out of the shadows. Getting ahead of prisoner radicalization," The George Washington University Homeland Security Policy Institute and the University of Virginia Critical Incident Analysis Group, 2006, http://www.health system.virginia.edu/internet/ciag/publications/out_of_the_shadows.pdf.

8. Al Baker, "New York City police report explores homegrown terrorism," *New York Times,* August 16, 2007.

9. Mira L. Boland, "Sheikh Gilani's American Disciples," *Weekly Standard,* March 18, 2002.

10. "Al Fuqra: Holy Warriors of Terrorism," Anti-Defamation League, 1993.

11. Ibid.

12. It should be noted that Padilla, a.k.a. Abdullah al-Muhajir, was ultimately released of charges that he had planned to plant a "dirty bomb," and questions remain about his connections to terrorist organizations abroad. He has since filed suit against former Justice Department Official John Yoo, claiming he suffered "gross physical and psychological abuse" while in detention.

13. Noreen S. Ahmed-Ullah, Sam Roe, and Laurie Cohen, "A rare look at secretive Brotherhood in America," *Chicago Tribune,* September 19, 2004.

14. Ibid.

15. Mitchell D. Silber and Arvin Bhatt, *Radicalization in the West: The Homegrown Threat* (New York: NYPD Intelligence Division, 2007).

16. Blaine Harden, "A Nation Challenged: American Muslims, Saudis Seek to Add US Muslims to Their Sect," *New York Times,* October 20, 2001.

17. Ibid.

18. Ibid.

19. In a May 24, 2009, article in the *New York Times,* ("Imams reject talk that Islam radicalizes inmates"), however, several prison imams argued that prison clergy itself was not to blame; rather, they said, Islam has been a "moderating influence." Some also stated that radicalization took place among the prison population itself, but not from the leadership. The Federal Bureau of Prisons has taken action in recent years to screen imams and their materials.

CHAPTER 21

1. "Civil unrest in the French suburbs," Social Science Research Council report, October 2006.

2. Steve Emerson, "The Creeping Homegrown Threat," *The Daily Beast,* August 1, 2009.

3. Josh Gerstein, Islamic groups named in Hamas funding case," *New York Sun,* June 4, 2007.

4. Mitchell D. Silber and Arvin Bhatt, *Radicalization in the West: the homegrown threat* (New York: NYPD Intelligence Division 2007).

5. Randy Kennedy, "The Artists in the Hazmat Suits," *New York Times,* July 3, 2005.

CHAPTER 22

1. Paul Cliteur, "The postmodern interpretation of religious terrorism," *Free Inquiry*, Feb/March 2006.

2. Senate Testimony of Dr. Michael Waller before the Senate Judiciary Committee (Subcommittee on Terrorism, Technology and Homeland Security), October 14, 2003.

3. Interview with Zuhdi Jasser, July 15, 2009.

4. Mitchell D. Silber and Arvin Bhatt, *Radicalization in the West: the home-grown threat* (New York: NYPD Intelligence Division, 2007), 10.

5. Ibid., 19.

6. Ibid., 71.

7. Waller.

8. M. Zuhdi Jasser, "Treason by any other name," *Family Security Matters*, March 23, 2007.

9. Thomas L. Friedman, "Green shoots in Palestine," *New York Times*, August 5, 2009.

10. As cited by Kenneth Mentor, JD, PhD, University of North Carolina, Pembroke, "Literacy in Corrections" (*Encyclopedia of Corrections*, nd).

11. Ellen Winner and Lois Hetland, "Art for Our Sake: school arts classes matter more than ever—but not for the reasons you think," *Boston Globe*, September 2, 2007.

12. John Dewey, *Art As Experience* (1934); reprinted by Perigee, 1980.

Index

Abu Ghraib, 213
Abu Zubair. *See* Bouyeri, Mohammed
Adema, Jeroen, 173
Aertszstraat, Pieter, 154
Ahmadinejad, Mahmoud, 197
Ahmed, Rabei Osman Sayed, 118
AIVD (Algemene Inlichting En Veiligheids Dienst), 10, 51–52, 79, 136, 150, 170, 189
Akhnikh, Ismail, 136–37
Al Faisal, Sheikh Abdullah, 159
Al Fuqra, 198–99
Al Qaeda, 113, 114, 164, 185, 195, 197
Al Qaeda in Europe: The New Battleground of International Jihad, 162
Albee, Edward, 227
Aldrich, Mike, 207
Ali, Rachid Ben, 169, 170
Ali, Tariq, 92, 94, 96, 98
Allah Weet Het Beter [Allah Knows Better], 137
Allochtone, 29, 72–73, 98
Al-Taymiyyeh, Ibn, 137
Al-Zawahiri, Ayman, 115
American Diplomacy, 160

American Islamic Forum for Democracy, 210, 218
American Jihad: The Terrorists Living Among Us, 207
American Journal of Psychiatry, 183
American National Adult Literacy, 222
American Pew Research Center, 171
Ammitzbøll, Pernille, 162
Amsterdam, 15, 17, 95; bicycle theft in, 20–21; Diamantbuurt, 153–54; housing in, 17–18; Jews in, 43–44; riots in, 62–64
Anti-Defamation League, 199
Anti-Fascism Action, 152
Antillean communit, 49–50
Arab European League (AEL), 67, 97, 98
architecture, 35–37
Arendt, Hannah, 227
Aristegui, Gustavo de, 114, 115
art, 37
Ascherson, Neal, 129, 130
Atatürk, Kemal, 227
Atta, Mohammed, 72
August Allebéplein riots, 62–64, 182, 183

Ayaan Hirsi Ali, 7–8, 10, 34, 35, 59,
    64, 77, 79, 84, 88, 90–91, 126, 132,
    177, 186, 210, 221; early life of,
    85–86; female suicide bomber
    attack to kill, 154, 155; on honor
    killings, 104–5, 107; letter of threat
    from Thaghoet Party VVD,
    144–147; on liberal Isalm, 127,
    128–29; marriage life of, 86–87;
    news of van Gogh's murder,
    149–50; pepper spray, 127–29;
    search for national identity, 178–80;
    study of psychology, 87; on
    Submission (film), 102–3, 133–34; on
    West, 89
Aznar, Jose Maria, 114
Azzouz, Samir, 178

Baak, Marja, 40
Balkenende, Jan-Peter, 120, 188, 192
Barot, Duren, 185
Beeren, Wim, 37, 40
Belgium, immigrant Muslims in, 98
Berlage, Hendrikus, 36, 45
Berlin Wall, 25
bicycle theft, 20–21
Big Brother (TV show), 34
Bijlmermeer disaster, 31–32, 33, 172
bin Laden, Osama, 113–14, 206, 223
Bin Talal, Alwaleed, 204, 205
Blair, Tony, 158, 161, 192–93
Bolkestein, Frits, 29, 57, 60–61, 62
Booij, Lennart, 9
Boom, Joeri, 74, 75
Boston Globe, 210, 223
Bouazza, Hafid, 5
Bouyeri, Mohammed, 11, 54–55, 62,
    137, 159–60, 223; arrest of, 139;
    murder of van Gogh and, 138;
    confession trial, 178; writings, 136
Boxtel, Rogier, 58, 60
Boyd, Daniel Patrick, 196
Boyd, Marion, 186
Brenner, Marie, 107
Buruma, Ian, 54, 216
Bush, George, 207, 211, 213, 216,
    219

Café de Jaren, 15
Canada, sharia law in, 186–87
The Capital Gang, 11
Cartoon of Mohammed, protest
    against, 162–64
Center for Information and
    Documentation on Israel (CIDI),
    96, 98
Central Council of Muslims, 187
Centre for European Policy Studies,
    25
Chicago Tribune, 201, 202
children, 185; of Dutch-Muslim
    populations, 59; hidden, 42–43;
    immigrants, 28–29; Islamic schools
    for Muslim, 50–51; plans for
    protecting, 185–86
CIVITAS, 187, 188
Clinton, Bill, 40, 174
Cliteur, Paul, 216, 217
CoBrA Museum of Modern Art, 169,
    170
Cohen, Job, 9
Cologne train bombs, 166–67
Consumentenbond voor
    Cannabisliefhebbers, 56
Corcoran Art Museum, 212
Council on American and Islamic
    Relations (CAIR), 208, 212
Council on Foreign Relations, 195
Critical Art Ensemble, 212
Cromitie, James, 197–98
Cuypers, Petrus Josephus Hubertus,
    35

The Daily Beast, 207
Datz-Winter, Christina, 187
De Stijl movement, 3
De Telegraaf, 189
"Defence of Poetry," 222
Delftware, 12, 36
Der Spiegel, 167, 168
Dewey, John, 223
Dickey, Christopher, 41
Dittrich, Boris, 118–19
Djezeiri, Sheik Abou Bakr Djaber El,
    130

Documenta 7 (1982), 38
Doncasters Group, 205–6
Donner, Piet-Hein, 186
Dubai Holdings, 206
Dubai Ports World, 205
Duisenberg, Gretta, 98, 99
Dulfer, Hans, 95
Dutch Amsterdam School design,
    36
Dutch National Coordinator for
    Counterterrorism, 159

education, 50–51, 52
Egoland, 119
El Al 747 jet crash, 31–32
el-Hajdib, Youssef Mahammed,
    167
ELISE Consortium, 25, 26
Ellian, Afshin, 49, 52, 77, 189, 227
Emerson, Steve, 208, 209, 213
England: Al Qaeda activities in,
    158, 160; converts, Muslim,
    160–61; new laws to prevent
    terrorism in, 161, 173; radical
    extremism in, 159–60; terrorism in,
    158, 185; using Internet to spread
    riots in, 162
ETA (Basque terrorist group), 112
"Eurabia," 115, 116
European Islam, 217, 218
European Monitoring Center on
    Racism and Xenophobia, 96

Family Literary Centers, 222
family reunification programs, 26, 28,
    53–54
Federal Criminal Policy Office, 167
Fitna (film), 191, 192
Flimkrant, 42
Fortuyn, Pim, 4–5, 80, 81–82, 83, 120
Frank, Anne, 12, 13, 44
France: immigration in, 151–52;
    threats from bin Laden to, 116,
    117
Friedman, Thomas, 221
Fuchs, Rudi, 37–38, 39, 40, 102, 176,
    177, 181, 223

gay marriage, 58
Gemeentemuseum, 40, 190,
    191
General Electric company, 206
*Generatie op Drift (A Generation
    Adrift)*, 110
Geneva Conventions, 219
George Washington University's
    Homeland Security Policy
    Institute, 198
Gezelligheid, 1
Gezelschaap, 1
Gilani, Sheikh Mubarik Ali Hasmi
    Shah, 198–99
Giuliani, Rudy, 191, 204–5
Goldreyer case, 38, 39, 40
Gonzalez, Alberto, 200
Groen, Janny, 10
Groningen museum, 37

Hals, Frans, 35, 36
Hampton-El, Clement Rodney,
    198
Harris, Owen, 196
Hasjkeurmerk, 56
Hassan, Muzzammil, 210
headscarf, 109
Heathrow airport, plan for attacking,
    165–66
Heijn, Albert, 182
Hera, Sooreh, 190
Herben, Mat, 217, 219–20
Hermans, Tilly, 88
Het Parool, 21, 34, 38, 40, 150, 171
Hetland, Lois, 222
Hezb-ut-Tahrir, 159
Hidden children, 42–43
Hizb ut-Tahrir, 209
Hofstadgroep, 11, 118, 136, 137,
    147–48, 153, 170
Holland: conviviality in, 14–15; crime
    rates, 20–21; decline from
    democracy, 4–5; drug laws, 56;
    economy, 2; establishing new
    mosques, 19; festivals, 95–96;
    HIV-infection, 56–57; honor killing
    in, 104–6; housing system, 17–18;

identification card system, 152;
illegal immigrants in, 32, 33;
immigration restrictions (Verdonk),
121–23; implementation of new
laws in, 152–53; Islamic schools for
Muslim children, 50–51;
Moroccan's in, 80; Muslims in, 3–4,
5, 10, 116; Portuguese Jews in, 21;
racial violence, 10; social culture,
2–3; telecommunication system,
17; violent youth Muslims in,
110–12
Holman, Theodore, 11, 189
Holy Land Foundation trial, 208
Homeland Security Commission, 208
honor killings, 104–7, 111, 134,
193
Hoofwijk, Esther, 27–28
Hooghiemstra, Erna, 108
housing system, 17–19
How To Be A Good Muslim, 10
Huis, Anne Frank, 13
Hungarian National Security office, 167
Hussein, Saddam, 19

Ibrahim, Yussef, 53
"In bloed gedoopte" ("baptized in
blood") testament, 138–39
International Organizations Staff
Association, 174
Iran, 190
Iron Rita. See Verdonk, Maria
Cornelia
Islamic Jihad, 115
Islamic Saudi Academy, 203
Islamic Society of North America
(ISNA), 201, 202, 208
Islamic terrorism, 219
Italian Supreme Court of Cassation,
187

Jahjah, Dyab Abou, 67, 97, 98, 119–20,
193, 225
James, Kevin, 199–200
Jam'yyat Al-Islam Al-Saheeh, 200
Jasser, Mr. Zuhdi, 210, 218, 219, 220,
221, 225

Jewish Bride (painting), 176–77, 181,
223
Jews, 25; in Amsterdam, 43–44;
German, 45; Portuguese, 21
Jihad, Incorporated: A Guide to Militant
Islam in the US, 207
Jodenkoekjes, 180
Johns, Jasper, 13
Jonge, J. De, 29
Jordan, Michael, 224–25
Joustra, Arendo, 189
Jyllands-Posten, 162, 163

Kennedy, Randy, 212
Khalil Gibran International Academy,
203
Khomeini, Ayatollah, 197
Koppelingswet. See Linking Act
Kopspijkers, 119
Kuper, Simon, 193
Kurtz case, 212, 213

Leefbaar Nederland, 81, 82
Lievens, Jan, 35
Lijst Pim Fortuyn (LPF), 82, 83, 88,
173
Linking Act, 33, 34
Livable Netherlands, 81
London bombing attack, 157–58
Luger (film), 136

Maastricht Treaty (1992), 56, 193
MacLeish, Archibald, 222
Massachusetts Museum of
Contemporary Art (MASS Mo CA),
212
Madrid train bombing attack, 113,
114
Marcouch, Ahmed, 183–84
Marlowe, Christopher, 180
marriages, 108–9; Dutch-Muslim, 59,
108; forced, 107, 193; Gay, 58
Maximilian, Emperor, 12
McGuinty, Dalton, 187
Mein Kampf, 191, 192
Merkel, Angela, 180
Miller, John, 208

Minhaj El Muslim [The Way of the
    Muslim], 131–32
Mohammad, Sheik Omar Bakri, 118
Mohammed cartoon, protest against,
    162–64
Mondrian, Piet, 3
Moroccan Essalam Mosque, 19
Moroccan immigrants, 21–22, 130
Moroccan Islamic Combatant Group
    (GICM), 113, 114, 164
Mufti, Grand, 192
"The Multicultural Drama," 72
Multiculturalism, 84, 216, 217, 224
Munich massacre, 166
Murder in Amsterdam, 54, 216
Murdoch, Rupert, 205
Murphy, Eddie, 224
Museum for African Art, 101
Muslim American Society (MAS). *See*
    Muslim Brotherhood
Muslim Brotherhood, 5, 52, 159, 200,
    201–2, 208, 220
Muslim Democratic Party, 98

Naches, 42, 45
NAG (Nieuwe Allochtoone
    Generatie), 99
Napoleon I, 2
Nasser, President, 5
National Coordinator for Counter-
    Terrorism, 184
Nekschot, Gregorius, 188, 189
Netherlands. *See* Holland
"The Netherlands owes its existence
    to the democracy of wet feet,"
    61–62
New York Police Department
    (NYPD), 67, 198, 202, 218–19, 220
Newman, Barnett, 41
Newsweek, 41
Nightwatch (painting), 176
North Carolina case, 196, 197
NRC Handelsblad, 5, 19, 54, 60, 79

Obama, Barack, 208, 219, 226
"The Obligation To Kill Those Who
    Insult The Prophet," 136

Ofili, Chris, 190–91
"Open Letter to Ayaan Hirshi [sic]
    Ali," 139–43
Operation Desert Storm, 25–26
Operation Freedom, 114
Organization of the Islamic
    Conference, 88
Orgu, Fatima, 150

Padilla, Jose, 199
paintings, 38–40, 169, 170, 176–77
Pan Am Flight 103,bombing of, 113
Pan-Arab Federation, 97
Paris Metro attack, 52, 53
Parks, Rosa, 174, 175
Paul, Christopher, 196
Peace Education Foundation, 96
Peninsular and Oriental Steam
    Navigation Company, 205
People's Party for Freedom and
    Democracy, 88
Pleij, Herman, 61
Poldergeist, 4, 5
Poldermodel, 1, 61
"The portal to Auschwitz," 44
Postal Telegraph and Telephone
    (PTT), 99–100
Provo movement, 3

Raad, Ad de, 129, 130
racism, 34, 60
Radu, Michael, 160
Rasmussen, Anders Fogh, 151, 163
Rembrandt, 12, 18, 24, 25, 35
Rembrandt Research Project (RRP),
    24
Republican National Convention, 197
Rietveld, Gerrit, 3
Rijskmuseum museum, 35–37,
    177
Roosen, Adelheid, 92, 93
Roosevelt, Theodore, 66
Rose, Flemming, 162
Rosen, Jay, 74
Rotterdam Code of 2006, 172
Rus, Carla, 109
Rushdie, Salman, 30, 60

Saenredam, Pieter, 35
Salafism, 51–52, 218, 220
Samenwerking culture, 4
Samenwoning culture, 4
Sarkozy, Nicolas, 152
Satanic Verses (Rushdie), 30, 60
"Satan's Mother" bomb, 168
Saudi Arabia, 202, 203, 205, 213, 229
"Saudi Influences in the Netherlands:
    Links between the Salafist Mission,
    Radicalisation Processes and
    Islamic Terrorism," 51–52
Scheffer, Paul, 72, 73, 74, 84
Schumer, Charles, 207, 209
Schwartz, Gary, 24, 123, 124
Sen magazine, 170
September 11 attack, 4, 35, 48, 67,
    68–72, 82, 206, 209
sexual abuse, 109
Sharia Islamic law, 78
Shelley, Percy Bysshe, 222
Shuaibe, Faheem, 203
Sidali, Salah, 27
Sinterklaas, 180
Smoot, Jeanne, 210, 211
SOFI number, 33
Spain, threat of terrorism in, 114–15,
    117
Spencer, Robert, 196, 209, 211–12, 213,
    225
Spruyt, Bart Jan, 150
Stealth jihad, 196, 203
Stedelijk museum Amsterdam, 37, 38,
    100–1
Stella, Frank, 37
Stigter, Bianca, 19
*Studio Thinking: The Real Benefits of
    Visual Arts Education*, 223
Submission (film), 8, 10, 102–3, 133–34, 191
Summers, Lawrence, 205

Takfiri, 52
Taliban, 191–92
Tamburlaine the Great, 180
Third Reich, 3, 43
Times, 39, 203
"To Catch a Wolf," 136
Trouw, 10, 78, 79, 88, 111, 173

"Trouwen Over de Grenz" [Marrying
    Across the Border], 108
Turkish immigrants, 21, 112

United Arab Emirates, 205, 206, 207,
    221
United Nations Development
    Program's 2004 Human
    Development Report, 129–30, 221
United States, 210; Islamist threat in,
    195–96; radicalization in prisons of,
    200
USA PATRIOT Act, 211, 212, 213

The Vagina Monologues, 93
Van den Oever, Martine, 178
Van der Graaf, Jolande, 83, 189
Van der Laan, Medy, 176
Van Doesburg, Theo van, 3
Van Gogh, Theo, 4, 5, 11, 41, 119–20,
    133, 172; Bouyeri's attack on,
    138–39; early life of, 135; interview,
    41–42; memorial for, 174; murder
    of, 6–7; people's reaction to murder
    of, 8–10; political background of,
    135–36; reasons for murder of, 7–8;
    writings of, 137
Van Gogh, Vincent, 24
Van Royen, Jean-Francois,
    100
Van Thijin, Ed, 73
Vanity Fair, 107
*Veiled Monologues [Gesluierde
    Monologen]*, 93
Veling, Wim, 183
Verdonk, Maria Cornelia, 9, 120–22,
    172, 173
Vidino, Lorenzo, 162
Vinas, Bryant Neal, 197
Vlaams Belang, 165
Vlaams Blok, 98, 152, 165
Volkskrant, 10, 81, 120, 135, 169, 170,
    176, 184, 192

Wahhabism. *See* Salafism
Wall Street Journal, 37, 39
Waller, Michael, 218
Washington Post, 164

Webeling, Pieter, 135–36
Werdmolder, Hans, 111–12
Westerkerk bells, 12–13
Whitlock, Craig, 164
Whitney Museum, 212
Why I Am Not A Muslim, 205
Wilders, Geert, 149, 150, 151, 171, 191, 192, 193, 194
William I of Orange, 2
Winner, Ellen, 222
Winter, Leon de, 42
Wolf, Frank, 207, 209

women, 151–52; immigrants, 28, 60, 110; views on Islam, 154, 155
World Trade Center, attack on, 48, 65, 66, 82, 198, 209

Ye'or, Bat, 116–17, 205
youth riots, 205

Zalm, Gerrit, 150
Zapatero, Jose Louis Rodriguez, 115
Zembla, 179

About the Author

ABIGAIL R. ESMAN has been called "one of the best writers we have when it comes to jihadism in Europe." An award-winning author and journalist based in New York and the Netherlands, Esman has written extensively about Islam in the West for various international publications, including the *New Republic*, Salon.com, *Foreign Policy*, and others. Also an art critic, she is a contributing editor at *Art & Auction* magazine and the author and coauthor of books on art and contemporary culture.